Low Budget HELL

MAKING
UNDERGROUND MOVIES
WITH
JOHN WATERS

ROBERT MAIER

FULL&PAGE
PUBLISHING

Full Page Publishing
P.O. Box 1416
Davidson, NC 28036 USA
www.fullpagepublishing.com

Library of Congress Cataloging-in-Publication Data
Maier, Robert G.
Low budget hell making underground movies with John Waters / by
Robert Maier. – 1st ed.
p. cm
1. Waters, John 2. Maier, Robert. 3. Baltimore
LCCN 2011934307
ISBN 978-0-9837708-0-0
10 9 8 7 6 5 4 3 2 1
First Edition

Dedication

This book is dedicated to Catheryn, my wife, who encouraged me at the beginning of this journey, stood with me the entire time, and whose delightful laughter at my stories around the dinner table convinced me this book was the right thing to do.

Acknowledgements

I originally thought that writing this book would be easier than making a movie, and it was, but not as easy as it seemed when I started with an empty page. I was surprised how many people it takes to produce a book. I learned that the Acknowledgements section is like the end credits of a movie, and most readers probably skip this section the way most people walk out on movie credits. I never walk out on the credits, even if the usher hints that I should move along by coming down my row with his broom and dust pan. So, here are my end credits, but at the top.

I greatly appreciate those who read the various drafts and made intelligent and insightful comments that I was delighted to incorporate into the final. They include friends, family, and professionals: Philip Maier, Emily Withers, Lindsay Planer, Kate Carmody, Evan Maier, Cliff Anderson, Frank Morgan, Audrey Anderson, Mike Martin, Bethany Niebauer, and Jason Frye. I especially thank Charles Roggero who not only lived through much of what happened in this book, but relentlessly encouraged me to begin and pushed me complete this book. I am extremely grateful to the talented Val Bochkov who designed the covers and Val Sherer, who did the interior layout design.

Special thanks goes to Victor Bockris, author of Warhol The Biography, who allowed me to use the excerpt that appears Chapter Six where I meet Andy Warhol.

Contents

1

Out on the Edge

· · · · · · · · · · · · · · · · · · · ·

I paid people to take off their clothes. I didn't mean to. I went to private school, and a good college, but I was a child of the 60s.

Summer, 1969. I was a scruffy college kid from Towson, Maryland, toting a backpack and hitch-hiking out Cape Cod's Route 6 to the very end, Provincetown. I wanted to be a hippie, and this was the summer of Woodstock, the upstate New York rock music festival and gathering of the hippie tribes. I had to be there.

First, I took a long detour to Provincetown, Massachusetts. A friend from college, Stoney, said it was a can't miss stop on my hippie haj. Provincetown, he claimed, was a village full of freaks, drug experimenters, and free souls. I knew nothing about it, but its remoteness probably enabled desirable hippie activities like pot smoking, public nudity, and head shops with vast arrays of drug paraphernalia—a hippie theme park.

Arriving very late in the evening, in the communal spirit of the time, I knocked on the door of a guy Stoney recommended, asking if I could crash there. He was not happy, but let me flop in a corner. It had been a long day and I slept into the next evening when the house's residents banded together and in an un-hippie like manner, kicked me out. On the street, I was greeted with a Disneyland culture, but not the one I expected.

Provincetown was the gay Disneyland. Instead of hippies, gaggles of gay men, hugging and holding hands, dressed in colorful Hawaiian shirts (or colorful dresses with perfect hair and makeup) packed the streets. Provincetown was a full-time gay pride parade, but gay culture was so totally foreign to me, I didn't get what was going on at all. One group, more colorful and flamboyant than the others, handed out flyers. One of them, a big woman with huge hair, gigantic tits, and thick makeup shoved one into my hand.

"Come to our movie premier tonight young man. You won't believe your eyes. I'll be expecting you," he growled in a husky voice, then winked, and rejoined his crew. Was that was a man? What kind of place was this?

"That was Lady Divine," a guy on the street told me. "The others are John Waters and his acting troupe, the Dreamlanders, like in Dreamland Studios, the name of his movie company. They make movies in Baltimore and show them here in the summer."

From a distance, I watched the leader, a tall skinny guy with shoulder-length hair and a thin mustache pasted on his upper lip. He wore big black sunglasses, even though it was night. Baltimore? That's where I'm from. Movies? But movies are made in Hollywood. Dreamland Studios? Never heard of it. What a bunch of weirdos.

I watched them move down the street for another minute, and then stuck my thumb out headed for the Aquarian gathering at Woodstock. If someone had told me that four years later I would be working shoulder-to-shoulder with John Waters on five movies, talking to him on the phone for hours every night, gossiping with him on bar stools for hours, and would be his movie date several nights a week, I would have dropped dead in the street.

We Meet Again, Four Years Later

I met John formally four years later at the University of Maryland Baltimore County (UMBC)'s tidy business park campus. He had come by UMBC hungry to find people who would help make his next movie, Female Trouble.

I had completely forgotten the Provincetown encounter. To prepare for this meeting, I had just seen his notorious gross-out movie, Pink Flamingos. When released in 1972, it was dubbed "the sickest film ever made." People would dare you to see it. It was beyond X-rated. They gave out vomit bags with tickets. Mainstream critics hurled the worst epithets at it, naming its most disgusting scenes, like an actor eating real dog poop, a beautiful woman with a real penis, and a man with a singing asshole. This of course only drew bigger crowds.

With this "Prince of Puke" reputation, when he held out his hand I wondered would he shake it or would he lick it? He warmly shook it, and it was the beginning of a hair-raising eighteen year ride through the world of low-budget, underground filmmaking.

I had worked in the UMBC film department for about a year; my first job after graduating from American University in Washington, DC. American U. had one of the few film and TV production departments in the country. I majored in literature, and as an aspirant to the hippie counter-culture, loved the books of Jack Kerouac, William Burroughs, and Ken Kesey. Halfway through I got interested in film when a roommate showed me his TV production textbook. Leafing through pages of lights, cameras, and microphones, I was blown away that you could actually study something interesting in college. I always loved messing around with stereos, electric guitars, cameras, and walkie-talkies. I experimented with the 60's drug culture—had even smoked banana skins—and signaled it with my long hair and scraggly beard.

John and I hit it off well. Surprising to me, he was extremely well-read, unlike most of his Baltimore friends at the time. He thought a techie lit major was an interesting combination, and he could relate to a fellow traveler in the drug culture. He immediately engaged me by asking friendly questions; what did I do at UMBC, where did I live and grow up, and was I doing anything fun that summer? This engagement endears John to everybody he meets. You expect a monster, but he could pass for an assistant Presbyterian minister trolling for church members. Even my father, a hard-headed arch conservative, liked him immediately—except for his haircut.

John, Divine, and I grew up in the Towson, Maryland, area, a few miles north of the Baltimore city line. I delivered the daily Baltimore News-American newspaper to an old mansion behind my house in Towson where Divine lived and his parents ran a nursery school. The mansion was famous because F. Scott Fitzgerald drank himself silly there while his wife Zelda was treated at the Shepherd Pratt Mental Hospital next door. I had my first cigarettes, beer and French kiss in the nearby woods where Divine's junior high school classmates kicked the shit out of him every day for acting like a queer. It was a historic neighborhood.

John and I ate in the same downtown beatnik restaurants. We were both regulars at Baltimore's Communist bookstore, and had graduated from religious boys high schools—he from the Catholic Calvert Hall and me from the Episcopal St.

Paul's. We even had a few friends in common, including Mark Isherwood, who made national news when he was arrested for public nudity during the filming of Multiple Maniacs. John was so pleasant it was impossible to believe he had made the weird Pink Flamingos I had seen the night before, in preparation for this meeting. He was an astute artist-businessman; an actor-showman who had his finger on the pulse of something and intended to go places with it. We hit it off like old friends, talking for a half-hour about Towson, movies, books, and Baltimore, ("Bumberg" he called it). I think I was especially endearing to him because I laughed enthusiastically at all his jokes and funny stories.

All About Me

Though I had aspired to the greatness of New York City since I was a young teen, I still lived in the Baltimore suburbs. My goal was to be a filmmaker, but I didn't have a clue how. It was an exotic career in 1972. Baltimore was not considered a place to make films—it was a place to flee.

I had made three short silent films in The American University's film program, but they didn't involve lights, sound, or even a tripod. They were like super-8 home movies, but shot with a 16mm wind-up Bolex camera and 300 feet of black and white film (seven minutes worth)—all you were allowed. We edited the original film with hand-cranked viewers—great training for how films were made in 1910.

When I was eight years old, I joined the professional boys' choir of Baltimore's Episcopal Cathedral, which rehearsed four days a week and performed on Sundays. It set me on a career as an entertainer. In high school, I sang and played guitar in a garage band that played mostly drunken bacchanals at Lumbee

Indian weddings and gay Johns Hopkins University frat parties. As a techie, radios, miniature TVs, tape recorders, and 16mm film projectors were beautiful art objects. After graduating from college, I applied for an audio-visual technician job in the Arts and Humanities Division at UMBC, which seemed to be a nice combination.

The dean was a laid-back, poker-playing former English professor and we hit it off well. He was impressed with my degree in literature, and not concerned with my technical abilities. Hell, I had been editor-in-chief of my college literary magazine, so I was perfectly qualified to be an A/V tech.

The main part of the job was to watch the brand new arts and humanities building in the evenings to protect its millions of dollars worth of equipment. The most important thing was a package of the best professional 16mm film production gear money could buy. To justify these grandiose digs, they couldn't just shut the building at 5 o'clock; an art school must be open late so budding young artists could create (and procreate) into the wee hours.

The doorman job was boring. Maybe a dozen students a night signed in, and I just had to make sure no one walked out with a stereo. But it was a good time to read. The film department had stacks of American Cinematographer magazines, which I devoured each night, learning ten times more about movie making than I had from my college classes. After reading a hundred or so magazines, I was itching to make movies. I had to get into the film department and get my hands on the real deal. I explained to the Dean I could be more effective if I came in earlier, and helped professors with various A/V projects. He agreed. I was off the door and free to do more important things like learn to operate the new $10,000 French 16mm movie camera.

My garage band, The Missing Links, in 1965, rehearsing for one of the gay frat party gigs we played at Johns Hopkins University (we were way under age). I started singing in a boy's church choir when I was eight, and got hooked on entertaining. For equipment geeks, my treasured Fender Mustang guitar, Ampeg Gemini 1 amp, and Beatle Boots were sadly lost.

L-r, Billy White, me, Pat Reilly, Pat Doherty and Charlie Stagmer. ©Robert Maier

The film department was purpose-built by the film professor, Lee, to produce professional quality Hollywood-style movies—stuff he wanted to make. He and his outside partner, Joe, partly inspired by Waters' success, planned to make low-budget movies, and maybe even break into Hollywood. Free access to UMBC's equipment would help them get there. This included the camera, a $4,000 Swiss tape recorder, camera dollies, light kits, and the best German-made film editing machines. The idea was that students, by working on these films would learn more than listening to boring lectures, or stumbling through their own painful films. Plus they'd be free crew.

In reality, students rarely used the good stuff. They were banished to a cabinet of rickety super 8 cameras and hand-cranked home movie viewers. If a student actually cobbled together a film, it was a miracle. A film got an "A" if it ran through the projector without catching fire. Classes consisted of watching weird experimental films while lying on a water bed Lee had secretly installed in the screening room. For the most part the students were quite content with the arrangement.

UMBC was a good bus stop for John. The gear was there and the people were open for anything. I was ready to jump into the world of movies, especially rebellious movies. I was hungry to help John Waters on the road to fame and fortune.

An Intro to John Waters

I got to know John better over several months. By the end of Female Trouble, we were spending many work and social hours together, and he happily regaled me with his life story. He grew up in Lutherville, Maryland, a few miles from my house. He started his entertainment career as a pre-teen giving puppet shows at local kiddie birthday parties, but did not fit so well with the upper crust neighborhood. As a confirmed homosexual in his early teens, John was labeled a misfit who read books during phys ed class softball games, ignoring the occasional ball that happened to plunk down next to him. His response to screaming teammates was a disinterested, "You get it." John hungered for the edgy elements of the gay community. He did not hang out with secretive queers who ran hair salons and cooked fondue dinners for gay friends. That was too normal.

Though John was not a secretive queer, he didn't wear gay pride buttons either. John seemed asexual when I first met him. It never occurred to me he was gay—naïve little me. He was just an odd character who worked hard to project an image—both in his personal life and in his films. I would accuse him of being enigmatic and most enigmatic when he'd fervently deny there was the slightest enigma about him. But there was that little wry smirk.

John was slightly effeminate, though not more than many heterosexual men I've known. His deep, authoritative voice contradicted the girly-man stereotype. His hair was Jesus Christ long; but greasy and uncared for. He called it his "bacon." John was bulimic-thin and tall, and moved like a bony house cat. Add his thin Latin lover-boy pencil mustache and you thought maybe the guy is a little swish, but maybe not. John wanted to be an outsider—a dangerous gay artist. His favorite coat was a ludicrous dog handler's jacket with a portrait of a smiling German shepherd's face, whose massive red tongue hung out like a "Hollywood loaf."

John's attention to his trademark pencil mustache was meticulous. If you thought this guy was your average hippie stoner, notice please the immaculately kept mustache, highlighted with eyebrow pencil that was the exact opposite of fashionably unkempt hippie beards.

John's huge bug-eye sunglasses hid his face as if he had running sores for eyes and had searched the world for the hugest pair to hide them. They added B-movie mystery to his look, suggesting he might be an incognito celebrity. When asked by anyone where he found such glasses he had a ready answer.

"Los Angeles. That's the only place I buy sunglasses. They have all the sun, so they have the best sunglasses."

John's contradictions made him difficult to typecast. Some were definitely practiced. Over the years I had learned he recited the same jokes and shocking comments to everyone he met, learning which punch lines worked and milking them for months—or years—even decades. This was his Shecky Green persona, he told me. Others seemed to come straight from the heart as truly spontaneous wit with no ulterior motive of projecting a certain image. This was John at his most promising and human.

John had made films since 1964, more than eight years before Pink Flamingos became a hit. Pink showed that one person could make a movie, get it distributed, and find a national audience—but, most importantly, get the mainstream press to write about it. John's films are proof that there's no such thing as bad publicity. In the defiant atmosphere of the 70s, a scandalized review from a mainstream critic could be sarcastically emblazoned on a poster to fire up the counter-culture. Pink Flamingos was a gas can thrown into the smoldering fire of counter-culturalism.

Before Pink, John carried his 16mm movie prints around the country in the trunk of his car, showing them at student film societies, church basements, and coffee houses. He lived off the meager ticket sales, and sometimes sleeping in his car to save money. His films, Eat Your Make-up, Multiple Maniacs, and Mondo Trasho were booked because the young and hip liked the term "underground movies," but unless you liked John's cockeyed view of the world, you'd likely leave halfway through, bored with the atrocious acting, the shaky, grainy, out-of-focus, black and white images, and distorted sound tracks. Most people went to underground movies to see bare breasts or psychedelia, not puking, murdering, and dressing in drag.

Pink Flamingos is obsessive and not so funny to me. The Nazism, torture, bestiality, and meanness are not meant to be funny, but to be leered at. The most memorable scenes involved the nudity underground audiences craved—David Lochary's sausage-lengthened penis, Elizabeth Coffey's soon to be removed penis, and the singing asshole guy. The most memorable scene, of Divine eating dog shit, was bad taste that shocked every single viewer, and was impossible not to talk or write about.

Because the pre-Pink audiences were small and scattered, the mainstream press did not write much about John. But when New Line Cinema, an honest-to-goodness distributor, decided to open Pink in a real New York theatre, the press exploded. Real money rolled in, and he no longer had to work out of the trunk of his car. He gave well-practiced interviews and public appearances, which were often more interesting than his films.

The early John was a frugal artist, in the hippie vein—though he despised the hippie ethos. He drove a big beat-up Buick, wore bizarre clothes purchased for spare change from thrift stores, and lived in bad areas of Baltimore where rents were ridiculously cheap, just like the hippies. He didn't eat much, saying he only ate because it made cigarettes taste better. His only extravagances were books and magazine subscriptions. With the real money from Pink, he could move to this next more complicated movie, Female Trouble.

2

Female Trouble

. . . .

A moonlighting local TV news cameraman with a single-system 16mm film camera was the sole technician on John's earlier films. The camera guy made a few adjustments and then John filmed, holding the camera with a brace on his shoulder. Single-system film was designed strictly for news stories and allowed only basic editing. It was barely a step above home movies. But John knew 16mm could be copied and projected in real movie theaters, unlike the grainy 8mm movies he first produced.

Sound had always been a problem for John's films. It is a miracle Pink Flamingos survived with any sound. The news camera recorded sound on a thin magnetic strip on the side of the film, so to add music or narration, John had to record directly onto the film. If he missed his cue and recorded over the original dialogue, it was lost forever.

Though John vowed he hated technology, he wanted his films to look like the ones in movie theaters. He realized Pink Flamingos' bad sound had to be addressed in Female Trouble. UMBC had double-system equipment where the sound and picture were recorded and edited separately, which solved the sound problems. This double-system thing was beyond the abilities of the local TV station moonlighters, but the owner of the local film lab advised him to contact UMBC's film department. They had been making deals with independent producers before, and he could probably get one too.

John was embraced by UMBC's freewheeling film department. Pink was notoriously made for $10,000 and edited by John in his attic. Female Trouble had the "extravagant" budget of $25,000. It was a tiny amount, but enough to make the leap to a more professional-looking movie, especially with the help of others

The UMBC deal gave John unlimited use of its production equipment—the cameras, lights, recorder, and dolly, and supplied competent people to run it. Lee and Joe paid themselves as "consulting producers" who made sure the equipment and crew showed up, offered a little technical advice, and encouraged students to participate, which justified not charging for the equipment.

Waters liked the idea of using Maryland State property to make his movie—especially considering his greatest nemesis was the Maryland State Board of Censors which made him cut the more explicit sex scenes from his previous movies.

If it weren't for this sweet deal, John might have ended up writing cult novels or directing demented plays in little hole-in-the-wall theatres. On the bright side, now that John is an international celebrity, he has more than paid back the people of Maryland, bringing millions of dollars in jobs and tourism to the State, not to mention his occasionally hefty charitable donations to Maryland non-profits. UMBC's film department still exists, but is now called "Media Arts." It has a snazzy website, touting the extensive academic achievements of the faculty, but I wonder if they know its history of launching John Waters into real filmmaking.

Female Trouble Begins

When the news of the film department's assistance to John became known, I was desperate to work on it. I knew the equipment well, especially the sound, and would have worked for free. Unfortunately, though shooting would be mainly on weekends, there would be a few weekdays, and it would have been too difficult for me to do my full-time work plus be on the movie crew. The Female Trouble crew initially consisted of Dave Insley, a teaching assistant at UMBC, who would be camera assistant and lighting guy. Richard, a real odd ball with a drinking problem was chosen to be the sound recordist, the only other paid job. Though an unpredictable character, Richard claimed he had met Jean Luc Goddard when he was a student in France, so he was allowed to operate the good stuff. However, he had little interest in sound recording, because he really wanted to be a director.

I was very disappointed that I wasn't offered the sound recording job, especially since I had been recording sound on several of Lee's and Joe's other outside films, and felt I was a real member of their family. Also, I got along well with John at our first meeting, and I had at least seen Pink Flamingos, which Richard had not, and said he had no desire to. Finally, Richard was a real flake who slept all day and edited film all night, but never really accomplished much nor displayed much reliability. I sensed John needed someone reliable, like me, because he seemed, even that early in the game, to be a tenacious businessman who didn't suffer fools lightly. Lee and Joe threw me the bone of doing some side jobs to support the production, so at least I would get some credit. They claimed I could be much more useful watching over the film department while they were out shooting.

Lee and Joe made sure there was electricity for the movie lights, that the crew had directions to the filming sites, and the right film stock was purchased. Occasionally students came to the shoots, but these were college students, and shooting required being on set at 7:00 a.m. Saturday mornings—a bad combination. They mostly carried the gear, and were forced to hang out in uncomfortable rooms away from the shooting because most of the locations were tiny. It became known that working on the John Waters film meant hanging out with weirdo extras in cramped, dirty locations with nothing to eat or drink. Running out to buy a pack of Kool cigarettes for John could be the highlight of the day, so the number of student helpers quickly shrunk to zero. So much for the justification of cooperation by the university, but the show must go on. One student did complain to the Dean that he could never use the good equipment because it was being used by the faculty on a "porno film." The student was placated by being promised exclusive use of the equipment after Female Trouble wrapped, but Lee was called on the Dean's carpet and ordered that whatever he was doing must stop as soon as possible.

The film's editor would be Charles Roggero, a sophisticated grad assistant in his late 30s who had grown up in Argentina, where his father had been a high government official. He had a privileged upbringing where they dressed in tuxes for dinner. After many trips to Miami, he got a degree in architecture from the University of Miami, which taught him plenty about American partying too. But Charles's passions were movies and music, not architecture, so he moved to Los Angeles, and discovered the movie business during a tour of UCLA's film department.

Charles focused on the music business in LA, formed a record company, and produced several records with seed money from his family. The company didn't go far, but involved him in the LA entertainment scene. An internship on Academy Award-winning director Stanley Kramer's 1965 movie, Ship of Fools, opened the door to the movie industry.

Charles partied, Hollywood-style, through the 1960s, which included three fashionably short and expensive marriages. After ten years, he had burned out on Los Angeles and needed a quiet place to re-consider life. Moving to Baltimore where his mother had been living for twenty years made sense. Being fluent in English and Spanish, he thought he might get a quiet job making propaganda films for the government in nearby Washington, DC. Joining Baltimore's underground movie scene wasn't on the radar screen of this sophisticated Argentinean.

Charles understood movie production, and spent many hours operating UMBC's fancy film editing machine, while working on a master's degree. He hadn't cut a full-length movie yet, but that wouldn't be a problem, because John insisted on sitting at the editing machine, overseeing every cut and making every creative decision. John would have happily edited the film himself, like his three previous movies. However, the double-system film editing method was a complex mechanical process, which John conceded, was way too technical for him. So Charles became the editor for a flat fee of $300 for three months' work. Such a deal.

In many ways, Charles was the exact opposite of John, and I wondered how they would get along. First, Charles was a completely heterosexual Republican; a preppy dressed in penny loafers and button-down shirts. He had impeccable manners and played tennis at the country club with Baltimore's old-money trust fund babies. Charles never smoked, never drank more than a small glass of wine, and hated drugs. He loved intricate modern Jazz and Bossa Nova, not John's trashy novelty songs like "Papa-Oo-Mow-Mow."

On the other hand they were similar. Charles attended private schools, drove the best cars, traveled extensively, and lived in sophisticated cities like Buenos Aires, Miami, and Los Angeles. John too came from a well-to-do family. He had grown up in a high-brow section of Baltimore and entertained the children of Baltimore's blue-bloods with his kiddy puppet shows. He and John were both polite, social people. They both loved movies, and they developed an amazing working relationship and friendship based on a mutual respect that John's movie fans probably wouldn't get. It lasted through three films, then collapsed miserably when New Line took over Hairspray and began the process of squeezing out the production team formed at UMBC. In a sad ending, Charles sued John and New Line for breach of contract, and actually won a settlement. Amazingly, it was the only time in his career John was sued.

Joining Female Trouble

The filming began, but I had to be satisfied sitting in an office, sad that I couldn't work on it. I jealously listened to stories about the shoot from Dave and Richard. Richard wasn't getting along too well. He was so authentically cracked even John was unnerved. He showed up late, hung over from all-nighters, reeking of B.O. and stale cognac. He chain-smoked French Galois cigarettes, lighting every new one from the smelly butt of the previous. Being the soundman was beneath him, and he fantasized about being the director—thinking if John died of a heart attack on set, he would take over because he had met Jean Luc Goddard. John, wisely concerned about how his money was being spent, badgered Lee and Joe about

Richard's indifference and unreliability. They did nothing, probably because they were scared of Richard, and didn't want to agitate him.

Very early one Saturday morning on a location shoot at Baltimore's old Polytechnic High School, Chuck Yeaton, a general aide to John and the husband of Pat Moran, the production manager, was searching for the continually disappearing Richard. He opened a bathroom stall door and found Richard shooting up. Chuck went back to the set to tell John and Pat, and they went berserk. Rule number one on John's sets was no drinking and no drugs. Those, along with all sexual activities, had to wait until after the shoot. It was the last straw, and Richard was man-handled out of the building.

Within minutes my phone woke me up. It was Dave Insley.

"You said you wanted to work on John's film; we need you, right now; Richard's gone; you gotta be here now," he said. "We're waiting for you."

"I'm there in fifteen minutes," I answered, thinking I might just be dreaming.

It was 7:00 a.m. I zipped downtown and was on the set in twenty minutes. Everyone was relieved, because the scene had twenty period-dressed and made-up extras on a difficult-to-get location, four major actors, and a half-dozen day players. I had literally saved the day, and at the end of it, John said he wanted me on the crew permanently. Lee and Joe weren't enthused, but they didn't have much wiggle room after the very public embarrassment with their first choice. As for my full-time job, I would call in sick on the few weekday shoots. No problem.

Richard was banished to Lee's office, where Charles had now started the editing process. Richard seemed happy to be away from John's movie and back to his own, but both Charles and Lee were looking for a way to make him disappear. At this point, Richard was actually living in the Arts building. It was easy to do. There were several unused offices on the top floor, lots of snack machines, and you could even shower in the dressing room attached to the dance studio. Richard had somehow wrangled his way into getting a building master key, so he became the Phantom of the Arts Building, hiding out during the day and appearing at night to edit his film after everyone had gone. For me, he was just a harmless crazy artist. However, one day, a maintenance man stumbled into the office where Richard had set up his little home with sleeping bag, reading light, various snacks, a huge ashtray overflowing with Gaulois cigarette butts, bottles of cognac and the sickly green French liqueur, Chartreuse. The dean was alerted and ordered me to get Richard out of the building immediately.

"What do you mean, I have to get out? I have no place to go," Richard said.

"I'm really sorry, but I don't have a choice. Dean's orders."

"I'm the only real artist in this building, and they're throwing me out?"

That was pretty presumptuous and not true at all.

"Just pack everything up, and leave. Can't you go home to your parents?"

"They're both dead; I'll have to go back to the mental hospital."

I was way too young and ill-equipped to deal with this and started feeling guilty.

"Why don't you go down and explain it all to the Dean. Maybe he'll do something."

On Female Trouble's Baltimore City Jail location just before Dawn Davenport (Divine) gets the electric chair.

Front Robert Maier with tape recorder; l-r John Waters (partial), George Stover, Divine, Pat Moran, Elizabeth Coffey, Mumme.

Photo by Charles Roggero ©Robert Maier

Richard pondered this for a minute and said,

"Yeah, I'll do that."

I took this as my exit cue, glad to be out of it.

A few minutes later, Richard appeared at the door of the Dean's office suite, barefoot and wearing his trademark black rain coat. A Gaulois clung to the corner of his mouth, and he held a bottle in one hand.

"The Dean's busy right now. You'll have to make an appointment," said the secretary.

"No, I don't," snapped Richard. He marched up to the Dean's desk and without a word, emptied the bottle of Chartreuse onto it covering all the papers with the sticky green liqueur, and stalked out.

I later saw security emptying Richard's stuff into a laundry cart. In my mailbox a note from the Dean informed me that Richard was permanently banned from the UMBC campus.

This was attention the film department didn't need, and would come back to haunt Lee and help scuttle his plans for a grand movie-making empire.

From our earlier conversations about growing up in Towson I had a comfort level John needed: reliable, educated, polite, sensible, and a techy, but also a suburban rebel who "got" John's humor and movies. Despite his underground, counter-cultural visions, John could also be as conservative as any of the uptight suburbanites he made fun of. Especially when it came to business, and filmmaking for him was a business, he wanted to work with reliable establishment people. His father was a successful small business owner, so it was in his blood. John wanted establishment people to like him too. Being accepted by successful people meant much more to him than idolization by the freaks who took his movies as gospel truth. He did not want to be known as an uncivilized geek who lived in a trailer surrounded by deranged misfits.

Shooting of Female Trouble was a sea change for John and the Dreamlanders (as they were known for being part of John's Dreamland Productions) culture. His first three 16mm films, Mondo Trasho, Multiple Maniacs, and Pink Flamingos were made by eccentrics and artists who had known each other for years and worked for nothing. With Female Trouble, suddenly a crew of straight-looking technical people had appeared. Nobody knew their backgrounds. Their knowledge of the technicalities of cameras, microphones, lighting, and the organizing of a shooting day was intimidating to the more laid-back artists. Suddenly the process was more complex than John shooting the camera from his shoulder with one light, and a friend pointing a mic in the general direction of the actors.

With the new production, wires were strung everywhere and imposing equipment was scattered around. Lights had to be nailed into ceilings, and they constantly blew fuses interrupting the shooting. Unlike John's previous films, if there was outside noise, shooting was halted until the offending source was found and stopped. Taking care of such persnickety details was so different from the earlier films, which had flowed uninterrupted like little plays. Now outsiders stopped the artistic flow to fix seemingly invisible little problems. Scenes were chopped up into different angles, or shot out-of-sequence, slowing the pace, and increasing the stress. It was confusing and stressful to people who had never been through this kind of movie-making before. Art Director Vince Peranio was particularly unsettled that the crew moved his props and sets around to position a light or get a different camera angle. His sets were meticulously designed, placed, and decorated with little consideration for the needs of lights, camera, and sound. These new guys were pushing them aside like junk.

John never let anyone watch the film after it had been returned from the lab, and didn't have time to watch it himself. Since he was the camera operator, he felt he already knew if everything was right with the shot. He was not concerned with clever blocking, lighting, or composition. If the person speaking could be seen and the lines were delivered exactly as written, it was a good take and we would move on, even if the composition was poor, lighting a problem, or the shot was out of focus. Watching Tim Burton's Ed Wood movie reminds me of shooting Female Trouble, especially the studio scenes in Plan 9 from Outer Space, when the producers were shocked

Ed ignored big problems, like grave stones tipping over, saying that audiences would never notice.

John's style was to plop the camera down and never move it, and he'd argue every time we tried to get him to shoot a close-up, reaction shot, or other cutaway. We gave up on the idea of shooting lots of angles and decided among ourselves John should be doing stage plays, not film—and we'd just go along with him. It's ironic John's biggest hit movie, Hairspray, was a much bigger hit as a Broadway play. He once said he wanted Desperate Living made into an opera. That made perfect sense to me.

Another bone of contention with the original Dreamlanders was that the film crew was treated a bit better than John's stable. Lunch, drinks, and snacks were never available on John's previous films—you brought your own. On earlier films, crafts service (a department that provides free snacks and water or soda to cast and crew to keep them from wandering away during set-ups) meant bumming a Kool off John. I think he smoked Kools because everyone hated them, which minimized the bumming.

Since the crew on Female Trouble was "professional," it was understood a cooler of drinks and lunch would be provided—at least for them. Generally it was a sandwich from the local deli, but who knew when the break would occur or what state the food would be in when you finally got it. Union niceties like meal penalties (money paid to union crews if the lunch break is late) and hot sit-down catered lunches were inconceivable concepts in John's non-union film days. John has since remarked that he loves unions because they make filmmaking so much more survivable.

The art department, Van, the makeup artist, Chris, the hairdresser, and even Pat had to go out and buy their own.

Five minutes for a Kool, a Coke, and a candy bar was lunch for John. When the original Dreamlanders grumbled about the new crew's special treatment, it was explained that the crew never had the opportunity to slip out for a quick bite to eat, the way actors or the art department could. If the cameraman and soundman stopped, everything stopped, and what a waste of time that was. It calmed things down, and the Dreamlanders didn't want to complain too loudly, lest they appear ungrateful for the opportunity to work with John.

John hated taking breaks on the set, and could barely be contained when the pace slowed. In later films, when I was the production manager in charge of the money, if the crew took a short break, or took too long setting-up, John slid up and whispered, "Dollar, dollar, dollar," in my ear. It was a regular joke, but only partially. Money was not a joke to John. Breaks for him should be at the end of the day, or better yet, not until the end of the movie, when people were off the payroll.

Another source of friction between the new crew and the old Dreamlanders was that the crew was paid by the day, and not a flat rate for the film. Vince, Van, Pat, the actors, and a few others were paid a flat rate. It was maybe a thousand dollars, which sounded like a lot, but worked out to be less than a dollar an hour. After the wrap, when I became good friends with him, Vince confided to me that unhappiness with the money deal had been growing since Pink Flamingos appeared to be making real money, and not because the crew seemed to have a better deal.

Despite the hidden grumblings, Female Trouble was absolutely fun, and unlike any movie being made at the time. I was from a suburban and academic background, and the people in the movie were a culture shock for me. Most hadn't gone to college, or paid much attention to education, which had been my life for eighteen years. They were friendly, approachable, and respectful; creative, informal, and funny. The key people, Vince, Pat, John, Van, Divine, and Chris Mason, had strong work ethics. No matter how early the call or how long the hours, they stuck it out, sober as judges.

The shoots were all business. Hangers-on were forbidden. Groupies and girlfriends or boyfriends wanting to rub shoulders with "movie stars" were not allowed. These clever "uneducated" people were a refreshing change from the stuffed shirts of the academic world I was now ready to bust away from.

Female Trouble was a guerilla production in the best spirit of the 60s-70s. We never asked permission to shoot on the street or in parks. To accommodate everyone's real job schedule, most shooting was done on weekends. But it was still a huge production by all of our standards. Considering it was partially a period film with dozens of dressed locations all over Baltimore, a large cast, hundreds of extras, fight scenes, shootings, heavy make-up, scores of original costume changes and multiple special props and sets, it is astounding that it was made for $25,000.

My first day on the set was exciting and eye-opening. The scene was in a classroom filled with teased-hair extras wearing nerdy late-1950's costumes. Divine was dressed and made up as the perfect Baltimore trashy teen with a sky-high bouffant wig. The dialogue, set, and cast created a perfect picture of a dysfunctional public school and Baltimore's class conflict that John adored. My first shot required me to lie down on the floor at Divine's feet, holding the mic just out of camera sight. The scene called for Divine, as Dawn Davenport, to unwrap a giant meatball sub hidden in his lap, and then gobble it down. The top student snitches to the teacher, who then insults Divine, which starts a hair-pulling girl fight. Divine is thrown out of the class, much to the entertainment of the other students.

Divine looked down at me on the floor with the sweetest smile as the camera was set up.

"Don't worry hon, I won't step on you," he whispered.

Considering his 300 lb. weight, it was a concern. He said it in a funny and friendly way, and I thought, "Wow, here's another notorious 'monster,' somebody who really did eat shit on camera, whose first words were friendly and warm." Divine chatted with me throughout the setups, asking if I was comfortable, or if was he speaking loud enough. I'd never been that close to anyone in full drag and got an eyeful. His makeup was an eighth of an inch thick; his legs were massive and shaved. My arm brushed against one, and it was rough as sandpaper. Though I never saw for myself, John assured me Divine was a very hairy fellow, so shaving every inch of his body every two days was a major undertaking. He had a full-body 5 o'clock shadow.

Female Trouble's locations included a dump, ghetto streets, a large nightclub, a hair salon, a courtroom, a nursing school, the Baltimore City Jail, Vince's home, and John's apartment. An empty room upstairs from Pat's hippie head shop was the "studio" and was dressed several times as Divine's living room. This gives Female Trouble a real dynamism. The first fifteen minutes race through Divine's difficult youth in a swirl of eye-catching locations, tragic/comic events, and wardrobe, hair, and make-up changes.

It was fun charging around Baltimore in a pair of cars, jumping out—usually in some hideous location—putting quick touches on Divine, and then rolling three or four takes of some ludicrous scene. Lighting was absolutely basic since there wasn't time and that wasn't John's directing style anyway.

Watching John direct was a fascinating exercise. He memorized every line of the script, mouthing each word in sync with the actor (shades of Ed Wood again). John insisted on operating the camera to be sure he captured the vision of his script. He wasn't the most coordinated person, so the camera movements could be pretty rough. Close-ups were out-of-focus, moves were jumpy, composition could be way off, and zooms were shaky. This sort of camerawork has become stylish, but Female Trouble's shaky, artsy look was completely unintended back in 1973. John operated the camera not to be artsy, but only because he had to be sure the acting was right.

It was equally impossible to convince John to shoot different angles of scenes for more flexibility in editing. It's funny considering how much he loved films, how many film books he had read, and how many film magazines he subscribed to, that he didn't seem to grasp basic film 101 directing and editing. It was all about content for him, not technique.

On later films, beginning with Polyester, when he was spending investor money and not his, he happily indulged in movie toys like cranes, catering vans, street lockdowns, lighting towers, animation, special effects, moving car shots, rain machines, gunshot effects, time-gobbling stunts, and big crowd scenes in expensive locations. Dollar, dollar, dollar became spend, spend, spend.

Dealing with the public on Female Trouble was always exciting. There was no such thing as a film permit in Baltimore. Except for John's films, no one could remember when a film had shot in Baltimore. Everyone thought it was way too ugly for glamorous movies. Being on the guerilla film crew, watching the shocked, bewildered bystanders was a hoot. One memorable shot was Divine "modeling" on a busy Baltimore street. He was in full drag wearing a shimmering blue sequined gown, with a big hairdo and Van's Clarabelle make-up. We filmed him from the window of a slowly-moving car, so bystanders on the street were clueless. Their reactions were as if Divine had been dropped from a flying saucer and was having an epileptic fit. Not a soul would think it was a scene from a movie.

The Christmas tree scene, where Divine beats up his parents, topples the tree, stomps on his presents, and then runs away because he didn't get cha-cha heels, was a memorable location shot. The runaway setup required our small crew to perch behind a bush outside the house. We had a very small profile, so the neighbors had no idea a movie was being shot in their quiet suburban neighborhood on that cool Sunday morning.

When Divine burst out the front door, howling at the top of his lungs, in his sheer neon-green nightie, we saw neighbors peeking out their front windows, wondering what the hell was going on. The next set-up was even better when Dawn's father flew out the door screaming, "Dawn Davenport come back here! You're going straight to a home for girls! I'm calling the juvenile authorities right now!"

He was a genuine suburban dad in his red plaid robe, bedroom slippers, and plastered wig. He was a short man, but could yell quite loud. In the movie, you can hear his lines echo up and down the street. After the third take neighbors began to poke their heads out their front doors. They were too shy, clueless and maybe even afraid to get involved. But they had probably called the cops to report a domestic disturbance, and we didn't need to be in the middle of that. Figuring three takes were enough, we piled into two cars—our entire "transportation department," and took off back downtown where we belonged.

Throughout Female Trouble, John delighted in shocking me by increasing my non-existent vocabulary of gay slang. For example, when Van, the costume designer, smeared brown shoe polish on the bottom of Divine's tighty-whiteys before the revolutionary sex scene where Divine played both the man and the woman, John informed me they were "skid marks." Skid marks came from the "Hershey highway." I learned heterosexuals were "breeders," that "chickens" were hairless boys, and "chicken hawks" were men who pursued them. "Chubby chasers" were people of any sexual persuasion who liked fooling with fat people. A "glory hole" was a hole carved in the partition between stalls in a men's bathroom, large enough to stick a weiner through. One that always gets a chuckle, and is not yet in the Urban Slang Dictionary, is a "payday," which is a turd left in the toilet by an inconsiderate non-flusher. John named his production company "Payday Productions" while trying to raise money for Pink Flamingos II but dropped it later in his more dapper days.

As part of his drag outfit, Divine wore a "cheater," a strap-on camel-toed fake vagina with an ample crop of curly black hair sewn on. It can be used to great effect, especially when worn under a sheer dress, like Divine's see-through wedding dress in Female Trouble's wedding scene.

Female Trouble's comic interludes were welcome because of the usually difficult conditions. As the sound recordist without a boom operator, I had to squeeze into tight spaces to pick up decent sound while keeping out of the shot. Dipping a mic into a shot was possibly the only technical error John loathed. It was a mistake that required a re-take and put me on a guilt trip for wasting precious film. Frequently, this meant lying on my back on a filthy floor and pointing the mic up from there. Pat proclaimed,

"Oh, he just wants to look up the girl's dresses."

Van chimed in, "No, he wants a close-up of Divine's cheater. I'll show it to you; you don't have to lie on the floor. You can borrow it for the night."

When I had to hide a lavaliere mic in Divine's blouse, between his gigantic foam rubber breasts, John teased, "You can make it snappy; they're not real you know."

The heat on the sets could be ferocious. Filming began in late August, and the room above Pat's store, which was dressed up to be Dawn's apartment, had no air conditioning. A 19th century row house, it only had windows in the front and back, and those had been painted shut with a hundred coats of paint. The hot movie lights turned the little room into a sauna. The cast could usually take a break in a cooler room, but for the crew, it was relentless. John had endless energy, and the crew was always moving, setting up, rehearsing, shooting, or tearing down for another set up. I was barely 23 years old, so it wasn't such a big deal, but thinking back, those little Baltimore row house rooms were a good taste of low budget hell. The non-stop pace was exhausting, and started affecting everyone's good moods.

No one thought about taking the time to provide water. Lunch was ordered from a sandwich carry-out around the corner. If we were in the middle of a set-up, which was almost always, the sandwiches, usually meatball subs, were delivered and laid in a pile until we managed a break. John seemed to survive on Kools, so food was not a big consideration. When we'd finally get to the meatball subs, usually at the end of the day, the sauce had soaked the bread to wallpaper paste and they were stone cold inedible. We finally got together with John and demanded a lunch break to get decent food, or we couldn't go on. He was miffed at the idea of stopping for food, but we gave him no choice. It was the first conflict, and at first John agreed with the other Dreamlanders about the crew's special treatment. However, in a few days, as we gobbled down our subs and Cokes, John, Pat and the others started to take breaks too. John added a large bag of potato chips to his three-Kool lunch break, and everyone acknowledged a lunch break was a good thing that improved the work and morale.

Hoping to push the borders of shock like he had in Pink Flamingos, John included a few notable ground-breakers in Female Trouble. One was filming a real main-line needle injection—not something fake with those hateful cutaways. It would be the first real mainline ever in a movie. Supposed to be liquid eye-liner, the dark-colored sterile water injection was given to Divine by a friend of Pat's, a "nurse" with a sketchy medical background. It could be dangerous, but good shock requires risk. Unfortunately, Divine's arm was so fat it was impossible to find the vein. John insisted on a good close-up of the fluid slowly emptying from the hypo into the vein, so the nurse kept trying. Poor Divine was stuck over and over like a pin cushion, with black fluid dripping all over his arm. It wouldn't happen, so John finally gave up. In the film, it's not very convincing, and witnessing it, I thought it must have been a much more painful experience for Divine than eating dog poo in Pink.

Another scene where Divine's acting required professional medical assistance was when Taffy (played by long-time Dreamland actress Mink Stole) first meets her father, Earl (played by Divine). Taffy finds Earl living in a hovel, drunk out of his mind, and tries to reconcile with him. Dirty Earl only wants to rape her. After grabbing her, he vomits all over the pretty new dress she had worn to impress him. John wanted this to be cinema's first real vomit scene ever. Movie vomit had always been an actor spitting out a mouthful of Campbell's vegetable soup, and always looked fake. John ideally wanted a quart of real projectile vomit rocketing out of Divine's mouth into Mink's face.

The "nurse" brought several vials of ipecac—a stomach-emptying vomit inducer used only in emergencies. To prepare, Divine ate a quart of vegetable soup and was about to burst. Ipecac is supposed to work immediately, so we shot all the coverage, set the lights and sound, and loaded a new roll of film to be ready for this historic cinematic moment. The nurse opened one vial, the normal dosage, and Divine downed it like a shot of Stolly.

We waited, waited, and waited. Nothing happened. Since Divine was so big, the nurse thought maybe he needed another dose. Always the trooper, Divine agreed, and tossed back one more. Again, we waited for him to signal he was ready to throw up, before rolling the camera. Ten minutes later, there was still no effect. We scratched our heads wondering if Divine might be immune to ipecac. The nurse had one more vial, and John and Divine agreed to try one last time. We sat down to wait, no matter how long it took.

Very soon, Divine said he felt queasy. He looked pretty green, so we rolled the camera. He grabbed Mink and made quiet gurgling vomit sounds, but only a little dribble came out of his mouth. John kept encouraging him, and the camera kept rolling, grinding through hundreds of feet of unusable film. Finally a small mouthful of vomit came out and spilled onto Mink's dress. But Divine was so ill, he could barely stand, and we had shot nearly a day's ration of film.

John said he could live with what we got, but it was not the ground-breaking projectile vomit he had hoped for. We wrapped, and while carrying a case outside, I saw poor miserable Divine leaning against a tree, puking his guts out. The ipecac was working with a vengeance—a half-hour too late.

Female Trouble was not a Screen Actors Guild-approved production. If John had tried these medical stunts with actors under a SAG contract, he would have been arrested for assault. Adding insult to injury, another shot in this scene required a close-up of Earl waving his penis—made-up with bruises and oozing syphilitic sores—at Mink; another John Waters shocker shot. Divine's own penis was deemed too small to fit this premiere role. For once John consented to use a stand-in. Pat's husband, Chucky, was volunteered, and Van dutifully applied the sickly make-up to his stand-in member. John took the camera with Chucky into a back room and discretely got the shot. I've always suspected it was really John's penis. No one witnessed the close-up filming, and John occasionally added secret biographical touches to his movies that only a few close friends would get. Maybe this was one.

I enjoyed observing the production activities like John working with the actors, the crazy beehive hair-dos, excessive make-up, tacky props, and the still photographer who always hovered in the background. I had time to do this because sound recordists on movies have notoriously easy jobs. Ninety-nine percent of the energy on a set goes into camera, lighting, set decoration, and acting. Some shots can take hours to set-up, so the sound crew sits around with little to do. Sound recordists purposefully have carts stacked with intimidating equipment and wires they can fiddle with, so they are immune to accusations of malingering. Astute producers, however, know that if a crew is grumbling, or the women are being delayed because they're being chatted-up, it's probably the sound department looking for something interesting to do.

"They're the only ones with time on their hands, so they're always the root of trouble on the set," a seasoned BBC director once told me.

Sound recording wasn't my goal in film production, nor was picking up girls or stirring up trouble. I did decent work, but met fanatical recordists with electrical engineering degrees who worshiped microphones and EQ curves. That wasn't me. Working on John's set I preferred to make mental notes about how all the things in production could be done more smoothly, with better quality, and cheaper, as I planned to be my own producer-director one day. I was fascinated with how John worked. He knew exactly what he wanted, and was very comfortable with being in charge. He had a strong authoritarian voice, alternately serious and humorous, and never lost his temper. So many directors and actors have screaming fits on sets, but John was always cool and persistent. Not that he didn't worry. When I managed his films, we'd talk on the phone long into the night after the shooting, discussing his worries, problems, and a list of chores he wanted me to do.

John's quirk of memorizing every line and mouthing it as the actors spoke was fascinating to watch, but made the acting pretty stiff, like the actors were puppets. Everyone's lines had the same stilted, sing-songy, delivery. John's usual direction was: "Here, say it exactly like this," and he recited the lines. Since the actors were basically untrained and inexperienced, they did their best to parrot him, but it came across as amateurish.

Divine was a big exception. He was a believable actor, because he had a natural sync between his body and words. In his memoir of Divine, Simply Divine, Bernard Jay, Divine's manager and agent, said he constantly complained about John's lack of direction, compared to other directors he had worked with in New York. He felt lost and frustrated on the set, when John told him, "Just do what feels right to you." I think this was because Divine's character was John's fanatical obsession, and the only character he really cared about. It seemed John modeled all his characters on Divine's persona, so Divine didn't need his lines recited to him, like Edith, Sue Lowe, Mink, and Bonnie, and others in the Dreamland acting ensemble.

John's films are peppered with gifted, talented, or at least notable celebrities in their own fields like Liz Renay, Pia Zadora, Ric Ocasek, Debbie Harry, Sonny Bono, Stiv Bators, Jerry Stiller, and Patty Hearst. But I'd cringe when they recited their lines. In Hairspray, New Line egged John on in his search for recognizable celebrity names to add to the marquee. It didn't matter if they couldn't act. They were firm believers in the Hollywood name cult; that a film could only be successful if it had "names." However, as these non-acting, but well-paid celebrities came and went, I thought the money could have been better spent on quality professional actors or maybe a few lessons for John on how to direct non-actors.

An ironic aspect of John's success is that he never formally studied film, writing, or acting. He never discussed film structure and critical thinking in an academic setting. He never watched other directors working with actors through difficult scenes. He never put in long hours of apprenticeship in an editing room. He never made commercials or puff-piece documentaries to hone his craft. Instead, he read Variety and Hollywood Reporter, learning that shocking scenes and familiar names got media writers' juices going, and notorious publicity was the best road to success. So much for film school. John learned to make movies by watching movies.

And he was right, to a point. John's financial success is not due to the box office income from his movies. He is a well-rounded entertainment entrepreneur who leveraged a raft of notable press quotes from his earlier movies into a lucrative career as an author, visual artist, and live performer. Outside the cultural urban bubbles of the Boston-NY-DC megalopolis, plus Los Angeles, Chicago, and San Francisco, John is hardly known except to the gay community. In one of our many conversations, when I asked him where he wanted his filmmaking career to take him, it wasn't to be an academy-award winning director.

"I want to be a fop," he said (fop: "pejorative term for a foolish man over-concerned with his appearance and clothes; a "man of fashion" who overdresses, aspires to wit, and generally puts on airs, which may include aspiring to a higher social station than others think he has. He may be somewhat effeminate.")

"A what?"

"You know what a fop is?"

"Yes, I was an English major, but why a fop? That's like an insult."

"Oh, but that's why I like it. I want to be a fop."

I looked at his stringy "bacon" hair and loud thrift shop clothes and thought, "He's got a long way to go." Now, when I catch him on late-night talk shows wearing his comic $2,500 Commes des Garçons outfits, his much-thinned hair pomaded to his head, shocking the hosts with his ludicrous opinions, and driving audiences wild with laughter, I think, "Damn, he made it. He is a fop."

Inside Female Trouble

One of the undercurrents during the filming of Female Trouble was money. With the success of Pink Flamingos, the original Dreamlanders began to feel strongly that John was making out financially better and better with each movie, but not sharing it. From Mondo Trasho and Multiple Maniacs, he had been receiving regular income that afforded him a bit higher standard of living than most of the Dreamlanders. Some of them survived with disability payments, maybe a little drug dealing, a little nude modeling, selling art and antiques, hoping a miracle might occur that would provide a comfortable income. Most felt John's movies would pay off one day, so no one wanted to rock the boat.

But with Pink, the money trickle from college rentals that had barely supported John before now turned into a steady stream. Suddenly Pink started playing in multiple theaters and getting regular national press attention. This midnight movie madness, which Pink shared primarily with The Rocky Horror Picture Show, was created by cult followers who saw a film so many times they could recite the dialogue and mimed the scenes on screen. Audience participation was part of the show, and generated a big buzz. Before long, Pink played consistent midnight shows in big-city theaters across the U.S. The houses were packed and lines stretched around the block. It was clear that tens of thousands of people across the U.S. and Europe were seeing this weird little project from Baltimore, and "somebody" must be making big money. How much trickled down to the Dreamlanders? Very little. At least in the beginning.

The trigger of the daily-paid crew on Female Trouble drove the key Dreamlanders, Vince, Divine, Chris , Mink, Bonnie, Pat, and Van to assemble as a group and inform John they deserved a portion of Pink's profits, especially if he wanted them to work on other films, including continuing with Female Trouble. With the earlier films, no written or verbal agreement existed between John and any person or entity. It was a big oversight for John, who was usually meticulous about business details. But since all the royalties were coming to John alone, it was tempting to ignore certain legal obligations to share.

John's actors never signed releases or contracts, and no commercial entity permitted its products or names to be used. While the Dreamlanders could have asked for the sky, it was fortunate for John their approach was mostly friendly and tentative. The situation forced John into finding a good attorney (recommended by his father, naturally), who strongly advised John to immediately lock up the intellectual rights of his work before he was broadsided with huge breach of promise or intellectual property suits. Having no corporation, production insurance or worker's compensation insurance, if something serious had happened on one of his sets, John could have been on the hook personally for millions of dollars.

John had lived a charmed life though. Considering the risks taken in his films: car-driving shots, guns on the set, Divine swimming in a freezing river, the Pink Flamingos trailer bursting into a raging inferno, nothing bad ever happened. From working on dozens of films, I know bad things do happen on them: broken bones, electrical shocks, major property damage, expensive lawsuits from angry neighbors and location owners, stunts gone wrong, car wrecks, drug busts, thefts, statutory rape, large runaway animals, disturbing the peace violations, air-space violations, trade-mark infringement, and child labor law violations. These happen with frightening regularity, and are why movies require tens of millions of dollars of property and liability insurance.

Early in the production of Female Trouble John signed formal agreements giving a generous-looking 25% of all of his films' profits through Pink Flamingos to be split among the original Dreamlanders. All films after Pink paid a flat rate, with no ownership or royalties. The hope was that if Female Trouble was a success, John could raise real money, and pay everyone a decent day rate—on the next one. In the movie biz, sometimes it happens, but usually not. The royalties did help those who were nearly destitute at the time—but it wasn't a living. The shared profits pointedly did not include other income from John's appearance fees at college screenings and film festivals, which increased steadily, and for years dwarfed what he earned from film royalties.

This was a one-time deal, and John was sharp enough to cut the Pink Flamingos pie generously so he wouldn't be considered a cheapskate. At least he did make a real deal. In most no/low budget films, it is extremely rare that anyone receives a profit percentage, even if one has been promised, even with a contract. There are too many ways to hide the profits. It is even rarer to receive a bonus after participating in a surprise success. John's sharing could be a mark of the innocence of the time—of the hippie philosophy that your friends will share with you fairly, even though he expressed distaste for anything to do with the hippie philosophy.

Speaking of taking care of people down the road, when Hairspray the musical became a Broadway hit, and John's celebrity and success reached a new high, New Line released a fancy boxed set of his re-mastered films. Though it had been more than twenty years since I had had contact with New Line, I received a copy in the mail one day, with a personal thank-you message signed by Bob Shaye. Bob had sold New Line to Time Warner/AOL for millions of dollars. He stayed on as the executive producer of the hugely-budgeted Lord of the Rings films. I would have preferred a $10,000 check signed by Bob Shaye in the box, thanking me for the thousands of hours worked on New Line's pre-big budget movies, when we squeezed every penny until it bled. Of my hair-thin share in the profits of New Line's Alone in the Dark, I never saw a penny. Ah, showbiz.

Personal money or the pleasure of travel was not much of an issue for John. In the bars, Dreamlanders noticed that he always had a fresh rum & coke in hand, while they nursed a .50 cent draft as long as they could, then went home because they were out of cash. Unlike other Dreamlanders, John had friends and admirers across the country, who wined, dined, provided drugs, and put him up on his frequent trips to the big cities where his films played. He never left a bar because he'd run out of cash.

With the flow of money and engagements increasing from Pink, John moved from his little row house in a bad part of Baltimore to a once-glamorous, but now worn-at-the-edges apartment building. His apartment was large and spacious, had private parking and a 24-hour security desk. Though in another bad part of Baltimore, it was a step up, and more befitting a rising celebrity. Some people were surprised at and maybe a little jealous with his quick leap from the ghetto. The apartment's desk clerk held an increasing flow of presents and letters from fans, as well as John's dozens of magazine subscriptions while he began to gallivant around the world. She also shielded him against the increasing number of occasional hopeful actors, admirers, and scary freaks who dropped by hoping for an audience with his eminence, the Pope of Trash.

A few Dreamlanders were not so sure of the Pink profit sharing scheme. David Lochary, living in New York City, personally witnessed the crowds attending Pink's midnight showings, the continuous press, and the buzz surrounding the film. Convinced it was making a fortune, he wondered loudly if John was hogging too much of the money. David worked on Female Trouble, but the new faces and sophisticated camera gear fanned his simmering resentment. David sadly died soon after Female Trouble was completed, embittered that the thousands of people who went to see Pink didn't translate into thousands of dollars in his pocket.

The movie business is notoriously sketchy about profits, and many huge successes never make enough "profit" to share according to a contract. Hoping to get an honest and detailed royalty report is a pipe dream. John warned me that New Line didn't send him a royalty check without his calling several times for it. He never understood their accounting and all the vague deductions for "distribution expenses." Worse, New Line's ogre-faced financial officer was a tough cigar chomping wheeler-dealer New Yorker, with a hair-trigger temper who made John's skin crawl. Of course that's who Bob Shaye required John to talk to when he had money questions.

"Everybody in New Line's office gets paid on time. How do they think I pay my rent? New Line gets its money for films that I made and I paid for. Why should I be the last to get paid?" he frequently complained to me. John, the astute businessman, realized that to make real money in the movie business, you had to get it up front. You could not depend on the dishonest food chain of ticket seller, theatre owner, sub-distributor, and distributor to pay fair and timely royalties.

This was the story with my short documentary about Edith Massey, Love Letter to Edie, which featured many of the Dreamlanders, including John. It played every night at the Cinema Village in NYC, and was distributed by New Line to college campuses around America for years. Though royalties were supposed to be paid quarterly, maybe once a year I got a report and a check for a few dollars from New Line. The report never mentioned where the film played or how much it had received in rental per site.

Five years later, when I worked at New Line's office on Union Square in NYC, a sales person told me that Love Letter to Edie was a big success and had gone out with nearly every rental of John's films (which amounted to hundreds of bookings). However, the sales people thought John had made it, so they threw in Love Letter as a freebee, and John got all the royalties. When I asked Sarah, the VP about it, she was shocked (shocked!) that such a thing could happen, and said she'd send a memo out telling the sales people to charge for Love Letter to Edie and credit the income to my royalty account. She didn't mention payment of past royalties due. Not wanting to be a crybaby, I smiled gratefully. Many years later, when I sold the Love Letter to Edie DVD on eBay by myself, I made more money in three years than I did from New Line in twenty-five. Showbiz royalties: as tangible as fog.

Although Female Trouble cost more than twice what Pink Flamingos did, there wasn't a big pay increase for the Dreamlanders. John convinced them that the budgetary increase from $10,000 to $25,000 had to go on the screen, for the better equipment, larger crew, and increased editing expenses. This would pay off eventually because it would increase the likelihood of its success. Sets, props, and costumes had more money with the idea that if every cent appeared on the screen, the film would be more successful, and that would benefit everybody. The Dreamlanders had to go with him again, since there were no real investors. The production cash came from John's pocket, and modest loans from a couple of his well-off Baltimore friends, not big, profit-seeking investors. It was a convincing argument, bolstered by the recent Pink profit sharing deal.

There was no real choice. John was the Dreamlanders' only path in town to fame and fortune. Even Divine, who was pursuing a live performing career in New York and San Francisco, needed Female Trouble to be a hit. Everyone thought movies were where the money was. It was this hunger that made everyone give so much and would make Female Trouble John's best film ever. Female Trouble had a raw, honest innocence and both a frightening and comic reality. It was a gritty, biting commentary on modern life, not so dependent on silly gimmicks like exploding wigs or cheap shocks like eating dog poo.

Female Trouble is the Dreamlanders' favorite film. It is untainted by big money and meddling outsiders from New York and Hollywood. Every scene in Female Trouble is funny or poignant. Divine's character of someone desperate to be famous and loved reflected his own inner-most feelings. Growing up, he was the "queer" who was beaten up and rejected by straight society, but he was now becoming world famous. He'd show those suburban jock bullies, who were probably now suffering through life as frustrated corporate office slaves.

At the end of Female Trouble, when Divine has reached his pinnacle of fame and fries in the electric chair—which was also the last scene shot—everyone on the set had tears in their eyes sensing that the top of a mountain had been reached and everything would be different after that. Indeed everything did change. It was like high school graduation, and it's no accident that the first thing you see when entering John's Baltimore house/museum is the electric chair from Female Trouble. It was his diploma showing that he'd finally made a real movie, just like in Hollywood.

Female Trouble completed shooting around Christmas. There wasn't a real wrap party. We were so green, we'd never heard of such a thing. On the last day, actually evening, after getting a few final pick-up shots, I was driving in a car with John, Divine, and Van and there was discussion of getting a few drinks to celebrate. Everyone was so cold and exhausted after ten full weekends of shooting, we grabbed a six pack of beer from a convenience store to chug-a-lug on our way back downtown. We just wanted to go home and get to bed, grateful that it was over. I hadn't had much time to get socially friendly with any of the Dreamlanders. We had a polite goodbye, and then it was off to my real job in the morning.

Not that there weren't parties. John and the Dreamlanders had held Christmas Eve parties for years. He loved the kind of Christmas that was colorful lights, kitschy decorations, visiting with friends and family, getting and opening piles of presents, and the license for extended drinking. Religion had nothing to do with it. Holy Communion at midnight mass was not on John's Christmas calendar. However, a psychological analysis of Female Trouble might find it full of Christian allusions. John's Catholic upbringing was fertile ground for his obsessions: the bizarre sexual implications of an immaculate conception, the absurdity of a baby savior modeling a jeweled crown, and Christmas' prophecy of Christ's betrayal, trial, last supper, bloody torture, and execution were all part of John's Christmas spirit.

I had always celebrated Christmas with my family, but many of the Dreamlanders did not get along with their families, so to celebrate John's beloved Christmas spirit, they threw themselves a Christmas party. John still holds one in his

Baltimore home, with most of the older faces still attending. He has another later one in New York where the New John's friends are found. After the Dreamland party, John scooted up to his parents' comfortable suburban home, for nicely wrapped practical presents of hardcover books and warm socks to be opened on Christmas morning. He had a big family dinner, where he could entertain with stories of hob-nobbing with celebrities. His family was supportive and amazed by his success, especially considering that his parents had never seen his movies, nor did he want them to.

Because I hadn't had any social interaction with the Dreamlanders yet, I was surprised when John invited me to the Christmas party held after Female Trouble. It was in the spacious and very feminine Fells Point apartment of Dreamland actress Mary Vivian Pierce. John, in a tradition he famously continues, paid for a nice spread of food, and intoxicants, but everyone had to bring a wrapped present. The gifts were put next to the "Christmas Chair." John, wanting to be humorously sacrilegious, decorated a chair instead of a tree with colored lights, tinsel, and ornaments. When he decided to decorate the prop electric chair, I'm not sure if he appreciated the irony of the grim religious symbolism of Christ's being born to die as a sacrificial lamb.

I had to bring a gift, and struggled for days about what it should be. Since it was a secret Santa party, I didn't know who would receive the gift. Should it be a book, or an record album? A bottle of booze? I didn't know anyone's tastes, so those could be bombs. They were such clever and artistic people, I was afraid that whatever I gave would be dismissed as stupidly suburban.

Sitting at my desk at UMBC a few days before the party, I noticed the clapper-board slate used on Female Trouble lying in a corner. Still stuck to it were the pieces of gaffer tape strips saying Female Trouble, Waters as director, and the scene and take numbers of the last shot. The slate was worn out, with deep scratches, chunks knocked off the corners, and a broken hinge. We had other new ones, and this one would be thrown out—but maybe it could be a clever gift. I took it home and wrapped it for the party.

I was the only person from the crew to show up to the party. Not knowing the people well, and still dealing with some remnants of the original Dreamlander suspicions about the newbies, I didn't mix very well. I felt that I was John's special guest, and not really a part of the group. At present-opening time, most were funny little gag gifts from thrift shops, and everybody enjoyed guessing who had brought what. Finally they chose the person who was to get my gift. I hoped like hell that it would be John or Pat or one of the stars at least. Seeing the trivial nature of all the other gifts, I realized that the slate was an important artifact from John's life representing thousands of hours of work by scores of people. It was not just a beat-up slate; it was a museum piece that should definitely go to John. I felt like crap.

I thought about sneaking up to the decorated chair, pulling the wrapped slate under my coat and slipping out. I could give it to John later. But it was too late. The package was handed to an extra who helped carry set pieces. When he opened it, people gasped like it was the unveiling of the Holy Grail. I saw John's and Pat's jaws drop. I was ready to die. Even the recipient said that he didn't deserve it, and tried to give it to John. Being the polite gentleman, John refused it. Of course it could only have come from me, no guessing needed there.

I expected a scene like in Female Trouble where the mother gets thrown into the Christmas tree. Would I be thrown into the decorated chair, tied down with the Christmas lights, and whipped? Would John, like one of his movie characters, jump out of his chair screaming "Gimme that! It's mine, and if I can't have it, nobody can!"

It was especially un-nerving to me because I badly wanted to continue working with John. I wanted to be part of the inner circle. Had I ruined my chance for that? Fortunately, it didn't carry any lingering baggage. I was new and learned an important lesson. John should be treated special, be deferred to, and get the best presents. I got it, and by the look in his eye, I think John knew I did too. By making the effort to come to this intimate party, John recognized my interest in continuing with him. He wouldn't make a scene or burn a bridge over a broken slate. That was not his style.

Female Trouble Post-production

By the time Female Trouble had wrapped, I had a good idea of how a low-budget film should come together. I wanted to produce movies, not just be the sound man. While I coveted Lee and Joe's production management job, it wasn't a sin, because they had made it clear that they did not see working with John as such a big deal. They wanted to make easy money, which John's movies were not. Since Female Trouble had caused trouble with UMBC's film department, it was clear that Lee could not use the university's equipment to make another low-budget movie anyway.

Female Trouble still needed to be edited and finished, which required many months. Lee had a large office which he rarely used, since he was rarely on campus. It had a brand-new $50,000 film editing machine, like the ones used in Hollywood. Lee threw it in as part of the Female Trouble deal, because, except for Richard's all-night editing sessions, it sat idle. John had exclusive use of it for the three or four months it would take to edit Female Trouble.

Charles began editing by himself right after the filming began. In the beginning, it was technical preparation work, cataloging the shots against the script, and matching the sound and picture tracks. Charles' work in Hollywood did not prepare him for the first shots he viewed of Divine strutting down Baltimore's sidewalks, dressed in sparkly drag with his signature half-shaved and half-bleached blonde hairdo. Charles thought it was interesting. Having met John earlier, and knowing that John was not a psycho, made Charles comfortable working with him—or at least intrigued.

John and Charles were both meticulous, prompt, organized, and dedicated workers. Despite Charles' conservative upbringing, he had an appreciation for the bizarre, just as John's enjoyment of being with sophisticated, educated people contrasted with his desire to be the Prince of Puke. Charles edited not only Female Trouble, but also Desperate Living and Polyester. He began editing Hairspray but left after being elbowed out by the new editors New Line brought from Hollywood.

Female Trouble's editing was a business-like process. John and Charles promptly started at 9:00 a.m. and worked through the day with a half-hour lunch before leaving at 5:00 p.m. No one bothered them, despite the fact that the editing room was located around the corner from the Dean's office and his four female office workers. To go to the bathroom, John walked by the department secretaries, and gave a smiling nod if they happened to look up at him. Nobody thought it was a big deal that a professional movie maker was spending months using the State of Maryland's filmmaking equipment. When I was

in the secretarial area and John walked by, I'd see them roll
their eyes or scrunch up their faces behind his back. John's
shoulder-length bacon hair and pencil moustache made it hard
for him not to be noticed. The prim and proper secretaries had
no interest in seeing Pink Flamingos, nor did they want to hear
anything about it—good West-Baltimore Catholic girls that
they were.

Sometimes when working after 5:00 p.m., a curious cus-
todian hung out in the editing room to empty the trash cans.
He looked over John and Charles' shoulders grinning, not at
the picture, but at the film moving through the sprockets of
editing machine. He didn't seem to care about the picture.

"Oh God, I love fil-um," he said in a unique Baltimorese
that put a heavy emphasis on the normally silent "l." "I love
showing dirty fil-ums. Seein' a piece of fil-um, any fil-um, just
touchin' it makes me want some."

It was an interesting fetish and I wondered, if we gave him
a short outtake, would he go to the men's room and abuse
himself? He was John's kind of Baltimore wacko, but he might
be dangerous, and John pantomimed to me behind the guy's
back: Get him out of here. Even now, when someone tells me
that they love films, I wonder precisely what do they mean?

Though working full-time for the arts division, I still had
technical jobs to help with the editing: transferring additional
sound takes, recording sound effects, or fetching editing
supplies. John and Charles never had screenings, nor did John
ever ask for anyone's opinion about the cut. His main demands
were that the movie be exactly 88 minutes long and that it
follow the script exactly. John told Charles precisely what
frame to cut. Charles' important work came when he had to
fix a sequence that had directorial errors—mainly insufficient
coverage. John's inexperienced camera operation haunted

him in the editing room. Mics dipped into frame, close-ups were out of focus, zooms were shaky, and sometimes critical elements were cut off in badly framed shots.

John shot a large amount of footage for a low-budget film, but it was not because he covered a scene from multiple angles, which is the standard movie-making trick that helps cover up problems in the pacing and performances. He shot endless re-takes because his amateur actors could not remember their lines. Edith Massey, the "Egg Lady," was the worst case. Though a sweetheart, she was much older, easily confused, and her short-term memory was pretty bad. This was all part of her charm, but it was difficult for her to memorize John's long speeches. Wasting a lot of film was part of the price to pay for having Edith Massey—who did have a substantial following, and plenty of ink spilled about her. As Newsweek said, "It's not clear whether she deserves an Oscar or a 24-hour nurse."

When we quietly suggested to John that he break up her speeches with close-ups, reaction shots and other coverage so the best takes could be pieced together—like in a normal movie—he absolutely refused. He wanted the wide screen interaction, like a play, with everyone shouting at each other up and down the line he had arranged them in. He wanted to see everyone, in their full costumes and make-up and the eye-shattering sets in the background. That's what his audiences wanted—not cinematic pacing and edited performances. At least that's what he said, but I sometimes wondered if he just didn't know any better. After all, John's first foray into the "arts" was presenting puppet shows at neighborhood kiddie birthday parties. Maybe he could not release himself from the staginess and the control-freak aspect of a puppet show.

My little post-production technical discussions and tasks for John and Charles grew into longer chats and more involvement. In John's earlier films, he always cut the original 16mm film. This left almost no margin for error. Once the original is cut, it can't be changed without cluttering up the image with ugly splice marks. Original film is very susceptible to scratching and dust marks, and can become unwatchable after going through projectors and editing machines hundreds of times.

To avoid these problems, Female Trouble was edited using a "work print"—a disposable copy of the original—so the original would remain untouched until all the editing decisions had been made. The work print, scratched and dirty, is only used as a guide to cut and "match" the original film stock cuts, frame by frame. This ensured a clean original from which the screening prints would be made. Matching was a crucial technical process in making a professional-looking movie.

I asked John if he wanted me to match Female Trouble when the time came. Matching a 90-minute feature was a big job that could take weeks. It was a rare skill in Baltimore, and an expensive one. I had learned how to do it with my earlier short films, so John jumped at my offer to do it for $200. It would have cost him ten times that outside. John turned all the original over to me, which was a big responsibility. The original film rolls represented nearly every penny spent on the movie. There was no back-up copy. If something happened to the original, that was it. I commandeered a lockable cabinet and stored Female Trouble's hundred and fifty 16mm film rolls there.

This joined John and me at the hip. I was in charge of his "original," and I would be the only one cutting into it—like a bris. Now he had something to talk with me about every day. "How is the negative?" "Is it still safe?" "How much more time do you need?"

This business talk turned more social. Charles had already been going to Fells Point to hang out with John, Pat, and other Dreamlanders. They said it was lots of fun, and that I must come down too. I first said I was busy, feeling a little shy, but they both persisted, especially John, who almost pleaded with me to come down and drink with him and the gang. I finally said yes. I would come down and hang out with them at Bertha's Bar. It was a decision that immediately changed my life in ways I couldn't imagine.

3

Getting to Know John

. . . .

John did not go out to bars during the week. After the day's editing, he might go visit Pat, or head home to work on his correspondence, make phone calls, read some of the dozens of magazines he subscribed to, or plow into one of his books. This was before cell phones, e-mail, the Internet, and answering machines (though John had an answering service—remember those?), so evenings were full of catching up. The days were blissfully uninterrupted by cell phone calls, texts, and emails.

Weekends were party time for John, especially Friday night, and Fells Point was the destination. The Point is one of Baltimore's oldest neighborhoods, a working class jumble of houses mostly built in the 1800s. Its cobblestone streets were built before the Civil War, and its industrial heritage was accented by freight trains that crept by on tracks in the center of the streets. When I lived there in the mid-late 1970s, it was home to mostly first and second-generation East European immigrants who worked at the docks, breweries and factories that lined the busy waterfront. They kept scores of tiny bars and shops in business. It was a real place with real people doing real jobs, not a gentrified tourist destination.

Fells Point was in a steep decline in the 1960s. Factories closed and the younger generation fled to the green lawns and suburban car culture. The last nail in the coffin was an eight-lane Interstate highway spur that was planned to run right through it. Urban renewal money purchased dozens of the red brick 18th and 19th century row houses for tear-down. An industrial bakery that still makes millions of McDonald's hamburger buns gobbled up ten square blocks of irreplaceable historic houses for its sprawling, windowless factory. Most other businesses had closed. A few slumlords picked up many of the buildings not yet taken by urban renewal, hoping to flip them for a profit as the road got closer. On its north side, Fells Point was bordered by scary, rundown housing projects that were havens for drug dealers and single welfare moms raising bands of at-risk kids.

It was an end-of-the-world scene, with a bleak future. But such negatives were positives for Baltimore's more adventurous (and broke) students, artists, and bohemians of the 1960s. The slumlords rented the artists houses, apartments, and storefronts for next to nothing, as long as they didn't ask for improvements or repairs. A few surviving bars catered to visiting sailors, and the quirky ethnic left-behinds, but with the influx of the young hipster artists, new places opened to cater to them. A little artist scene quickly developed, with a night life unique to Baltimore, that combined a post-modern end-of-the world setting, cheap drinks, and interesting locals to gawk at. These artist bars like Berthas, The Horse You Came In On, and Ledbetters had a very temporary feel. Plaster walls crumbled exposing old brick. Torn out ceilings exposed old wooden rafters, and strings of Christmas lights were the main lighting. 1950s style juke boxes filled with tunes from the 30s through the 60s were turned to max volume, so all conversations had to be shouted. It was Baltimore's own Greenwich Village, but only about two blocks big when I first visited.

A local group, which had rescued a few of the older buildings banded together in the 70s to save Fells Point. They stopped the road, and it became an upscale, gentrified tourist destination famous around the world, complete with water taxis, a Ten Thousand Villages store, and gelato bars.

One of the first artist settlers in Fells Point was John's art director, Vince Peranio. He and a few of his young friends from the Maryland Institute of Art, looking for a large cheap space for their painting and sculpture projects, rented an abandoned industrial bakery space in the heart of Fells Point. It was a classic artist find, and the price beat New York hands down. The bars and lunchrooms were ridiculously cheap. But because of the planned road, none of them envisioned a future there; you had to go to New York to be an artist anyway. But in the meantime, it was cool being in a funky old neighborhood, right on the waterfront, where on a foggy night, you could imagine glimpses of Edgar Allen Poe stumbling down the old cobble stone streets grasping a bottle of amontillado in one hand.

Fells Point's development in the 1970s and early 80s was a slow transformation. Initially it was more about hippie kids escaping the suburbs. Its central feature was a municipal market with a dozen vendors selling meat, fish, vegetables, and baked goods. They served cheap, locally-made Polish sausages from Pollack Johnny's, and "coddies"—a Baltimore-style deep fried potato and fish ball.

Fells Point had everything. It had its own porno movie theater. Across the street was the Broadway, which showed second-run films, and hosted live music shows. It had a little community theater, a stripper bar, one of Baltimore's few lesbian bars, country music bars, Spanish, Greek, Polish, and seafood restaurants, genuine pan-handling bums, a nationally-known abstract-expressionist painter, Grace Hartigan, after-hours clubs, a head shop, and several thrift shops. It was a perfect nurturing spot for the Dreamland ethos.

For his film, Multiple Maniacs, John needed a giant prop lobster and heard that Vince Peranio and his two brothers were handy metalworkers with an artistic flair. John took a trip to Vince's Fells Point studio, fell in love with the little art colony, and hired Vince to make the prop lobster, named "Lobstora." This began John's enduring relationship with Vince as his art director. The look of John's early movies is probably 90% Vince. The garish wallpapers, tacky furniture, and cheesy home décor are all Vince. Vince grew up in working-class Baltimore, and was infused with its kitsch, which combined with his private art school education, has made him one of the most original art directors working in edgy movies and TV, ever.

When a local community group dedicated to saving Fells Point started making headway to preserve the historic neighborhood, real estate values and rents began to rise. The bakery decided to renovate, so Vince found a very cheap, very rare wooden house from the 1700s on a tiny alley street and moved in with his girlfriend, a flamboyant clothing designer, Delores DeLuxe, who had just returned to Baltimore from Los Angeles. This ended his long-time romantic relationship with Mink Stole, though they remained good friends, and Delores and Mink actually shared a chic collectable business in Fells Point for a while.

Word spread about this new little group, and many of the Dreamlanders moved to Fells Point. Edith Massey had moved there well before Vince. She worked as a bar maid, and her friendly, unassuming manner charmed the artists who drank in her bar, Pete's Hotel. Pete's was a spare little place that opened at 7:30 a.m. to serve cheap Baltimore-brewed "Natty Boh" beer to the third shift dock workers and alky down-and-outers who wandered through the Point.

Dreamlanders Mink, Bonnie Pierce, George Figgs, Bob Adams, Sue Lowe, Paul Swift, Chris Mason, and Peter Koper lived within a few blocks of each other. It was Fells Point's café society. Notably missing were John and Pat, who preferred the more refined, more gay-influenced uptown culture. John had moved to his apartment building because of its better security and anonymity. He didn't like the idea of living in the cramped Fells Point row house culture, and of continually displaying his higher income to the people he needed to make his movies. His ability to eat every meal at a restaurant, always have gas in his car, and go to movies every night would cause friction with the Fells Point Dreamlanders, most of whom in those days could barely buy food, or afford a car that ran more than a few blocks without breaking down—much less spend summers in Cape Cod, like John. The best they could do about Baltimore's hot and humid summers was to visit "Tar Beach"—the flat roof top of their row house, and squirt each other with a hose.

John and Pat, however, did like the Fells Point night life. Bertha's bar and restaurant was their meeting spot. It was the Dreamland Country Club clubhouse, and everyone was there. Every Friday night, from about 10:00 p.m. to 1:00 a.m., John and Pat held court in Bertha's, catching up with friends, and meeting out-of-town visitors. Bertha's had cheap drinks and the tiny restaurant in the rear served pretty innovative food by a friendly gay chef. I think he introduced vinaigrette to Baltimore. They were also famous for their "Eat Bertha's Mussels" bumper sticker, a badge of double-entendre edginess that signified the time and place.

Becoming Chummy

I'd never been to Fells Point. The idea seemed a bit too wild for a settled suburban guy who preferred staying at home with his girlfriend and a bottle of Mateus; whose idea of an evening out was a quiet suburban mall bar for a few beers with friends. But John pressed the issue, asking that I come down, telling me how much fun it was. I first went down with my girlfriend. Bertha's was full of artist types, and everyone had a pose or costume totally estranged from the "real" world I had been occupying. My world admired sensitive, earthy, people like Arlo Guthrie, Bob Dylan, and Joni Mitchell. It was bearded guys with flannel shirts who ate homemade granola, and played lap dulcimers. The women were mostly braless hippie chicks with long skirts and ironed blonde hair who wrote poetry. This was not Fells Point's Dreamlander culture.

Bertha's was a thin row-house bar, packed shoulder-to-shoulder on weekends. Its loud jukebox, heavy drinkers, smoky air, shrieking laughter, and wildly dyed hair was another world. The wardrobe required was gaudy-flashy for the women, and selected thrift shop cool for the men. My flannel shirt was definitely o-u-t.

John was genuinely pleased to have me there. He met my girlfriend and was very nice to her. She was smart, articulate, had survived a troubled blue collar family, was a little butch, and chain-smoked. John liked those kinds of people. But it was not her scene, and though she admired John, she preferred having him over for a quiet dinner party. The Fells Point bar scene was too visceral and over the top.

To me, the music, smoke, loud chatter, and dim lighting was a refreshing circus that stimulated every sense. I loved the absurdity of shouting into each other's ears, trying to be heard over the jukebox. I loved how the busy bartenders worked the large crowd. I had been stuck in the suburbs for about a year and a half, watching my big dream of going to New York slipping through my fingers. I wanted excitement. I loved to travel, I loved to hang out in bars and cafes, and I'd been to Europe four times, the last time bumming my way from Paris to Istanbul and back. I wanted adventure. I'd hook high school and ride the train to New York City to look at electric guitars on Music Row. I'd spent four years in DC and thought my next stop would be New York. Suddenly Fells Point re-awakened my urban dream.

John clued me in right away that if I tipped the Bertha's bartenders a quarter for every drink, I'd receive immediate attention and get every fourth one free. I immediately felt like a seasoned regular. Tequila Sunrise was the fashionable drink, but John stuck religiously to rum and coke. He was pleased to see that I liked them too, but I didn't want to mimic him, so I stuck mostly to the Tequila Sunrise, or a gin and tonic. A huge glass of jug wine was a buck, which is what we drank when feeling particularly arty. A bottle of Pabst the same. There were no suburbanites, jocks, or girls in Hunt Cup hats and pink dresses with nice hair. It was a new city crowd; people on the edge. I loved it and couldn't wait to go back.

My girlfriend let me know that she would not go back, and this was a big turning point. Every Friday night from then on I was in Fells Point with the Dreamland gang soaking up the funky Baltimore arts scene alone. Eventually people stopped asking why she was never with me. In a way, it was a business decision, so I didn't think it would influence my relationship very much, but within a year, we developed two sets of friends, and finally decided to split.

On weekends, the Dreamland group started at Bertha's, around 10:00 p.m., and soaked up the booze until it closed at 1:00 a.m. They'd shoo us out and we'd walk almost as a group to Zeppies, a very un-artistic waterfront Polish bar that was usually nearly empty, that is until the circus of Dreamlanders and their entourage charged in the door for the last hour.

Zeppies was dull, but it was open until 2:00 a.m. and by 1:00 a.m. everyone was pretty drunk. As a bonus, Zeppie's drinks were half the price of Bertha's. You got a Pabst draft for a quarter. Hardboiled eggs on the counter were a dime, and bags of Utz potato chips were a nickel. We were tossed out in the street at two, but you could buy a six pack of Natty Boh for a buck and a half and take it with you.

Leaving Zeppies with our six-packs, we stumbled over to Eddie's place. Eddie Peranio was Vince's younger brother and a budding singer/actor who lived in an ancient sail-makers' loft a few doors down from Zeppie's. We'd go there for a few more drinks, and maybe a little pool played on Eddie's stained and lopsided pool table. Eddie played his beloved collection of Rockabilly music on a big stereo with ripped speakers. Friday night ended around four in the morning when most people had passed out.

The ground floor of Eddie's loft was the Fells Point gate company where the Peranio brothers had a metal working shop. It was grimy and we had to stumble over greasy piles of twisted metal to get to Eddie's loft. It was a real let down— Bumberg at its worst—a real shock that no, you weren't in New York or Hollywood, but Baltimore's smelly waterfront with Polish alkies and mean bikers. Eddie's loft was a long way from a cozy loft in Soho or the Mudd Club in New York, where I'd be spending late nights a few years later.

John usually disappeared from Zeppies, after a few more 50 cent rum and cokes, avoiding the genuine tawdry Baltimoreness of Eddie's loft. It was rumored that he cruised the meat rack along Eastern Avenue. His mysterious exit ended the camaraderie, and it amazed me that John could turn it off and on so quickly; to disappear into the night into his own private world, after being so public and chummy all night.

It was during these many nights in Fells Point that John told me most of the public stories that can be read in his two books and many articles about him. He told me how he grew up with stiff, regal parents in the most historically significant mansion in the wealthy district of Lutherville about ten miles from the Baltimore City line. His parents had tried to insulate him from the city's bad influences as a child. But Baltimore's suburbs were actually full of boys and girls itching to break bad. The ideal was to have sex, cigarettes, and alcohol before you were a teenager, so as not to waste one minute of fun. In the baby boom generation there were plenty of bad examples in every neighborhood more than happy to show you how to have sex, inhale a cigarette, snitch a $20 from your mom's purse, and drain your father's liquor bottles a quarter-inch at a time.

The youthful anger and resentment in the 1950s created the sassy "Drape" culture that Waters admired and made a part of so many of his movies. Drape was Baltimorese for "greaser." They were guys who wore black leather motorcycle jackets, dyed their hair black, and styled it with Wildroot Cream Oil in a classic 1950s duck-ass. They might have had a motorcycle, but more likely a customized hot rod. They smoked unfiltered cigarettes, drank whatever they could find, wore jeans as tight as a second skin, and were way-cool bad role models for the tweeners. Crybaby shows the mythic Drapes vs. Squares conflict that defined much of John's teenagerhood.

I grew up in that same culture with John: educated suburban family but attracted to the wild lower-middle class culture. It appealed to John, but I lived in a lower-class neighborhood, and I couldn't get away from it. My mother, a liberal educated Protestant whose parents had grown up in Wales couldn't wait to get me away from the neighborhood of Irish Catholic bullies, alkies, petty thieves, and two-faced perverts. My neighborhood was full of Eddie Haskells. The worst girls disappeared to nunneries to have babies in secret. The worst boys disappeared into military school after punching a teacher or getting caught in a b&e.

I didn't get along so well with that crowd. My family had violated one of its cultural taboos. My mother had graduated from college and taught school instead of staying home doing laundry, watching soap operas, and beating the hell out of her children for not going to Friday night confession. I'd been typecast as a pansy, and been beaten up too many times because my mother taught French to find the mean Drapes very appealing.

John's upscale neighbors weren't the kind to beat him up because his mother had a toney accent, or his father owned a big company. He would have been a very different person if he had had the shit kicked out of him as much as I had by the bullies in my neighborhood. Divine, who came from a working class family was beaten up for being a "swish" by the same groups.

Nevertheless, when John told me of sneaking out at night with friends, hooking school, drinking, smoking cigarettes, and having sex at first opportunity, and I identified with it. In fact some of John's friends were some of the older hellions from my old neighborhood. Growing up less than 10 miles from each other was a bond.

Ironically, most of the key Dreamlanders had good relationships with their parents. John and Pat loved when my father visited the sets and got into conversations with him. My father, a traditionalist who worked for a finance company and wore a suit every day, frowned on artists or beatniks, generally, but John was a success; respectful, well-spoken, and obviously well brought-up. To my father, all could be overlooked if you were a success.

Many of the kids I had grown up with had horrible relationships with their parents. They had regular screaming battles and even fist fights in their front yards with them. They stole from them, and ultimately separated themselves from them completely, often to escape their alcoholic rages.

But John, Pat, Vince, Divine, Mink, and Bonnie maintained peace with their parents, and enjoyed meeting their friends' parents. Given the nature of Waters' films, you'd think parent-child relationships would be train wrecks—like Divine and her parents in Female Trouble, when she pushed the Christmas tree on her mother because she didn't get cha-cha heels for Christmas. Dreamlander parents didn't actually hang out with the kids, and certainly not when they were acting up. They wouldn't see John's films, but the parents were delighted to share in their kids' success and were there when the kids had a major health or financial setback. Many dutifully visited their parents on Sunday afternoons, almost as a respite from their frantic weekday lives as over-the-edge artists. If you hated your parents, and they hated you, you would not fit into the Dreamland crowd.

Saturday night was usually a night away from Fells Point. John, Pat, and Charles never showed. It was movie night or art opening night, or just time to stay home, avoid the crowds, and recuperate. I would often go out with Bonnie Pierce (better known as Mary Vivian Pierce, John's earliest best friend, actress, and muse) on Saturday nights. She loved the high culture of opera, ballet and symphonies, and I was one of the few friends who appreciated them too.

Many times we didn't have money for such high-toned entertainment, and she taught me the fine art of "second-acting." We would dress up in our finest clothes, and hang out at Bertha's for a few drinks. Around 8:30 pm, we'd jump in my car and race up to the Symphony Hall. When we got there, we'd stand out front chatting and smoking cigarettes. A few minutes later the doors would burst open and people dressed in their symphony-appropriate finery would pour out onto the broad sidewalk and light up too. We'd blend into the crowd, and when the intermission ended we were swept back into the theater with them. The ushers never checked ticket stubs, and we'd hang back until just before curtain and then race down the aisle to pick a pair of great seats that had been abandoned by a couple who didn't like the show. We'd frequently get dirty looks, being new faces and obvious seat stealers, from people sitting next to us, but it was always an exhilarating experience, and we never got kicked out.

Sunday morning was Dreamland breakfast time in Fells Point. John, Pat, and Chuck had breakfast at Jimmy's, a wonderful Greek greasy spoon right next to the tugboat dock. Before I moved to Fells Point, I made the trip downtown for breakfast with them. John insisted I attend this most inner circle gathering. About eight came to breakfast, but they were mostly Pat's friends from uptown. Eating breakfast out was unaffordable for most of the Fells Point Dreamlanders, even at cheap Jimmy's. Plowing through their bacon and runny eggs, John and Pat regaled the group for two hours with gossip, their takes on current events, the arts and fashion scene,

Baltimore's gay culture, and new press reports about the films. Pat was a tough Baltimore character and a true eccentric. She never learned to drive a car, but was a fearless and daring entrepreneur with flaming red hair and a hair trigger Irish temper. Pat's razor sharp wit was poetic and original, and appeared to be one of John's major inspirations. Charles and I thought many times that Pat's words of wry cynicism, outrage, and shock were the seed of John's scripts, and he was merely taking dictation.

We were all twenty-something and felt on the cusp of a new and exciting art movement. I got to know John, Pat, Chuck, Peter Koper and the rest of the breakfast club very well, and they honestly welcomed me, tightening up to make room at their table, including me in their conversations, grilling me about my past, and asking about my future plans.

I seemed to be a safe friend. I had a full-time job at the university, was financially secure, didn't look like a monster, and was well brought up. Above all, I was going out of my way doing an increasing amount to help John through Female Trouble's post-production, for which they were grateful. They all knew he was special and wanted him to succeed.

Post-production of Female Trouble ended without much incident. We did introduce several basic cinematic technologies to John. First was dialogue "looping." For some reason, a dozen of Divine's lines as Earl had been unusable. John panicked, but we assured him the lines could be easily re-recorded in a few minutes in a studio. Several short scenes with other actors needed audio re-takes, so one day we all piled into John's old brown Buick and drove to one of the few recording studios in Washington, DC that could do looping. The recording engineer, Nelson Funk, a buttoned-up audio geek with a small studio in Georgetown, usually recorded sound for government training films. Now a pack of America's weirdest filmmakers, including Divine himself had arrived to brighten his day. We wondered if he would throw us out when he saw what the film was all about.

Nelson didn't know what to make of Divine's redneck screaming of "Oh go fuck yourself. I don't owe you nothin'!" He handled the session very professionally though. John wrote a check for the bill, and we arranged to return for Nelson to mix all the sound tracks. He surprised us by saying he looked forward to seeing the whole movie. He said his next job was a film for the CIA—one of his more usual clients, who were waiting in their suits and ties in the lobby. Their eyes bulged when our troop walked past them.

Three weeks later when we returned for the four-hour sound track mixing session, Nelson enjoyed it thoroughly and laughed out loud in all the right places. It must have been the most fun job he'd done in a very long time. It was a good sign, since he was the only "test" audience Female Trouble ever had.

As he did with his other films, John pulled the soundtrack music from 45 rpm records in his friends' collections. He didn't know about the federal copyright law that required licensing music. Dreamland Studios was such an outlaw operation that it couldn't be bothered with getting permission to do anything—that would violate the whole spirit of the operation. It is amazing that Pink Flamingos played around the world for decades without paying for a license to use the infamous music on the sound track. But in a big way, John's using twenty-year-old obscure novelty pop songs for a sound track was ground breaking. In the 1970s, after a pop song fell off the charts, it was gone. There was no such thing as "oldies" stations, and song writers and publishers apparently couldn't be bothered to chase down money for usage of their back catalog. They were blind to anything but current hits. John's films played in dozens of theaters every day. Some songs were well known like the Rivington's Pa Pa Oom Mau Mau, which accompanied the singing asshole scene and How Much Is That Doggie in the Window, used as background for Divine's dog-doo eating scene. New Line, a multi-million dollar company worried a little about it, but not enough to get permission and pay licensing fees. It was just so new, no one thought that much about it.

George Lucas changed mainstream sound track music when he used clips from nearly 40 songs in American Graffiti, released in 1973. It was a huge success and gave everybody the idea to pad soundtracks with oldies. It woke the record companies up to the fact that their vaults were goldmines, and the awareness of the practice and the price tag went up quickly. Suddenly the thought of being sued started keeping John up at night. We talked about this a lot. When he learned that the record companies could come after him and it could be really expensive for him, he was shocked. He didn't have the money to buy rights for anything, much less hire a lawyer to negotiate a good deal. He hoped that the songs he had selected for Female Trouble were so obscure that even their copyright owners would have forgotten them. It seemed a safe bet.

Theater owners, who were making big money from the new midnight film thing, assumed the music had been licensed, and colleges would be the last to rat on an underground hero. New Line Cinema's lawyers knew there was a problem, but thought John was a fluke, and swept the music problem under the rug. No doubt, John had signed a contract with them assuming all liability for licensing any way. Nobody wanted to rock Pink's money-making boat, so it was left alone for another day.

After Female Trouble, John was so stressed that he vowed to do only original music on his future movies. Unfortunately, his audiences loved his crackpot collection of oldie novelty songs, and the music was a big part of the success of his films. Desperate Living and Polyester had cheap, but lush, post-scored symphonic tracks that sounded very Hollywood, which John insisted on. But they were both box office disappointments, and no one ever mentioned the music—though it was produced by two very talented groups. John learned his lesson, and built a large music licensing budget into Hairspray to win back that portion of his audience. And it worked.

John finally hired an attorney and bought music licenses for his films when DVDs became popular, and more Hollywood movies used nearly forgotten tunes from the 50s-70s as hip soundtracks. Overnight, record companies realized there was big money in their back catalogs, and started checking every DVD to find violations. John knew the jig was up, and paid a lot to license the tracks for his old movies. By then, he could afford it. John was making big creative fees per movie, and New Line was raking it in on the Nightmare on Elm Street series. They made it seem like an honorable thing, but the longer he waited, and the bigger the celebrity he became, the more he would likely have to pay. In my most angry hours after being pushed from John's movies after Hairspray, I contemplated reporting the piracy. But I could never stoop so low.

Female Trouble's title song (called Female Trouble) was its only piece of legal music. With Divine's growing performing career, John thought an original song would help the movie, and maybe one day become an income stream. Charles offered one of the many songs he had produced when he was in Los Angeles, trying to break into the record business. He still had reels of high-budget, professionally written, arranged, and recorded tracks stored in an LA studio, and agreed to give John a song for free, if John wrote the lyrics, and they would equally share any royalties. Divine was in LA at the time, and took a taxi one afternoon to the studio to overdub the vocals. John and Charles listened to the session on the telephone from their editing room at UMBC; another technological breakthrough for John.

Unfortunately, Divine only occasionally hit the right notes. He was basically tone deaf. For the camp audience it was great, but Charles' producers were mainstream Hollywood award-winners. Seeing the 350 lb. Divine with his shaved head, in his usual flouncy pants and oversized shirt, and listening to John's psycho lyrics like "I'm berserk, I like it fine, As long as I'm making headlines," they thought Charles had lost his mind and was working with a Manson-like cult in Baltimore. The producers worked hard to make Divine sound professional, using thick reverb and doubling his tracks, but they couldn't change the many flat notes (this was well before Autotune). To finish with some semblance of professionalism, they resorted to Divine reciting the lines, not singing them, making Female Trouble one of the first rap songs ever—accidentally.

The music had been acquired, the original had been cut, and the first print had been struck. Female Trouble was finally ready for its big Baltimore premiere. Having cut the original, I was in charge of the first and only print, and delivered it to the projection room of a downtown college auditorium where Pink had premiered two years earlier. John, Pat, and other friends had spent the days and nights before "wild posting," that is taping and stapling Female Trouble posters around town—a Dreamland tradition. Three shows were scheduled that night. Lines were around the block, and the audiences were dressed to the nines and high as kites.

It was a big hit. The script carried the audiences along, laughing where we had hoped, and in several places we hadn't expected laughs. John's experiment with moving away from his "freak show" premise and toward a solid story with complex (if totally nutty) characters seemed to be a success and we felt he had moved up the next rung on the ladder of success.

John's brother ran the box office. I had never met him, but with $10,000 cash funneling in that night, John only trusted family for that job. John didn't have to share the take with anyone; not his cast, crew, distributor, sub-distributor, or theater-owner. He would make back nearly half of the film's budget in one night, and there was still the second night's take to come. In 1974, that was a year's salary, so it gave John plenty of financial breathing room. Although he had a distribution deal with New Line for Female Trouble, he had reserved the income from the Baltimore and Provincetown premieres for himself. Given the reality of most distribution deals, it was probably the only money he would see from Female Trouble for a long time.

With John's next film, Desperate Living and all of his future films, when investors needed to be paid back, the cash cow premieres were eliminated. But, John began to receive a guaranteed salary, a cash advance, and most important, worldwide distribution backed by advertising and PR, and free trips to dozens of premieres and film festivals. This would open the door to book deals, personal appearance fees, acting jobs, art shows, and magazine article commissions. These are the perks of America's celebrityhood empire. They would dwarf the royalties he earned from his films. Maybe one day John will lend his name to a perfume line. John Waters' #2 maybe?

Despite the good vibes, Female Trouble was still an underground movie, destined to play only in colleges and big city art houses with 16mm projectors. Blowing it up to 35mm was not considered an option because it would cost more than the production budget and New Line mainly distributed to colleges and art houses anyway.

Although it did well, Female Trouble didn't have the cult repeat audiences of Pink Flamingos. Audiences enjoyed it, and the underground press liked writing about it, but it did not reach the level of Pink's big three shocking scenes: beautiful Elizabeth Coffey's half-removed dick (before his sex change was complete), the singing asshole, and Divine's dog shit chow-down. With Pink, audiences returned time and again because they couldn't believe their eyes the first time, and dragged their friends along too, promising a "you won't believe this" experience. Female Trouble was a much more intellectual film, with a real plot and character development, which pushed it more into the realm of lower-grossing art movies.

New Line was not looking for an art movie, but was pleased enough with the reception, and happier that John was heading in a more respectable direction. He had proved he could follow-up with a better looking, almost professional production. Most important, Female Trouble didn't have Pink's graphically distasteful content that would embarrass New Line's Upper West Side friends. Female Trouble was witty, had intellectual content, and social commentary—and it got good reviews. Maybe John could become more mainstream and help Bob Shaye obtain his goal of becoming one of the world's most successful movie producers.

As New Line's golden boy, John started writing his next film, hoping to shoot within a year. New Line promised to put up a good chunk of the money. John had crossed the Rubicon, but it was not going to be an easy path to fame and fortune for either him or New Line.

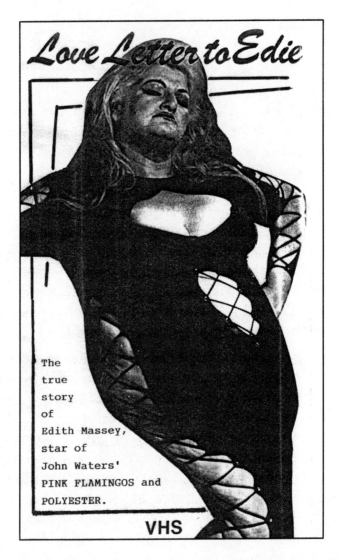

*My first home-made cover for my Love Letter to Edie VHS
video that I photocopied in black and white and advertised in
Rolling Stone magazine's classified ads. I sold 100 copies before
it went to a distributor who sold many hundreds, but never sent
me a penny in royalties. I have sold "Director's Edition" DVDs
on e-Bay for several years and made more money than I ever
received from any of its distributors.*

Love Letter to Edie

After the release of Female Trouble, I continued my job at UMBC, but was restless to move on. I continued partying in Fells Point, even though John was away at screenings many weekends. I had made new friends there, especially with Edith Massey, who ran a little thrift store/junk shop, Edith's Shopping Bag, three doors up the street from Bertha's bar. I had saved some money and got the idea after listening to Edie's stories to make a little documentary about her life. She was in her late 50s at the time, and had a lot of problems. She was overweight, ate terrible food, had rotting teeth, and barely survived on what she earned in the store. Bob Adams, an original Dreamlander, shared the first quirky shop with Edie. He was a sharp antiques and collectible dealer. As a "movie star," Edith drew the weekend bar crowd. Bob sold old baseball cards, movie star portraits, Pink Flamingos posters, T-shirts, and antique toys, and especially campy "junque" he found by prowling Baltimore's many thrift shop gold mines of bad taste collectibles.

Edie had led a unique life. She grew up in an orphanage in Colorado during the Great Depression, where they skimped on food but the rod wasn't spared. She bounced from foster home to foster home until she ran away as a teenager to Hollywood to see if she could get a job in the movies. That didn't work out, but she did get involved in the underworld of LA's strip joints, bootlegging, prostitution, and organized crime—and made it her life. Edie fled a couple bad marriages and worked her way east, waitressing in mob-run bars, and was a madam in a brothel outside Chicago. She even had a bar of her own in Tishamingo, Okalahoma, but couldn't make a go of it. She headed to Baltimore in the late 50s because she heard "nothing but bars were there."

This was when the notorious "Block" of stripper bars, porno peep shows, and dirty book stores was packed with sailors, travelling salesmen, and curious diplomats from Washington, DC. The "Block" was anchored by the infamous stripper and mistress of Louisiana's Governor Huey Long, and Edith worked at many of its clubs, as bar maid and a B-girl. A "B-girl" was a sexy chick who perched on a bar stool and convinced drunken rubes to buy her $50 bottles of champagne. The champagne was actually ginger ale, and the b-girl split the $50 with the house. For independent-minded gals in Baltimore, it was a respectable living, with higher status and much less risk than a hooker.

Edith began to lose her looks, figure, and teeth, and besides, as she said "the cops got hot against the girls for soliciting drinks," so she figured it was time to move on. She landed in Fells Point serving beer to night shift workers at Pete's Hotel bar when it opened at 7:00 a.m., and eventually the new artist crowd in the evenings. This is where she met John, and because of her old-world charm and world-worn looks he asked her to be in his movie, Multiple Maniacs. Of course, this fulfilled her secret life-long dream of acting in the movies. Her bold manner, tucked into her short, round frame, along with her goofy nearly toothless smile gave her a charm that John pounced on, and earned her millions of fans around the world. What a great subject for a documentary. I decided it would be my first real film—Love Letter to Edie—after the hundreds of fan letters she received from her role in Pink Flamingos as Edie the Egg Lady.

I wanted to make a dramatic film, so I decided to re-enact Edie's funniest stories interspersed with a few interviews. I didn't have enough money to make a feature film, so I aimed for a short, about 15 minutes long. Maybe it could play with his films, and I would include many of John's stable of actors as bit players.

When I asked John what he thought of the idea, he was initially nervous. He had been working with his exclusive troupe for nearly ten years, and I was the first to intrude with this request. Though I had become close, it had only been for a few months, and they weren't sure of my motive or how Dreamland would be portrayed. John said OK, but insisted I show him the cut before I finished.

The Dreamlanders jumped at the chance to work with a different director on another movie. Mink Stole and Pat Moran played Edith's evil step sisters. Vince Peranio, his brother Eddie, Delores Deluxe, and other Fells Point characters had parts too. Dawn Davenport's home set from Female Trouble still stood in the room above Pat's store, so we shot an interview with Edith there. John did a short sincere statement in front of Pete's Hotel praising Edie as a great American character. Edith thought it was her great chance for celebrityhood, and was game as always, for anything.

I spent many Saturday mornings in Edith's store, doing research on the story, and she happily prattled on about her life while I sipped a cup of coffee. I sat back pretty far, because her store cat, Lovey, sat like a guard dog on the counter. If I got too close, Lovey would hiss and growl, and Edie would jerk her leash to keep her in line, like a lion tamer. Lovey was like this with everyone. Assuming that Edie would only keep a nice cat on the counter, customers would reach out to pet Lovey and get the same hissing and growling treatment. Edie would shout at them not to touch the cat "because it's mean." Lovey was not so lovey after all.

I scribbled notes on my yellow pad, and then typed short scripts for the re-enactments and her interviews. Edith was a fearless video interviewee, and could go on for hours. Pity that film was so expensive and I couldn't afford more than one hour of 16mm film for the whole project. When people tell me I should make an extra for the DVD with the outtakes, I say there were none. We used it all but the slates—and even used one of those.

I got very close with Edith. My house in Fells Point was a few blocks from hers. I gave her many rides when she needed them. I visited her when she was sick; brought her sandwiches and cups of coffee. Her home was a miserable row-house apartment filled with junk and feral cats rescued from sewers and dumpsters. They ate from giant bowls, overflowing with the cheapest cat food pellets. They perched on any blank space, copulated right in front of you, and fought screeching fights, while Edith yelled, "Stop that Mr. Purr, be a nice kitty!"

The air was choking. Edith liked warmth, so the big gas space heater burned full blast, drying the air out like a sauna; literally vaporizing cakes of dust off the threadbare overstuffed furniture. Coupled with the poop and piss of a dozen cats, and the insect spray she used against giant "cock-a-roaches," the air was like mustard gas. I spent as little time as possible in her house, sure that one day I would visit, and she'd be lying on the floor, mummified, while the cats perched high on her belly patiently waiting for their dinner.

When Love Letter to Edie was nearly finished, John came to UMBC for a private screening. He thought the film was OK, but very different from his films. He might have been a little jealous seeing his cast acting with such gusto in a different film. I wanted to cut one reality scene in Edith's store where a couple of the tough Dreamlander friends confronted a black guy who they suspected of stealing something (not that there was much worth stealing). It was very real, and you expect to see fists fly as Edith pleads for them to stop. I told John I thought it didn't fit, with its racist tinge, but he thought it was the best scene in the film. Confrontation and violence was good box office. It was a scene the press would write about, so I should definitely keep it in. Not wanting to ignore his advice it stayed. It is one of the most noted scenes, and people regularly ask if it was scripted. When I say it was real, they're not sure what to say, they're so shocked. John's touch.

Soon after, I set up a private premier screening for Dreamlanders-only in Eddie Peranio's loft, the Dreamlanders' unofficial after-hours club. They applauded loudly at the end, and it broke any remaining barrier to my entering the Dreamland inner circle. Their fears that I might make them look dumb, mean, silly, and incompetent were proven wrong. It was a big relief to me, and encouraged my impossible dream of producing John's next film.

John helped me get Love Letter into theaters. We started with the Cinema Village in New York, where Pink had been playing midnights for years. The theater owner loved Love Letter and booked it as a short subject with Pink. I was in seventh heaven. I was paid maybe $5 a showing, but in the weekly Village Voice ad for Pink, he kindly included "with the short film, Love Letter to Edie by Robert Maier." I was finally famous, except only I knew it. I've learned that getting your name in the paper doesn't mean much, unless it's every day in a hundred papers. For instance, outside the big East and West Coast cities most people have never heard of John Waters or Divine, except maybe Hairspray—and mostly because of the Broadway play and Travolta movie. Count the number of New York Times subscribers, and you'll get a rough estimate of John's fan base (though some fans disagree and say it's much more).

John also recommended Love Letter to a theater-owner in San Francisco who distributed it to a handful of West Coast art theaters, and regularly sent me a couple hundred dollars' royalties without prodding. After some arm twisting, New Line picked it up, complaining they didn't know what to do with a short film, since it would be the only one in their catalog. They paid for a half-dozen new prints to be made by the film lab in Baltimore, but screeched about the cost, saying they could get prints made for half the price from their fly-by-night lab in New York. They considered the cost of the prints to be a cash advance, so it was years before I saw a penny in royalties. Bob Shaye wrote a vague 3-line letter of agreement that royalty checks would be sent twice a year. As a "Waters" film, and a short, they didn't see it worthy of a real contract.

Edith kept trying to succeed in show business and partnered with several musicians who encouraged her to sing with their band as a novelty act—"The Incredible Edible Eggs." John Mellencamp became friendly with her and she posed on the cover of his album Nothin' Matters.

But real success eluded her. After Polyester was completed, Edie began to get sick. She needed frequent visits to a doctor, and John and I alternated driving her to doctor appointments for a few months. Her health steadily declined and she was invited by several friends to move to southern California and its healthier climate. She tried to open another thrift store, but her health got worse, and she died of cancer soon after the move, and was buried in Hollywood. She deserves a book of her own, but sadly not even a plaque marks the spot of her store, and her huge collection of photos were accidentally taken to the city dump after she died.

With Love Letter to Edie as my Dreamland confirmation certificate, I decided it was truly time to break from my

Edith Massey and I posing during a short break in the filming of "Female Trouble." ©Robert Maier

suburban life. I found a tiny Fells Point house to buy with a mortgage that was cheaper than rent, packed up my few belongings, had a friend drive them downtown in his pick-up, and unlocked the door to my new life. I was ecstatic. I had my own bohemian digs and a film playing in New York. I could prowl the Fells Point bars every night, and had a promising future with John's movies.

The house, built around 1860, was a wreck. Ancient plaster and dust crumbled from the walls and ceilings, the floors tilted, the windows rattled, and it had only three electric outlets. Two scary gas space heaters kept it tolerable in the winter. I didn't care. I didn't plan to entertain. I expected to move to New York in a year or two, and all I wanted was a cheap crash pad in a fun neighborhood.

Vince and Delores came over soon after I had moved in and were appalled. Delores said it looked like Travis Bickel's apartment in Taxi Driver and I would go insane if I didn't decorate it. As passionate decorators, they dragged me "thrifting" and convinced me to spend $150 for a 1930s era dinette set, flowered wall paper, and linoleum that transformed the grubby kitchen into a colorful Vincent Peranio movie set. They even spent two days hanging wall paper and laying the linoleum. I loved the new neighborhood and friends and the new life.

4

Dating John Waters

John and I grew more and more friendly. In the three-hour Friday night bar sessions, we sat shoulder to shoulder, and he shouted stories in my ear. I'd never laughed so hard in my life. The guy was a certifiable comic genius, and from the beginning, I felt privileged to be getting to know him so well. John raved about how he loved to go to trials. "Trial hags" were an important subculture to him, and I was amazed that he would fly to a distant city where a notorious trial was proceeding and wait in line for hours to get a seat in the gallery.

John ate every meal in a restaurant, because he hated to cook and even worse to clean up. He gleefully said he didn't know how to wash dishes, and in the rare instance he used his few dishes to serve carryout, he'd toss them in the trash rather than wash them.

He loved Provincetown, where he worked summers in bookstores. He filched books from them to build up his library.

He told me about his regular jail visits with Manson Family members Tex Watson and Leslie Van Houten, and the excitement he felt being in prison surrounded by convicted felons and their families on visiting days. I think he genuinely felt sorry for them, but he also got a charge out of chit-chatting with famous criminals like most people chit-chatted with next door neighbors.

John had known most of the Dreamlanders for ten or more years. They knew his obsessions by heart, and nothing surprised them. On the other hand, I was a clean slate. I was also pretty close to his social class and background, so political correctness could be put on the shelf. John could be racist, sexist, jingoistic, blasphemous, prejudiced, criminal-minded, deviant, and sexually honest without fear. I had been around enough to get most of his jokes, and understand his ironies, wit, and obsessions. It was a Baltimore style of communication where insults were never taken seriously, but tossed out like a tennis ball to test your wit and ability to return with a good comeback. It's something that should not be tried among people aspiring to politically correct discourse.

I was impressed with how well-read John was. At that time, not many Baltimoreans in his circle read the New York Times, Film Comment, Daily Hollywood Reporter, Women's Wear Daily, and Andy Warhol's Interview. Not that I did, but I had at least heard of them, and subscribed to many of them, as a dutiful apprentice. John needed to be in New York or San Francisco for the intellectual stimulation he craved (but denied he wanted). His public image is the "king of sleaze" who praises the attributes of biker-redneck-bum bars in Baltimore's blue collar neighborhoods. But he'd prefer a tony club in New York or Paris if given the choice. John told me the stories that later appeared in his books Shock Value and Crackpot, and he still tells in his stand-up comedy act. I first heard them when they were shouted in my ear in Bertha's.

We talked frequently about sex. John let me know right away that he was gay, and always had been, but he didn't like the stereotyped mincing gay blade that he called "Marys." He liked the rougher side, which is obvious in all his films. Most of the gay sex jargon he introduced me to went over my head, as he delighted in enlightening me about gay culture. I first thought that maybe he was trying to hit on me, except there was always an intellectual distance, as if he were instructing me how to tie my shoes, and not exploring sexual possibilities. John said he was a "hetero-hag" and I was a pretty obviously a confirmed hetero. I was becoming his new #1 hetero friend.

I felt comfortable with John's sexual conversations, because he never tried any obvious (at least to me) come-ons. The only physical contact we had was his lips brushing against my ear so he could be heard over the noisy bar. His pencil mustache scratched like an old tooth brush, and I'd find myself leaning away to minimize contact with that itchy trademark. I knew for sure I couldn't be gay when talking with John, as sure as he had known he wasn't hetero when he first stuck a hand down a girl's pants and was disturbed to find only a "gash."

"It was like grabbing open heart surgery," was his colorful description.

When I innocently asked John how he could be so sure he was gay if he had never had sex with a woman, he said he had a girlfriend as a teenager, and experimented with her, but didn't like it much. He actually was relieved when she caught him in bed with a guy one day, and broke up with him on the spot. That sealed the deal, and he never looked back.

John increased my vocabulary even more with terms like Hollywood loaf (a semi-erect penis) that made me laugh out loud. He claimed many gays have their first experience at summer camp with older counselors.

"That's such a cliché, no way," I said.

"That's how most gays get started. It's always somebody older," he winked.

"Like scouts, church groups, school trips…" I asked.

"Yep," he nodded. "But they don't make you gay; you can't make anyone gay; you're born gay, and they just help a little."

I challenged John, which he liked. Why was he so obsessed with excessive make-up (it makes you more interesting), why the mustache (it makes him more interesting, and honors several of his mustachioed heroes: Little Richard, Captain Hook, and Vincent Price). I said that his praise of Baltimore's own shocking characters, including men who air their beer bellies on the sidewalks on summer nights, women with ossified beehive hairdos, toothless bums who wove down sidewalks clutching a pint of Ripple in a skirt (brown paper bag), and the extreme butch lezzie bars, had a touch of meanness, like a rube who laughs at pink-ass baboons in the zoo. He vehemently denied it, but I never knew for sure what was said for effect or was an honest belief. I thought maybe his greatest success would be as a performer.

With Female Trouble in distribution, John wasn't so busy. Female Trouble wasn't a smash hit, so his career grew slower and he focused on writing Desperate Living. I still lived in Towson with my old girlfriend, and we were drifting further apart as John and I became more of a "couple." One night, John called to see if I'd go to the movies with him. He loved going to the movies, but hated to go alone. Most people he knew were tied down in a relationship, or didn't have the money or desire to see two or three movies a week, like John did,—or they weren't the type John wanted to be seen with. Plus, it was hard to find people who wanted to see what John liked. That would be films like Ilsa: She Wolf of the SS; Scream Blackula Scream; or Russ Meyer quadruple feature nights with titles like Mud Honey, Common Law Cabin, and Mondo Topless. I had the time and the money, was happy to see the B-movies John obsessed about, and was happy to get to know him better. John told me he had a usual date, Roger, Chuck Yeaton's brother, who was single, straight, and easy-going, but he didn't really like the movies. He also looked old enough to be John's father. As a hetero 23 year old movie person, I was a much better escort.

In the mid-1970s, Baltimore still had a handful of 1930s deco-style theaters scraping a living from dwindling audiences. They played B-movies that were slightly violent and sexually suggestive (though revealing nothing more than the occasional topless woman). Admission was a buck; the refreshment counter sparsely stocked, and the popcorn machine was usually broken. Usually an usher in a stained maroon uniform took tickets and sold boxes of stale Goobers, Raisinettes, Hot Tamales, and cups of flat soda that tasted like dishwashing liquid. The aisles were so sticky with countless spilled sodas, they nearly tore the soles off our shoes. Some of the velveteen seats were so encrusted with squashed candy they gleamed.

John poured over the Baltimore Sun's movie listings every day, and called to let me know what movie he had picked. These were the days before VHS, DVD, cable, satellite, or Internet. To see a skin flick, or any weird, obsessive film you had to go to a movie theater. They generally only played a day or two, so catching them required a sharp eye and an encyclopedic knowledge of B-movies. John subscribed to Daily Variety and Daily Hollywood Reporter, so he knew what was what. If a Russ Meyer film like Vixen or UP! was in town, we had to see it. He dragged me all over the city, and I discovered theaters I never knew existed. Many were in Baltimore's blue-collar northeast corridor, along Harford and Belair Roads. While the theaters have all closed, John still visits the local biker bars in that area to be with the people for whom these movies were made.

John usually picked me up and drove because he knew the obscure movie theater locations so well. He was always 10 minutes early and sat in his big old American car of the moment listening to a black radio station, puffing on a Kool and tapping the steering wheel with his nervous energy. In the laid back 1960s hippie culture, arriving early was not a common trait, and I knew if I was to stay on his good side, I would have to be early too. It was a good life lesson.

We only went out weeknights, and were usually the only people in the theatre. One couple might be in the very back row doing who knows what. On our first date, I was shocked at his behavior. We walked down the aisle and plopped in the center seats about ten rows back from the screen. John ripped open a box of candy and had poured the last bit straight into his mouth before the previews ended.

"Dinner," he grinned.

I had been taught to eat one Raisinette at a time to make them last for the whole movie, and marveled at John's flouting of this rule. But that was only the beginning. Next, he put his long legs up on the seats in front. This was a shameful act. I had been taught to never put my feet up on the back of a theater seat. I'm sure John had been too, but he was always thrilled to break any parental rule. About five minutes into the film, since it had been about fifteen minutes since his last cigarette, he pulled a Kool from the pack in his shirt pocket, and fished his lighter from another.

"You can't smoke in a movie theater John!" I whispered.

"Oh sure you can," he said with great conspiratorial glee. "Watch this. Duck down to light it, and make it fast."

He put his head down between his legs, and with a quick flick of his Bic, lit the cig in a brief unnoticeable flash.

"Now you have to shake it while you hold it so the smoke doesn't go straight up, and they can't tell where it's coming from."

I thought, like, we're the only people in the theater, who the fuck do you think they'll think is smoking? Then he said,

"Cup it when you take a drag, to hide the glow." Which he did, "and blow the smoke down into your lap to spread it out." I watched his well-practiced ritual a few times and sure enough, it worked—kind of.

"Go ahead, have one too, they won't catch us," he whispered.

Game for anything, I lit up, and there we were smoking cigarettes in a movie theater, wiggling our hands like palsy patients to disperse the smoke. John looked at me with a triumphant smile—he had once again corrupted his innocent little hetero date. Smoking in a movie theater with John Waters—what was next?

Sometimes we got caught smoking. An usher would appear at the end of the aisle and flash his light at us.

"Are you smoking?!"

John would shout "No!" hiding the still-lit butt under his seat.

"If I catch you, I'm gonna throw you out," the usher shouted back. And get your feet off the seats!"

John would lazily move his feet and sneer back. After checking over his shoulder to see if the coast was clear, he'd take a fresh puff, and put his feet back up. Usually the usher never came back. Sometime later, when John had returned from his first trip to London, he told me how wonderful it was because smoking was allowed in the movie theaters. "They have ashtrays built into the seats," he said with the great reverence usually reserved for Buckingham Palace.

Besides the white rough-neck titty-films, John also loved the Blaxploitation movies that were hitting in the mid-1970s. Blaxploitation movies were action movies featuring violence and soft-core sex scenes that were a big hit for the urban audience, usually made and distributed by black companies. They played only in the big old downtown Baltimore shopping district theaters like The New, The Town, and The Hippodrome. These theaters once played mega hits like Gone with the Wind, The Wizard of Oz, and It's a Wonderful Life. Now, the shopping district had fallen victim to suburban white flight, and the magnificent rococo theaters limped along with Blaxploitation titles like Monkey Hustle, Hell Up In Harlem, and John's all-time favorite, Mandingo, which I think we saw three times, and actually broke through to the white suburban theaters.

The Blaxploitation theaters were pretty scary. We were always the only white people in the audience, which was made up of a combination of 1970s pimped out Shaft wannabes and ghetto punks in big Afros with Afro "pick" combs stuck in them. Even as a pre-teen, John idolized black culture, and he fearlessly spent as much time as he could at black music clubs, record stores, clothing stores, etc. Baltimore's edgy black AM radio stations like WSID with rule-bending unashamedly honest black DJs like Fat Daddy drew John out of his comfortable white suburban cocoon, like millions of emerging teen baby boomers nationwide. They offered a 24x7 siren song of a sexy, dangerous lifestyle that satisfied the white kids' itch to escape their parents' 1950s conformity.

John was comfortable in the black theaters with his secret soul brothers. To the brothers and sisters, many of whom probably participated in the Baltimore race riots six years earlier, we were probably white rich hippie kids trying to "signify" (black slang for being nosy or misrepresenting yourself) and slumming in their territory. From the minute we stopped at the box office, I felt all eyes on us wondering "who are these muthafuckers?" While I fancied myself a liberal, when I was eleven, I had been beaten and robbed of a couple dollars by a gang of downtown black kids while waiting for a ride. That first-hand experience with Baltimore's racial issues made me a little more aware of how one of these Blaxploitation movie dates could go bad.

We never had a bad incident, and sometimes got into good conversations with brothers who were proud of our efforts at integration and thanked us for our appreciation of black culture. I really liked the movies with their daring chase scenes, wild wardrobes, and flaunting of white cultural mores. To me, they were better than the cheesy colossal-breasted Russ Meyer girls of Beyond the Valley of the Dolls.

These B-movies usually played as double or triple features, so an evening extended between three and five hours. There wasn't time after to go for a beer or a bite to eat. We both were early risers—me to go to my job, and John to write. Anyway, seeing these movies was really work time. John was growing more comfortable with the idea of my taking on the line-producer/production manager chores on Desperate Living, and I wanted to understand as much as I could about his tastes. Besides being fun, we learned we could trust each other, and the foundation of our business relationship was laid.

Our movie dates lasted about two years. They ended when I got a new girlfriend who didn't think much of my spending two or three nights a week with John, and John was spending more and more time on the road giving lectures anyway.

5

Desperate Living: Let's Make a Movie!

· · · · · · · · · · · · · · · · · ·

The good old days at UMBC were definitely at an end. A new dean took over with the idea of making the Arts Departments a satellite of New York City's experimental theater and performance scene. To the film department it was a kiss of death. Famous experimental New York filmmaker Stan Van der Beek, the new department chair, thought the dramatic movie production department we had built was a waste. He had no interest in underground movies. Experimental video was the new wave, and he explored the idea of selling all the film gear to buy the new generation of video camcorders and editing machines. He wanted to make experimental dance films. He wanted to project abstract videos and laser lights on steam screens. He wanted to bring his New York friends to Baltimore to teach the Baltimorons some cutting-edge culture.

When the Dean who hired me resigned, a NY experimental theater producer took his place. He was a good buddy of Van der Beek, and supported his move to change the film department. It was definitely the end. Dave Insley headed off to Iowa to graduate school. I bickered constantly with Van der Beek, who told me to my face that he wanted an experimental video engineer, and asked me to resign, because I wasn't buying into his vision. The film students were in open revolt. They wanted to learn how to make a living in film, not depend on grants.

I had been applying for months for jobs in the film department at Maryland Public Television, getting only occasional freelance gigs there, mostly as a sound mixer. It was a cool, professional group, several of whom went on to successful Hollywood careers.

The end for me at UMBC came quickly when I stupidly signed a petition presented by the film students asking the administration to stop the shift to experimental video and fire Van der Beek. I was summoned to the Dean's office the next afternoon to meet with him, Van der Beek, the assistant dean, and the head of the Art Department, which administered the Film Program. Amazingly, that same day, the head of the Film Production Department at Maryland Public TV called. A new program, Up on the Farm, had received funding, and they wanted to put me on full-time staff. It was a local public TV bore, but it was real Television. Could I start next week? Hell yeah!

Feeling all pumped up, I went to the meeting at the Dean's office, where they pounced. The Art chair screamed with his pipe clenched between his teeth that I was staff and must obey the faculty, not mere students. Signing a student petition was a huge breach of protocol. I would change my attitude, or get out, which would it be?

"I'll get out, if you don't mind. I resign today. I've been offered a job at Maryland Public Television, and I accepted."

It was like throwing a firecracker in the middle of the table. Though it was their dream come true, the reality was like a dog catching a bus. Now what? None of them had technical or organizational backgrounds. They were artists, and depended upon practical people to run things and do the heavy work on their hare-brained projects. More than a quarter-million dollars of advanced gear was in the building, and they barely knew how to turn on a light switch. They had no idea about inventory, work-study students, maintenance contracts, keys to the dozens of studios, wiring, supplies storage, facilities scheduling etc.

I agreed to give them two weeks' notice, but not a day more. Van der Beek blew multiple gaskets, and put together a long list of chores and requests that would take a month to accomplish. He threatened me with all sorts of vague consequences if I didn't complete them. But I was mentally already out the door. No one in the professional production industry gave a hoot what some artsy-fartsy academic said. If he had spent more time around the department instead of running back to NYC for this or that event to enhance his international reputation, he would have understood how to run an academic film department.

Fortunately for the department, a diligent student assistant I had been training, Richard Chisholm, who later became an A-level globe-trotting documentary videographer, wanted the job and they hired him immediately. While I wouldn't give Van der Beek or his cohorts the time of day, Richard was a good guy, and I told him to call me anytime he couldn't figure something out, and I would definitely help him.

John and I had discussed Desperate Living at length over the preceding months. He knew that the UMBC deal would never work again. Lee, the film department head, barely held on. The new regime made him miserable because he had to come in on time and teach classes himself. They watched like hawks for the slightest excuse to can him. But Lee had tenure, and that was gold; if he could remember how to survive working for a living.

John wondered if I could production manage Desperate Living, with my new job at Maryland Public TV. He would have gladly stayed with UMBC, because he loved the familiar path. Jumping into the unknown again made him crazy. I was confident everything would go well. I didn't care about working seven-day weeks. I was 24 years old and ready to rock 'n roll. I could work cheap because I had a full-time job, and I was between girlfriends so I could be focused. Since we would still be in an ultra-low budget mode, the production work would be part-time, shooting mostly weekends. I reminded John that Maryland Public TV had a more extensive film department than UMBC, which might be helpful—though it couldn't do a formal equipment or facility agreement like UMBC.

Because he had known me for over a year, had entrusted me with big responsibilities on Female Trouble, and I had become a reliable and trusted friend and colleague. I was the only heir apparent. Over the past 18 months, we had spoken nearly every day, and I was the only film person he could possibly consider to help with his next movie. He would be terrified if I couldn't help him and he had to find someone who not only knew filmmaking, but could deal with his multiple insecurities, paranoia, and obsessions.

A great advantage of working with MPTV was that they were pretty lax about hours worked by the film crews. Nearly all of my work was on location. Frequently I had night shoots that lasted from 5 p.m. to 10 p.m., so I could work all day with John—scouting locations, going over the budget, etc. Sometimes the MPTV days would go long, and I'd rack up enough comp time to take off a few days in a row. It was a great arrangement.

One important assist provided by the MPTV connection was a middle-aged lady named Lane. She was a production secretary who was an expert in typing scripts for the staff TV producers. This was ten years before word processors, and typing a script with all its indents, centering changes, and parentheses was a big chore. John had always written his scripts in long hand on yellow lined legal pads in his marginally readable script, and photocopied those for his main cast only. He hated all machines except his car and 45rpm record player, so he never learned to type. When I suggested that Lane would probably type his script for a reasonable fee, he was at first skeptical. "But she'll have to read it. What will she think?" I agreed to a point, since most of the scenes in John's films featured felonies, cruelty to animals, pornography, and criminal insanity. Could we risk opening the tight Dreamland circle to a prim and proper public TV typist?

I spoke to Lane about freelancing on the side (everybody working at MPTV did), and she said she would be delighted. I moved to the more delicate subject of bad language and questionable content, and asked if she might be offended by profanity, gross-out scenes, violence, or perversions (the last one, mumbled under my breath). She cheerily answered that she wouldn't be bothered at all. They were just words on a page to her, and she only paid attention to proper spacing, spelling, and punctuation.

As a trial, John gave me a sheaf of the first ten pages of the handwritten script. It was nearly illegible to me. When I gave it apologetically to Lane, she said she'd seen worse, and would have it tomorrow. The results were astounding. All the scenes and pages were numbered, characters named, all the standard movie script margins, and indents were there. John was ecstatic. It was a drudge job he didn't have to do anymore. And it made him look much more professional—which he always strived for. From then on, Lane typed all his scripts with a smile. She never commented on the content, which included multiple disgusting murders, lines like "Seize her and fuck her!" or a scene that today would get her arrested for child pornography. We never asked her how she liked the script either.

I spent many hours reviewing the script with John, mostly meeting in his apartment. John is now a bon-vivant with exquisite tastes developed in great restaurants around the world. Back then, he ate in crummy diners or from Chinese carry-out boxes. His refrigerator had only a few jars of pickles, a six-pack of coke, and a few carryout food containers of unknown vintage. The pantry had a few bags of potato chips, his other favorite food. After my first glance into the fridge, he confessed he really didn't like to eat at all. He shoveled his food into his mouth and swallowed it as quickly as possible, to get to that infinitely more satisfying cigarette.

The apartment building, named Temple Gardens (because it was up the street from an imposing old synagogue) was built in the early 1920s for Baltimore's upper-class Jewish population who were very cultured, status conscious, and rich. Details included a maid's room with her own toilet, and an electric bell in the spacious dining room to summon the cook if something wasn't quite perfect. It was lush with molded plaster and decorative hard-wood floors. But the neighborhood had become a ghetto after WWII. A convenience store across the street that sold cigarettes, beer, candy, and other junk food featured the first thick Plexiglas clerk protection station I had ever seen. I made many visits there for lunches of bags of peanuts and pretzels, because John never had any food when our meetings went into lunch time.

The streets were among the most unsafe in Baltimore, especially at night, but a well-lit parking lot right next door ensured that you probably wouldn't get mugged. Nevertheless, at night, I'd scan outside the door seeing if the coast was clear, then dash to my car. While editing Desperate Living one night, Charles was blocked by a small group, while trying to exit the parking lot. Very frightened, he floored his car and headed to the exit as the gang scrambled out of the way. He said it was a miracle he didn't kill two or three of them. This was the main reason the rent was so low. Besides the low rent and 24-hour desk security, John liked it because it blended danger with old-world elegance. With its arches, columns, moldings, and deco light fixtures, it was an ideal pad for a fop.

John's Temple Gardens days were in the times before he could afford to fill his walls and floors with pricy modern art that had deep meaning to him, but looked like children's doodles or street junk to a non-connoisseur. His 1970s art consisted of paintings given to him by his non-famous artist friends. He had a few kitschy full-size movie posters including Russ Meyer's Faster Pussycat, Kill! Kill! A fan had sent him a full-size formal portrait of a famous, serial murderess scowling at the world. I was alarmed at one piece, a toy helicopter painted in LSD- inspired hallucinatory patterns by Manson murderer Tex Watson in his California maximum security prison cell. It was my first exposure to John's insatiable fascination with crime and criminals. Though it was the plot and theme of Female Trouble, facing the realities that John wanted to live with portraits of serial killers, and considered the criminally insane Tex Watson a friend and admirer was perplexing.

John guided me through his library of hundreds of books. He bragged that many had been stolen when he clerked at various bookstores—the only real job he had ever had. Several rooms had floor to ceiling shelves crammed with hardcover books. He said he hated using libraries, because he never wanted to give up a book after he read it. He was probably banned from Baltimore's Enoch Pratt Free Library system before he was a teenager, due to chronic non-return of books.

John refused to read or buy paperback books. He would only have hard covers, and if he could get one autographed, that was golden. On trips to New York, he loaded up with new releases marked down 50% from the Baltimore hardcover price. I'm not surprised that John now has more than 8,000 books lining the walls of his uptown Baltimore mansion—all perfectly catalogued and spotless, no doubt.

John had so much time to read because he hated TV. He owned a rickety black and white set from the early 1960s, but kept it only in case the world was ending, and it was being covered live. Disliking TV was part of his disdain for all bourgeois pastimes like sports, gardening, cooking, or walks in the park. His hobby was sneaking cigarettes at the movies. TV was also a machine with confusing dials, which he couldn't be bothered to learn with fifty new magazines and four new books to read every day. Turning a page was as high tech as he ever wanted to be. He initially resisted computers, but now he has e-mail and a Blackberry phone that he religiously attends to. Many of John's books were detailed biographies of famous murderers. I feigned interest, but murder was something I never took much interest in. When I was seventeen, two good friends were shot in a Towson sandwich shop, while lying face down on the floor. One was killed instantly. The other received a severe head wound. He was never quite right again, and bragged about the little round scar where the bullet had entered and grazed his brain. He became a cop, so he could hunt down murderers, but he was just a beat cop and delighted in showing me nauseating crime investigation photos of car wreck victims.

The family of the friend who died was shattered. His brother died of an OD after several years of terrible heroin addiction that tore his mother apart. His father committed suicide in a police station after years of complaining that the cops had done nothing to find his son's killer. That was my knowledge of murder and its effects. It was not very pretty and I did not get that part of John. Though I felt I knew him well, I was never absolutely sure that one day he wouldn't try something he obsessed over so much. He assured me it was only an intellectual fascination. He did not envy the perpetrators or their acts, but wished they would sublimate their tendencies and turn them into art—like he did—well, at least for now I sometimes worried.

John also showed me disturbing letters from fans. He received hundreds of cards and letters from people who took his early films to be gospel truth or documentary footage of the Dreamlander's real lives. They shared John's fantasies, and were grateful that someone made movies out of them. They wanted to be his friend, murder chickens with him, shoplift steaks with him, and try out painful sexual activities with him. They sent him gifts including tufts of pubic hair, photos of their physical deformities and sex change operations, and pamphlets on extremely rare sexual obsessions like foot fetishism and telephone scatology. Many of them disturbed him, and I don't blame him. I occasionally received similar letters from fans of Love Letter to Edie, and changed my mailing address to a post office box.

These were real misfits who completely missed the irony, comic hyperbole, and satire of John's work, people whom neither of us wanted as friends or fans. The last thing he wanted was for some nut case to murder ten children and say he was inspired by John Waters' movies. From the letters, it was plain he was walking a thin line in that department, but in many ways, John was an eternal optimist. He could safely be a "villain voyeur," and get away unscathed. Amazingly, for all of his great risks and taboo breaking, he has escaped not only unscathed, but has had a wildly successful career.

One of the biggest oddities of John's apartment was his collection of magazine subscriptions. They included news, fashion, art, entertainment, gossip, and underground cultural news like The Village Voice. He claimed that the daily and weekly subscriptions to Variety and Hollywood Reporter, which alone filled his apartment with one cubic foot of newsprint a week, should pay him rent.

It seemed impossible to me that anyone could read five hundred pages a week of periodicals, and still have time to read all the books he bought. But this was before the Internet and cable TV, and was the only way to keep in touch with the intellectual world. They were a business expense, but still cost thousands of dollars a year. When he'd go away for a week, he needed a shopping cart to haul the mail up to his apartment. He said every time he came home it was like Christmas, and he'd spend hours poring over the magazines and fan letters. Many were displayed in an old barber shop style magazine rack by his front door, and made a big first impact on purpose. You weren't dealing with some stoner hippie here—but a mainstream media executive. I doubted Ben Bradley, the editor of the Washington Post, had as many subscriptions as John.

In the beginning, John's apartment was sparsely furnished, and always impeccably clean. John was a neat freak. His clothes were always clean and pressed. Though he always said he had greasy hair, he looked like he showered twice a day. He shaved daily, except for the trademark moustache, which he trimmed and accented with eyebrow pencil—often several times a day; usually excusing himself to visit the facilities to do so. With Pink and Female Trouble achieving such success he could relax financially. I was surprised during an early meeting in his apartment to see a black woman open the door and say good-bye to John. "Oh," John said, "This is my maid, Clara. Clara this is Bob." A maid!? The Prince of Puke has a maid? How could that be? John said he was getting too busy to keep things neat and clean, and needed someone mainly to keep the dust off his books. It was the first time I saw him in this light. He was angry and rebellious about nearly everything bourgeois, but beginning with Clara, I began noticing cracks in that façade.

Planning Desperate Living required lots of talk about money. In the early films, the budget was not set considering actual projected costs, but how much money John felt comfortable about investing and raising. He always wanted to be cheap to reduce the financial risk. John approximately doubled the cost of every movie, because, well, it sounded right. Pink cost $10,000, Female Trouble cost $25,000, so Desperate Living should cost $65,000, according to John's math—considering that the previous films went 10-20% over budget. This one could not go over budget. Because investors were paying for most of it, the contingency was built-in.

My job as his friend and colleague was to come in on budget. This one had to be a great leap forward in looking like a professional movie too. It was virgin ground. People didn't make professional-looking $65,000 movies then. With a great stock of youthful ignorant confidence, I assured John I could bring DL in on budget—but what the fuck did I know? He didn't know how to direct a $65,000 movie either, so we decided to learn together. I was 24 years old, and hadn't produced a film longer than 15 minutes, so Desperate Living would become an appropriate motto for John and me through the next ten months of production.

Desperate Living was a much more complex film than Female Trouble, because it was a Wizard of Oz type fantasy where a whole village had to be built, both interiors and exteriors. Everyone had to wear a custom-made costume all the time, and everyone had to be made up by one of John's ugly experts. Always cost-conscious, John cleverly created a slew of nudist characters, to trim the wardrobe budget—and hopefully give the critics something to complain about. Ninety percent of his previous films were shot on location, and only a few special props were needed. With Desperate Living, ninety percent was shot on built sets.

John purposely wrote the script so he didn't have to buy expensive props and sets. Mortville (as in mortified, one of John's favorite words of the time) was the main setting of the film. It was an ugly fairytale village ruled by a despotic queen, which sheltered society's castoffs and escaped criminals. It would mostly be made of scavenged junk. Any old broken TV, smashed stove, or ratty sofa Vince happened to find on a Baltimore street would be added to the props and sets department for use later on the Mortville set. It was a brilliant money-saver.

The big expense was Queen Carlotta's castle, a cheesy false-fronted castle made from cheap plywood. It was twenty feet high with kitschy fairy-tale towers and a drawbridge gate. None of us had built such a monstrous structure, but that didn't mean a thing. We'd forge ahead and do it. Thank God we were out in the country and wouldn't be subject to building codes.

Another budget threat was music. John realized that he could not lift music he liked for the soundtrack any more, and the funky songs he had used in his other films would cost three times Desperate Living's entire budget. We decided to find a young composer looking for a big break, and pay a few thousand bucks for a basic soundtrack. But John was entering his dark Douglas Sirk mode, and wanted a rich symphonic score with strings, woodwinds, tympani, and lush piano solos. This was way before symphonic electronic synthesizers. All of it would have to be recorded with professional musicians. With its world-renowned Peabody Conservatory, Baltimore might be a good bet for this, but it would be difficult. The composers had to be good; they would need a copy of the film to compose to, arrangements had to be written, decent musicians hired, and a professional studio had to be booked for the recording and mixing. We would definitely have to depend on the kindness of strangers, and crossed our fingers, hoping that these things would be found, and there would be enough money left at the end of the editing to pay for this original symphonic score.

Divine Goes Missing

Much has been written about Divine's absence from the cast of Desperate Living. Most histories say he was too busy "touring." It is true that after Female Trouble he was recognized in the underground and gay entertainment world as a greater talent, and desperately wanted to make it in the big time as a legitimate male actor. He was tired of the clownish female impersonator psycho role. He had eaten dog shit in Pink. In Female Trouble, he was shot-up, forced to puke for real, swam across a cold river in the middle of winter, was mutilated by acid, and finally electrocuted—wasn't that enough?

Divine had been working in New York and San Francisco in a few off-off-Broadway plays, where he played a female impersonator but got to work with other directors, and saw a difference between John and seasoned professional directors with a wider range of experience.

Money was an issue too. Though John shared 25% with the main Dreamlanders, and it was OK for Fells Point, Divine's share didn't go very far with his New York and San Francisco lifestyles. He now had an agent who arranged decent paying, regular personal appearances in gay clubs across the country. Desperate Living's whole $65,000 budget couldn't come close to compensating him for what he and his agent now felt he was worth.

For one thing, Desperate Living's budget was so low, it might be a piece of crap that would do more harm than good to Divine's expanding career. While John was invisibly writing away in his Baltimore apartment and Female Trouble just doing average business, Divine was out working on stage nearly every night in the big cities. People wrote articles about him, and his fame was expanding. When I spoke to strangers about my working with John Waters, they frequently asked, "Isn't he that fat transvestite?" Divine was possibly eclipsing John.

John was also motivated by the need to know he could make a hit movie without Divine—that he wasn't a one-trick pony ridden by a fearless transvestite. Like many film producers, John was star struck and boob struck. He felt his movies couldn't grow without a name star, preferably a blonde with big tits, who wasn't afraid to show them. This was New Line's point of view too. A movie couldn't make money without sex, drugs, violence, and rock 'n roll. As far as New Line being an "art movie" distributor, they stumbled on the burgeoning college art film circuit, scooping up the sub-titled Euro-art films that were beneath the notice of major distributors. New Line's executives made good livings, but shifted their "art film" mission and vision when they saw the real fortunes to be made with movie box office hits. The Nightmare on Elm Street series, whose theme was that favorite puritanical threat to American teenagers: "have sex and die," was where the money was. So John struck out to find his own sexy blonde "bankable" star.

His first choice was an ex-stripper and girlfriend of a mobster, Liz Renay. Liz fit most of the criteria: she was blonde (or had a big wig that was), had huge artificial breasts, and a sexy Jayne Mansfield look. Unfortunately she was a 50-something grandmother on her way out of show business, and not the budding ingénue that could be hyped by New Line to a press that was drawn like a magnet to young pretty blondes. Liz was a name—well in some quarters. She had been in the news, mostly because she was a girlfriend of gangster Mickey Cohen and spent 27 months in Terminal Island prison for perjury. Liz had little professional acting experience, but had written a book titled My First 2000 Men, which helped maker her irresistible to John.

On the positive side, Liz wasn't in the actor's union, nor did she care to be. Most quality actors or big names, even newcomers, were in the Screen Actors Guild. There was no way we could afford a union contract, which requires every actor, including extras to be in the union, and would have easily tripled the budget. There might be money to pay a union name actor for a few days, but union rules forbid work on non-union films. Actors violating this rule could be tossed from the union and/or fined thousands of dollars, if caught—and they were almost always caught. How do you hide when you're on a movie screen?

This was a problem not only with John's films, but in all the low-budget movies I worked on. I got to know the unions well and probably came closer to being physically assaulted and murdered in my dealings with them than in any other aspect of my work on low budget films. They are tough customers, and it was imperative to avoid them on Desperate Living. Polyester and Hairspray would be different stories. On our side was that unions want to steer clear of $65,000 films. Pickings were way too slim. They might hassle and threaten a little. Getting into six figures? Then watch out.

Everyone was nervous about the choice of Liz as the new box office draw, and her being able to replace Divine in the eyes of John's fan base. For readers of gossip and scandal mags, she might be a name because of her stunts like streaking down Hollywood Boulevard and her relationship with Mickey Cohen, but her fan base—if she actually had one—was not the young, rebellious thrill-seekers who went to John's movies.

Liz also took a sizable chunk of the $65,000 budget. She was in town for just a few shoot days and her scenes had to be tightly scheduled in that short window. She was sweet and likeable, and a real trooper, but if you were paid $10,000 for an all expense paid trip to appear in a few movie scenes you might be too.

This is the way with most movies. Big names are paid big bucks to bring in big bucks, but so often it doesn't work that way. If John had really wanted to use Divine, and Divine really wanted to be in Desperate Living, they could have worked around Divine's not really so busy schedule. I think the main reason was both John and Divine wanted to see if they could stand on their own. It was a test of their egos, and not a bad thing at all. In the end, both Desperate Living and Divine's stage career stalled, so when New Line found backers for his next film, Polyester, John and Divvy agreed it was in their best interest to re-unite and re-kindle the fire in their core audience.

Desperate Production

After casting, the next big decision with Desperate Living was the Mortville exterior set. It had to be built in a quiet isolated area so that on-lookers or vandals wouldn't get into it. The nude scenes alone could have gotten them busted if irate neighbors complained. An old Dreamland friend, Peter, had recently bought a farm about 40 miles north of Baltimore. It was a gorgeous piece of land with a 19th century brick farmhouse, barn, wide stream, woods, and long winding farm road. Peter and his girlfriend, Laurel, a talented artist, planned to live a quiet, creative life there after spending several frantic years in Fells Point. Where they got the money, I never knew for sure, but this was the 1970s, and people made good money in new ways you didn't talk about much. Being a good friend, Peter allowed the ugly little fantasy village of Mortville to be built on his farm. Its Main Street was a dirt farm path that skirted a creek, which would eventually get us into some trouble. It was a bucolic setting that would soon be unforgettably changed.

Mortville's interiors were built and shot on the second story of a downtown Baltimore loft building, which at first seemed ideal and convenient. Situated on one of Fells Point's noisiest corners, it had some hellish quirks. A suburban ground floor multi-purpose industrial building, with reliable utilities, good parking, and easy access would have been ideal, but Fells Point was where Vince and the art department lived, so it was very practical, considering the amount of set building that would

On a Baltimore street shooting a scene from Desperate Living, winter of 1976.

l-r Tom L'oizeaux, John Waters, Robert Maier, photo by Paul Hutchins, © The Baltimore Sun

be required. It also had the creative Fells Point vibe, so a few essential modern conveniences wouldn't be missed—we thought.

The building dated from the 1900s, and was about as unsuitable for a film studio as possible. There was not enough electricity, no heat, water, or toilets in the shooting area. Thick wooden columns continually obstructed camera and lighting angles. The street noise from tractor trailers that idled and gunned their engines when the traffic light changed rattled the entire building. Everything had to be carried up two flights of stairs because there was no elevator. This included set flats, furniture, large props, movie lights, cables, chairs, water, food, and wardrobe. The loft was maybe 5,000 square feet, and was jam-packed. There was no heat, and we thought that all the people and movie lights would keep us warm, but many days the 20 degree outside temperature crept inside forcing everyone into jackets and sweaters. In some close-ups, the vapor steaming from actors' mouths was so thick that we resorted to the old trick of having them suck on an ice cube before delivering their lines. It just made the actors colder.

But this was low-budget filmmaking, and we were willing to move heaven and earth to get the shots done. Only occasionally did the conditions seem impossible, and they were major situations that when solved, seemed like miracles from above.

On Female Trouble I was the sound recordist; and given the still ridiculously tight budget with Desperate, I decided I could be both the production manager and sound recordist at the same time. It was insanity, but made sense to both of us because it was a cheap solution. The reality was like combining a 12 hour a day job with a 14 hour a day job. Plus I worked 40 hours a week at the TV station—at least I was supposed to.

Juggling it all was a huge learning curve. In meetings with John, he was much more organized than anyone in Dreamland, because he kept all his notes on file cards. Each person on the movie was assigned a different set of file cards. My method was not so reliable. I first tried remembering details, without writing anything down. That didn't work too well. Sometimes I wrote a note on the nearest piece of paper and stuck that into a pocket. When I got home, I'd pull out the bits of paper, look them over, and then make the phone calls and preparations I had discussed with John.

This was not good production management procedure, and caused me many problems. Little details were getting lost; nothing disastrous, but there were warnings. John called me in the evenings and gave me even more notes. I'd find myself waking up in the middle of the night realizing I had to pick up something, go to the bank, or buy a camera accessory. I'd jot it on a scrap of paper, and then put the paper on the floor where I'd be sure to see it in the morning. It got to the point where I'd wake up and twenty scraps of paper with important production notes littered the floor. Oh my God, how could I deal with this? How could I keep them all in one place? They didn't teach me this in film school.

I was reminded of elementary school note-taking and then it hit me: the three-ring binder. Eureka! I would get a binder and have it with me at all times. The little pencil pouch inside would hold several pencils, a few paperclips, a note pad, business cards, receipts. Perfect. Every note would be written directly in the book. Photocopies could be triple-hole punched, inserted, and never lost. I'd have a permanent record of every task and scratch it out when it was done. I would never lose a phone number or an address. I quickly advanced to adding section dividers for art, hair/makeup/costumes, production, money, legal, and contacts. I bought a bright orange binder so I couldn't possibly lose it. It was a God-send, and suddenly I was even more organized than John. File cards could get lost, but my book was forever. Unfortunately, the Desperate Living book has disappeared, but I still have Polyester, Hairspray, and Crybaby. I'll review the lists of chores and crises—anything from obtaining a Maryland First Class Fireworks permit to George Romero's phone number—like some people look fondly at baby pictures.

Desperate Living's crew was all new too. Dave was at graduate film school in Iowa, of all places, so I asked Tom L'oizeaux, a cameraman at Maryland Public TV and social friend from before I got involved with Waters to be the director of photography. Tom shot Love Letter to Edie for free and was a quiet and persnickety techie, known far and wide as one of the first long-hairs in Towson. His father and uncles were oddly famous for controlled demolitions of huge buildings around the world, like skyscrapers and massive derelict housing projects. If John had known, he'd have loved that. But Tom was not into building demolition, instead preferring playing Beatle music, and taking moody black and white photographs. His wife wrote children's books. As sensitive artists, they didn't fit with the Waters crowd. In fact, Tom didn't like much about John's movies—I don't think he ever even saw Pink. But Tom was a polite, refined, and very knowledgeable technician with a good eye, and worked extremely hard for almost nothing. His interest was getting a Director of Photography credit on a real movie.

A few days before shooting began, Dave Insley called. Hating Iowa, he had dropped out of graduate school after three weeks and was back in Baltimore. He needed a job, so I put him on as assistant camera. Both Tom and Dave eventually had busy careers as 2nd camera operators when features or TV series came to town, but their careers never fully blossomed, because you had to live in Hollywood to get on the A-list. They were nudged aside by Hollywood DPs when John moved into the multi-million dollar Hollywood realm, occasionally doing camera operator or second unit work for John, which paid the bills, but must have been at least slightly humiliating.

To help me through the production manager/sound recordist duties, I hired a sound assistant, Richard Ellsberry, who knew nothing about sound, but was qualified because he was happy to work for five dollars a day. Kevin Weber, a former UMBC student and tireless eager beaver did most of the grunt work laying cables, hanging lights, and moving the camera.

Dissatisfied with the money in the low-budget film world, Kevin disappeared from the Baltimore film scene soon after.

Since we couldn't get a deal on Maryland state equipment, I had to sleuth out the cheapest equipment to rent. I had bought my own sound recording package, which I rented to John for a song. For the camera, I found a network news cameraman in Williamsport, Pennsylvania, (home of the Little League World Series) who was building an equipment rental business and had several of the French Éclair 16mm cameras, like the one used on Female Trouble. It was a three-hour drive from Baltimore, but he gave an incredibly sweet deal for the eight week shooting period. Only one place in the area rented lights, but they were in DC, and their customers were TV networks and the federal government, for whom money was no object, and their prices were too high for a low-budget movie. I bought a portable kit of eight lights, and that would be it for the whole movie—what a joke. I rented them to John for about half the cost of what I paid for them, figuring I could sell them used, or keep them to rent on other shoots, and maybe break even. As pathetic as the little light kit was, it was more than he could afford on the budget, but at least it was more lights than Female Trouble had. On later movies, I'd rent a tractor-trailer load of lighting gear with more than a hundred lights. Though the rental bills that were stratospheric, I can't say it always looked that much better.

Tom was meticulous and not happy with taking risks. Many times the lights were not sufficient to get a reading on his light meter. He would stand in the middle of the scene to be shot, wave the meter around and swallow hard. He'd shake it, and then tap it with his finger, but the needle didn't budge. Every light had been used, the cast was finally in full costume, and make-up was ready. John paced around, puffing on his tenth cigarette of the morning, and all were hoping that Tom could work a miracle and get a decent exposure. Finally, he'd roll his eyes as if offering a little prayer and say "OK." He'd throw me a panicked glance and tell Dave "Open it all the way," meaning set the lens for the most exposure. This was dangerous because it made focusing more critical, especially when blowing up 16mm to 35mm, when any focus problems would be magnified 400%. Dave and Tom worked out complex focus pulls with most shots to keep at least something in focus. Any photographic problems would be blamed squarely on Tom, and he did not want his first feature film to be grainy, underexposed, and out of focus. He continually begged me for more lights, but there was no money. I said, "Just make it work."

The first dailies from the "studio" shots were stunning. The colors were rich, and the focus sharp. The lack of lights made Tom push for a more "arty" high-key film noir look, where certain spots were lit in contrast to darker areas. It reinforced the dark foreboding theme of the movie, and made the colors of sets, costumes, and make up ring out. After seeing the dailies, I paid less attention to Tom's cries for more lights. It was by far John's best looking film.

I learned on other movies I produced that no matter how many trucks-full of lights I rented it was never enough. Gaffers (the crew people who hang and adjust the movie lights) joked with me that a scene was never lit until every light was off the truck—and therefore rented. I never found it that funny.

Because the Desperate Living loft was ancient, we had to re-wire it to handle just our measly eight lights. Luckily Vince's father-in-law was a licensed electrician. He tapped into a big power line and built us a portable circuit breaker box with a thick 100 ft. extension cord that we dragged around from set to set. It threaded along the floor like a big white snake and was so delicate and dangerous we warned people to never step on it. It violated every building code, and if it had shorted while someone stood on it, it would have launched them straight up and embedded their head in the ceiling. It was such a menace I threw it out at the end of the shoot though it had cost hundreds of dollars to make.

Vince built all the sets in the loft. More than a ton of lumber, building supplies, and furniture was carried up the two flights of stairs to our studio. Because the loft was on Fells Point's noisiest corner, we stuffed the large loft windows with fiberglass insulation. The thick brick walls still resonated with diesel engines throttling up after idling at the red light, 50 feet from our set. We often had to shoot only during red lights, so it would be quiet enough. With the windows permanently blocked, the air was poisonous. Everyone chain smoked, except Tom L'oizeaux, who came to me many times to say he might leave the film because he couldn't breathe. I finally made up a story that no one could smoke near the set area because the smoke soaked up too much light, and we needed every little ray. John backed it up, but as director, he was made an exception. Every fifteen minutes, he walked about twenty feet away, lit up a Kool, took 4-5 furtive puffs, and then blew the smoke away from the set. It reminded me of our sneaking cigarettes at the movies.

The cast was holed up in a tiny green room where they huddled under blankets to keep warm. They had to walk down a set of creaky wooden stairs to use the bathroom, timing their visit to when the sound wasn't rolling. This was tricky since there was no way to know—no red flashing lights and no warning bells like real studios. They'd hold their bladders painfully long to avoid getting yelled at because a loud stair creak would ruin a take. We were outlaws holed up in a building where we couldn't make a sound, there was no daylight, heat, food or water—and few places to sit down. The general quiet was punctuated only by the scripted screams of one or another actor reacting to some horror inflicted upon them.

One of my duties as production manager was feeding the crew. I didn't know anything about catering or crafts service (the table of free snacks and drinks provided on all movie sets). The cast was on their own for even water. The crew, having worked professionally, was spoiled and would not tolerate buying their own lunches. The argument for catering is that productions don't want their crews or cast to wander away from the set and get caught in long lines or slow restaurants, thereby delaying the whole production. Better to spend $1,000 on lunch than pay $5,000 on overtime because the assistant cameraperson's waiter was slow. John didn't buy this, because we weren't paying overtime, but I prevailed. Six hundred dollars in a $65,000 budget for crew lunches would keep them happy, allow short lunch periods, and pay off ten times in productivity. I finally got a $20 a day lunch budget—for the crew of six. It was almost always pizza, because a pizza joint was right across the street, and it fit the budget.

Since we didn't have production assistant go-fers, at lunchtime, I had to put down my sound gear and run downstairs to order pizzas, wait fifteen minutes for them to be made, and carry them back up to the loft. Lunch break was almost over, so we'd gobble the pizza, and get off our feet for ten minutes. The actors, who all broke away for lunch, usually in costume, and make-up, were quite a sight standing in line for their pizzas or hot dogs in the nearby food shops. Many could take longer breaks, because their shots were scheduled later. Pat's husband, Chucky, or another close friend would run for a slice of pizza for John and Pat, and they usually ate quietly together discussing actor and casting issues.

My hands were always full, keeping track of the sound tapes and exposed camera rolls, discussing equipment problems and needs with the crew, working with Vince and his art department needs, and Van and Chris Mason with wardrobe and hair issues. Money was a big concern, because everyone had extra needs. Light bulbs blew out, a roll of film would get spoiled, more gaffers' tape was needed, or a tripod part would break. An important day player might have car trouble, and we had to reimburse her cab fare. The loft was so cold we bought a Kerosene heater. Sometimes the days lasted twelve hours, and I'd have to buy a dinner round of pizza and cokes to keep the crew from passing out. All these things cost money, and most weren't budgeted. John didn't believe in the standard 10% contingency fund at that time, so every little unexpected item was a hassle between him and me. Pat Moran handled all the complicated casting and talent issues, including hundreds of extras quite handily, which was a huge load off my shoulders.

I had desperately wanted to be the production manager of Desperate Living, and now that I had it, I was caught in a tidal wave. There was a little tussle between Pat, John, and me for the title. Pat ended up with the production manager title, and I got unit manager. Actually, they are slightly different titles for the same position. Pat had been titled production manager on John's previous films, and deserved it, but was more of an associate producer, as well as casting director, and second assistant director on Desperate Living, because she didn't deal with the technical aspects at all. She was primarily involved with the cast, since the art, make-up and wardrobe people were pretty self-sufficient, but she did work closely with Van and his myriad costume needs, and Chris with all the wigs and "hair don't's." Pat liked being a manager, but I needed a manager credit for my resume. Not wanting to create friction, I conceded the production manager title to her. We did split the production management responsibilities, even though scheduling, money, equipment, production crew, and post-production were my responsibilities.

The difficulties in the "studio" were multiplied many times over on the rural Mortville location set. Vince began constructing Mortville with Queen Carlotta's massive (at least to us) castle. The walls were 16 feet high and painted white. False lookout towers were stuck on. It was not a charming fairy tale castle, but the cheesiest collection of code violations you'd find in some God-forsaken West Virginia holler. Due to lack of money for sufficient structural lumber, and Vince's very modest engineering skills, the castle walls were propped up in the rear only by a few 2x4s, and were in constant danger of toppling over. People were advised to stay away from it. A gusty thunderstorm could have knocked it right down, and all we could do was hope it wouldn't fall on anyone when it did.

I noticed Peter's first stabs of regret when he returned home the day Vince and his crew had erected the main 2-story wall. But that was just the beginning. It was time to start the Resurrection City-style slum of tarpaper, demolition debris, cardboard boxes, and plastic sheeting. Peter's next shocker was when a dump truck emptied a load of junk from Baltimore street corners on his beautiful grass pasture.

"What the fuck is that?" he asked.

"Those are my set building materials," said Vince, "we'll need two or three more truckloads."

On the Mortville set of Desperate Living.

l-r Kevin Weber, John, Richard Ellsberry ©Robert Maier

"Okaaaaay," said Peter doubtfully, "but make sure you haul every scrap of paper away when you're done."

"Oh sure, you won't know we were ever here, it will be in better shape than we found it," said Vince with supreme confidence.

*Me as the soundman on
the Mortville set.*

*Me as the production manager
worried about the Mortville set.*

It was a line I would use many times as a production or location manager on dozens of later productions, usually to seal the deal, but too often not fulfilled. One time I arrived on a set to find the grips had cut down a whole 20 ft. tree in someone's front yard without permission. Another time they had chainsawed a 4x6 foot hole in the side of someone's house—to get a better camera angle.

Support facilities at the farm consisted mostly of personal cars—since there were no auxiliary buildings, and we couldn't afford a large tent, much less trailers or motor homes for the cast. If you wanted to sit down, warm up, or dry off you had to duck into your car, turn on the engine and hope for a few minutes rest before being called back to the set.

On the first shoot day, we discovered that the house's ancient septic system could not handle the dozens of cast, crew, and busload of extras. It overflowed in the house's bathroom and then the septic system in the front yard. Peter and Laurel were horrified, and the movie people were banned from using their facilities. They had to use the woods as their lavatory until a porta-pot was brought in a day later. The trip to the farm was a long one. The extras were met by a rickety, unheated rented school bus in Fells Point. Many of the extras were street bums from the Fells Point Mission who were looking for something a little different from walking the streets, and also a free meal. Curious hipsters who had answered ads to be an extra in a John Waters movie filled the other seats on the bus. Though most had cars, we forbid their driving. If they had their own transportation, too many would leave halfway through the day, and we'd never get our shots done. Having to ride the bus insured that they would be stuck on the farm until we didn't need them anymore. It rumbled through the city, past the suburbs and into farm country and took well over an hour. The extras were cold and shaken and not terribly happy when they arrived to discover no warm shelter awaited them, and things didn't get much better.

To feed the extras on a tight budget, Laurel and a few other Dreamland friends teamed up to talk me into subsidizing their making huge batches of chili. It seemed to be a good idea because of the cool, damp Baltimore fall weather. Laurel wasn't much of a cook though, and the servings were tiny. The busload of bum extras were delighted, but the crew instantly rebelled. Again, I had to make a pizza run into the town, which was several miles away. This extended the lunch break, which upset John. He didn't understand why the crew couldn't eat the chili, thinking they were primadonnas who weren't into the low-budget spirit. When everyone got terribly ill from the chili one day, the crew never slowed down and John stopped complaining.

I also befriended the little country pizza parlor, and made a deal to call them with a pre-order, and then rush to their store, pay, and return. But by the time I returned to the set, the pizzas were usually pretty cold and messy. Not having a production assistant to run errands like that, and not being able to leave the set because I had to record sound was a painful education.

Here was the production manager extending the lunch—what an abomination! I could never solve this lunch problem, because there was no money for a PA, and at that point in my career I hadn't realized that PAs would be happy to work for free, just for the experience. John didn't think it was a big deal and never recognized I might need help. But I absolutely resolved that on any of my future productions, I would always do one job, have PAs to run errands, and always pre-arrange a catered lunch on site, or I would get out of the business completely.

The farm had no accommodation for the extras. It was cold, and they mostly just stood around smoking cigarettes and shivering. John got the idea to build small fires in trashcans so they could get a little warmth. The smoke enhanced Mortville's desperate look too. It polluted the air though, and we'd change camera angles frequently, because the crew got smoked out every time the wind changed. One positive was that the extras didn't need much acting ability to look miserable. They already were. The nudist extras and day players had it the worst, and it's amazing that they put up with it for no pay at all.

It rains a lot in Baltimore, and the Desperate Living exterior shoot days were no exception. Mostly it was a cold drizzle, and every person was wretched, because we had to shoot, rain or not. Mud was a problem. It sucked the shoes right off your feet. Vince added thin board sidewalks so we could at least navigate the set. Van, the wardrobe designer also added trash bags and plastic sheeting to many of the costumes to give the extras more protection against the weather.

In the middle of one week, a downpour flooded the creek that wound through the set. Peter called John with the bad news that he couldn't even get his own car to the house, and half of Mortville appeared to have floated away. Vince, John, and I quickly drove out to assess the damage. Luckily, the castle held, and the worst was that a few shacks and junk that decorated the streets had to be retrieved from the trees where they had hung up, and everything was quickly put back together. But it alerted us that a heavier rain could be an absolute disaster. The set was built along a creek that could flood thirty feet on each side in a heavy rain. We realized there that we could lose everything and we had to wrap out of there as soon as possible. We had no insurance and no contingency. Another big consideration was that Liz Renay was being paid a huge (for us) weekly fee, and we couldn't pay her for extra days if we added extra days due to a set washout.

One Saturday morning in Mortville, the rented 16mm movie camera suddenly quit, and of course we didn't have a back-up. Like every day, a big scene was scheduled with dozens of extras, day players, and all the leads. But once again, the State of Maryland came to the rescue. The Maryland Public Television station where Tom L'oizeaux and I worked had several cameras sitting on a shelf. Being Saturday, the station would be dead. It was also less than thirty minutes away. Tom gallantly offered to drive to the station, secretly grab the camera and then race back to the set. He was so well known and trusted, the security guard wouldn't think a thing of it.

We took an early lunch break, and Tom returned less than an hour later.

Knowing we had violated a cardinal rule at the station, I asked him if he had run into any problems. He looked a little ashen-faced, and said while he was in the camera room, one of the sound guys on duty asked him what he was shooting. Tom said he wanted to test the camera, because it had been running a little funny. He told me he hoped the guy bought it, but he had a sinking feeling that maybe not.

Monday morning when I came in, I was immediately summoned to the film department head's office. He already knew Tom and I were working weekends on John's film, which was OK, but it was strictly against station policy to use its gear for outside projects. The sound guy had told him about Tom's taking a camera, and he knew it had to be for John's film. We were caught red-handed. But the department head was cool, and said though he could fire us on the spot, he knew we were sincere hard workers, and didn't want to wreck our young careers. Tom had already explained it was an emergency situation that would not be repeated, and the film head said he'd forget it if we promised to absolutely not do it again, because if it got up to the higher administration, he'd lose his job too.

John seemed to have a charmed life. None of the risks we took had bad endings, and most people were willing to cut us a break. There were bumps in the road, but we always made it through the bad situations, I guess because they sensed that doing what we were doing for next to nothing was really commendable.

Desperate Living ground on. People were tired of the lousy food, the lack of shelter, the mud, the ugly set, the smoky fires, pathetic extras, insufficient equipment, and tiny crew. There was no assistant director or continuity person to help John get through the days. I was tied up recording sound on every take, so I couldn't help smooth things along or anticipate problems like a unit manager should. We were all trapped in Mortville, and couldn't wait to escape. We knew we were taking great risks every day, with no back-up. The only solution was to get the job done and get out of there.

The only effect I noticed of this pressure is the lack of close-ups in the film. This was similar to Female Trouble, but to a much greater extent. Nearly every shot is a single wide master with dialogue bouncing from one side of the screen to another. It is like a filmed stage play. Then again, John always told me he wished it could be an opera. Sometimes there is a silent reaction shot close-up, but there are so many missed opportunities for great close-ups of people delivering hilarious lines, the electrifying costumes, and genius set details.

Desperate Living had many more stunning details than John's previous films. The costumes and sets are an amazing multi-colored visual feast. The real locations are interesting and rich in natural detail. Maybe the biggest problem was there was not enough time for shooting multiple angles. I had procured an expensive dolly that we paid for only on the days it was used, but only one dolly shot appears in the whole film. There was never the time or space to plan and execute dolly shots.

The overall camera operation suffers too. Even on still shots, John unconsciously shakes the camera, just enough to irritate on the large screen. When an actor stands up, there's either too much headroom or too little. The occasional zoom is always wobbly.

The last shot of Desperate Living was a grand dance on Mortville's Main Street celebrating the overthrow of the evil

Queen Carlotta. John wanted this to be a spectacular shot, and we planned it well in advance. First, to see all the action, we put the camera on top of a truck. This was revolutionary because John's camera was always at eye-level; no tricky high or low angles for him. But the final shot was to begin with an extreme close-up then move to an extreme wide shot with a very slow zoom that revealed all of Mortville. John was saving his establishing shot for the end—a little weird.

The end credits would roll over this scene; another very fancy touch for John. Tom, Dave, and I begged John to let Tom operate the camera and perform the difficult zoom professionally. John was adamantly against it, until I said, with the smoothly rolling animated credits, the background shot had to be mechanically smooth, or it would distract the audience and they wouldn't be able to read the credits. That he understood, and let Tom get the shot. John had always gotten the "filmed by" credit, and this would be the first exception. Tom's shot was perfect. Ironically, John would never operate a camera again on any of his other films. It was real breakthrough.

Unfortunately, though I had rented extra lights to capture the big finale night shot, there wasn't enough electricity, and you can't see much of the town. This was probably for the best, because by this time, it was almost impossible to find extras who would take the freezing cold 60 minute-one way bus ride to the set to sit in the mud and rain all day for a bowl of chili and cup of coffee. The big dancing scene would have looked pretty pathetic if you could see how few people were actually in it. But that was Desperate Living. In hindsight, if someone said here's $65,000 to make this costume drama, I would have told them to take the money and jump off a bridge; they'd have a better chance of success.

As soon as I got home after every shoot day, John would call and we'd review the day for an hour or more. He worried about everything. People were sick from the food; it was cold and wet. Was Liz Renay happy? Would we have enough film? Would I be able to help with post-production working at the public TV station? Actors were balking at having to eat real roaches, do nude lesbian love scenes, deal with multiple dead animal props, or perform ludicrous sex scenes they knew they would probably regret to the end of their lives. They wanted to be actors, not side show freaks.

Edith, who had a big part with lots of lines, could not remember them with any amount of coaching. We were burning through half the film stock budget on her. This stressed John, which ratcheted up Edith's stress, and shortened her memory even more. Over the phone, I again suggested we break up her scenes and assemble them together in the edit, but he shouted,

"No, I want her to say her lines in one take; Edith is not going to force me how to direct my movie. We'll do it until she gets it right; I don't care how much film it takes."

Edith's absolute worst day was a throne room scene, where she never got it right even after 20 something takes. In the take that appears in the film, she flubs the line, stops, goes back, and repeats a couple words. John was steady to the end. No cutaways; just master shots; the flub is in the film, but I'm sure it only enhances dear Edie's reputation.

One of the backers of the film was a bored guy who made John uncomfortable. He started hanging around the set most of the day, which broke a primary Dreamland rule. John ordered me to call the guy and find a way to explain that the set was closed to everyone, and that this was my rule, not John's. John didn't want the guy mad at him.

The investor initially wanted to video tape the shoots. The first day he brought a crappy little black and white video deck, but got in everybody's way, and drove John to the edge of distraction. Since he had loaned John money on several of his previous films, it was a touchy situation. I said I could bar him from the set, but he'd probably never invest in another of John's films again. I called the guy and explained that he was distraction, as kindly as I could, and though I think his feelings were hurt, he said he understood and never came again. Apparently he never felt any animosity, because he never complained to John about it. Mission accomplished.

New Line was pleased with how John's films were going. They were proud that he had Desperate Living up and going so quickly after Female Trouble and had suggested that they might want to fund his next film with real money. No more begging friends and family, and emptying his own bank account for the chump change required to make hellishly cheap movies that had a budget line for everything but him.

It was during these long phone calls that John and I were closest. John was making a huge financial leap with his film. He wanted to go big time, to make a big production with real production values: dozens of costumes, big sets, a real crew, and an original symphonic music score. It would be blown up to 35mm so it could be screened in real movie theaters around the world. He had to be legit. Everything had to be bought or rented, not borrowed or stolen or snuck under the table. And because the money wasn't there, he depended on me and the others to keep him out of trouble and get the job done. We had to complete the film with tenacity, money from our own pockets, connections, huge risks, and ultimately the kindness of others. John knew that many, many low budget films failed. They were abandoned halfway through due to under-funding or mismanagement, could not find a distributor, were ignored by the media, or flopped so badly at the box office that they were immediate career enders.

John needed sympathy, someone to say don't worry, everything would be alright, and you're in good hands. I got your back; whatever you need done, I'll do it. I was that person. I'd finished college. The crew members were my friends; I knew where to get the right kind of equipment at the right price. I was the pathfinder through the jungle.

That might sound like bragging, but the reality was that I kept going out of sheer ignorance of the odds against success. This was my first movie, and every day was brand new. I was bullet-proof only because I was 24 years old. I didn't know yet what could go really wrong on a movie. I would find that out on future movies and look back on Desperate as a quaint experience where we were unbelievably lucky.

Desperate Living Post-production

Desperate Living ended quietly, with a huge sigh of relief. I don't remember a wrap party or other celebration, except that it was probably absorbed into John's annual Christmas party. Charles busily assembled the miles of 16mm footage. He had purchased his own 16mm flat bed film editing machine. To save money, he suggested to John that they edit in the basement of the small suburban rancher where he lived with his elderly mother. The basement was typical suburban Baltimore with a washing machine, workbench, boxes of Christmas decorations, and a toilet for the black maid. It didn't fit John's quest for chic, but John was not yet so famous that he could make foppish demands. He still lived in a ghetto, drove a crappy car, crashed with poor friends when he went to New York, and had not developed a taste for transatlantic travel. He was spending his days in a tract house basement in Catonsville, Maryland, wondering if it would ever be worth it. And he was fortunate to find another dedicated supporter in this Baltimore basement who would help him achieve his dream.

Charles gave John a great deal, editing the entire film, including his new $7,500 editing machine, for $7,500 flat, no matter how long it took. So, Desperate Living's entire post-production budget was $7,500—excluding music. Charles was not a greedy person. He enjoyed working with John, and after all, $7,500 was a gigantic step up from the $300 he had received for Female Trouble.

A strict editing schedule of 9:00 a.m. to 5:00 p.m. was set, which suited John well. He was an early riser and was early for every appointment in his life. He told me he was even born two months premature. When meeting John somewhere I would find him sitting in his car reading a magazine and listening to his favorite black radio station in a fog of cigarette smoke, wishing everybody else would hurry up and get there. He wanted to start editing earlier, but Charles was strict about 9:00 a.m., not wanting to rush his mother through breakfast.

John usually got to Catonsville a half-hour early, but didn't want to park in front of Charles' house, smoking cigarettes in his unwashed 10 year old brown Buick. The neighbors would surely call the cops. So, he would stop first at a local convenience store, buy a donut and a Coke for breakfast, and a jar of pickles and bag of potato chips for snacks, then read in his car until five before nine, when he dashed the last 5 blocks to Charles' house. He had to use the back basement door, and Charles opened it at nine sharp; you could set your watch by it.

John and Charles ate lunch in the kitchen upstairs with Charles' mother, who fixed sandwiches. This 9-5 routine, plus a 30 minute lunch break with Charles' mom, would be a much more believable Baltimore situation if these two guys were working on a model train set in the basement, instead of an X-rated movie with lesbian rapes, do-it-yourself sex change operations, and baked rat dinners. As usual, John charmed Charles' mother, and she thought he was a perfect gentleman. This is such a contrast to his films. He is like a split personality. In his writings, he goes to great lengths to claim he is only a humorist and is shocked when people ask him questions like "Do you have parents?" or "Do you live in the woods?" thinking he lives in a trailer eating cold beans from a can and pulls wings off flies as a hobby.

The funniest editing situation happened when a couple of Charles' friends who worked in Baltimore City's Mayor's office came to visit. They were black, and dressed in business suits, and as Charles had instructed them, walked around the back of the house to the basement entrance. A neighbor noticed them and called the police to report black people were prowling in the backyards. John and Charles heard shouting, looked out the basement window and saw several policemen with guns drawn shouting "freeze, get down on the ground."

Charles and John ran out, and the cops cooled down when they saw the Baltimore City Mayor's office IDs. I wonder what the cops thought of long-haired John and straight-laced Charles running out of the basement. If they'd had a clue an X-rated movie was being cut there, they'd have arrested everyone.

John loved the excitement, and was awed at how fast the cops arrived to a call of "black people in the neighborhood." It was a classic example of Baltimore racism, and confirmed an essential thematic element of John's films—that suburbia was a scary, dangerous place for those who didn't fit the mold. Charles' black friends were used to racism and brushing themselves off, said they wished cops came that fast when called to their neighborhood.

The editing moved along very well. Charles moaned about the lack of close-ups and coverage, which slowed the film's pacing. John never wanted to cut tails off scenes, or rush the dialogue. His words were too precious, and he wanted the audience to savor them. This was as frustrating for Charles as it was during the shooting. He told John that it was like a recording of a stage play, but he just brushed it off.

The experience of recording the musical score was fairly routine. John wanted a lush symphonic score, like a Douglas Sirk tear-jerker. He hired two local classical music students to write and arrange the music, who in-turn hired several string players moonlighting from their union jobs with the Baltimore Symphony Orchestra. Charles spent a lot of time setting up a "click-track" to get the timing roughly in sync with the picture, but it wasn't sophisticated frame-accurate post-scoring. There was no picture at the recording session. It was all done to Charles' list of time cues, so it wasn't much more advanced than dropping in background music from a pre-recorded library.

Though it was recorded in a basic studio in the back of strip mall music store, it was still way more expensive than lifting music from friends' record collections. To keep the price down, the recordings were rushed. The players never quite got the parts down. They never really got their instruments tuned. All the instruments were recorded together, and the engineers were extremely rushed, so the mixes are pretty raw. The composition and arrangements were clever, but there was not enough music for a sound-track album, and symphonic music was so unfashionable, no one thought it would sell on its own. Ultimately, the music suffered from the same malady of the rest of the film. It showed promise, but was too ambitious for the budget, and at the end of the day, couldn't quite deliver the goods, and feels pretty cheesy. To many, that's the charm of John's movies, and Desperate Living is their absolute favorite, warts and all.

After slogging through nearly a year of production, from Lane's first typed script page to the first virgin print out of the film lab, Desperate was ready for its Baltimore premiere. John was the most insane I had ever seen him, mainly preparing to deal with the Maryland State Board of Censors. The Board, created in 1916, was a leftover of Maryland's odd combination of 1950s Puritanism and enraged Catholicism. Its job was to protect the morals of pious Marylanders by physically cutting out potentially sexually arousing scenes from projection prints of offending movies. John actually has a three foot strip of 16mm film snipped from one of his earlier movies, accompanied with an official receipt from the Censor Board for "one cunnilingus scene."

All movies shown in Maryland required a certificate of approval from the Censor Board. Its members were politically appointed, mostly religious zealots who represented everything in American culture John rebelled against. That they could snip scenes from his movies drove him mad. I couldn't change his movies, Tom L'oizeaux couldn't, Charles Roggero couldn't, New Line Cinema couldn't, and the American press couldn't. But the Maryland State Board of Censors in flagrant violation of the U.S. Constitution could. The Board was led by the infamous Mary Avara, a middle school dropout and proprietor of a bail bond agency who claimed she "wore the armor of God" in protecting innocent Marylanders from the likes of John Waters. John could fight them in court, but it would cost hundreds of thousands of dollars. The arrogant

State of Maryland would defend its blessed Censor Board with millions of dollars in taxpayer money, all the way to the U.S. Supreme Court. John knew it, and it made him insane.

He'd call me nightly in the days before his appointed screening with the Board. I suppose he could have shown the movie without approval, and have the police raid the theater where it would premiere, chain himself to the print reels, and be dragged off to jail. It would have made quite a splash in the world press—like when one of his actors was arrested for public nudity. But that wasn't John. He was a creative artist, not a dedicated political activist. He'd rather write about something than take a public action. He never really wanted to spend a night in jail, or pay a huge fine to the State of Maryland. That would put him over the edge. Instead, he complained to me on the phone.

His two previous films went through the Board with a few short snips. The audiences roundly booed the Censor Board seal at the head of his movies, and John's favorite Baltimore target, Mary Avara, was the butt of countless cruel comments from John in the national media. In a way, Mrs. Avara, a loony with a bad wig and thick Bawlmer accent was John's frenemy, and an endless source of comic material that probably helped more than hurt.

After all the wailing, the Censor Board amazingly didn't cut one frame from Desperate Living. They knew they were on their way out with the cultural changes of the 1960s and 70s, and John would never suffer their indignity on another film. I met John for drinks after the screening (he said he needed several), and he was crushed from the fact that he had to submit the film and grovel before "those cretins." His eyes welled with tears, and I could only think: "Hey, you finished a torturous film, New Line is embracing it, and you have crossed a minefield; get over Mary Avara."

The last step in the process was making a 35mm blow-up from the 16mm original, which New Line was funding, so it could open in regular movie theaters, and not just the few art houses with 16mm projectors. John and I went to New York to oversee the process, which meant sitting in a lab all day and then schlepping the brand new 35mm print over to a screening room New Line had booked for the first press viewing. It was a hot, humid July day, and since the screening room was a block away from the lab, John decided to save the cab fare and carry the film ourselves. Where a 16mm feature is two small reels of film, a 35mm feature has nine heavy reels that fill two wide cases that weigh about 30 pounds each. When we picked them up, John said he'd never make it, and we should take a cab. When we hit the street, it was about 100 degrees. Traffic around Times Square was in gridlock, with no empty cabs in sight, so we had to hand-carry the film anyway. Halfway there, we were about dead. The sun blazed and John's clothes were soaked through with sweat—something I'd never seen before. We stopped five or six times to take a break from the heavy film cans that looked like they were relics from the 1930s. Their jagged edges ripped John's chic designer linen pants. The thin metal handles cut into our hands. In the midst of weaving through Times Square's taxi gridlock, the lunchtime shoulder-to shoulder crowd of bums, and the sidewalk hustlers we stopped to wait for a light to change, about to collapse. John gave me one of his most crazed looks.

"Look around. We are in hell right now. After all I have to go through to make a movie, now I have to drag the fuckin' film five miles through Times Square in a 150 degree heat. We're in low budget hell, Bobby."

John's Change of Life

We made it to the screening on time, and the press was shocked and impressed, and many wrote positive reviews. Everyone felt good, and New Line was delighted.

New Line's embracing Desperate Living boded well for our futures. It was definitely better produced than John's other films, and it had a "name" in Liz Renay. They hired one of New York's biggest PR agencies, John Springer Associates, who handled Liz Taylor and other biggies. With Liz Taylor's press agent, John felt he had hit the big time, and he knew he was moving away from Bumberg's Mary Avara and its pinhead movie critics. After years of bumbling with John's early films, New Line was finally paying attention. More private screenings for the international press were scheduled in New York's poshest theaters and screening rooms. John's schedule was thick with interviews, and Desperate was booked in both uptown and downtown mainstream theaters.

This cost a lot of money, which the film's gross income had to pay back before anyone saw a penny. However, New Line and John could both hitch their stars to the media splash. It wasn't so important to these young companies that Desperate have a huge box office gross. This was a loss leader. The big NYC opening cost a fortune in posters, print ads, press kits, screening facilities, luncheons, invitation-only champagne-doused parties, agency fees, flying celebrities around, making 35mm prints, and guaranteeing the theaters a minimum in ticket sales. In one of the great ironies of low budget filmmaking, the promotion and distribution costs were way more than the film's $65,000 production budget. Of course, New Line charged its own overhead fees against the film's gross—as did John. Though this was on a much smaller scale, it is why the star of a blockbuster movie sues the distributor because she never received a penny of the profits she was promised. So many expenses are charged against movies that frequently no profits are seen at all.

Desperate Living did not do well financially. It closed faster than anyone expected at the NYC theaters, which discouraged theater owners around the U.S. from jumping in line, despite all the press. It played mostly in John's regular outlets, to his regular audience. Without Divine though, it struggled even in those markets. In the early days, Divine drew the big gay audience, not John. The younger movie-going generation didn't care much about Liz Renay or Edith Massey. On top of that, John made his only sexy ingénue, Bonnie Pierce, horribly ugly. The few quick foreign sales didn't yield much profit. Desperate Living was an ugly, obsessive movie, that could have been funnier, but John focused on the gross-out.

Female Trouble maintained a good balance between shock and humor, which is why many think it's his best film. But since it didn't do well in the box office either, John experimented with Desperate Living, testing his audience's capacity for his most outrageous fantasies. Except for a group of hard core fanatics, most Waters fans chalk it up as a transitional work with strokes of brilliance, but ultimately not as satisfying as Pink or Female Trouble.

On the positive side for John, it showed him as an emerging force in American culture who could handle the press and delight audiences—in personal appearances, either as a late-night TV guest or well-paid lecturer on the college and arts circuits. John Springer's publicity machine opened many important doors to the national celebrity glitterati of visual artists, actors, gallery owners, fashion designers, and writers. I won't list them here, but you can buy John's book, Role Models, to experience the avalanche of name dropping that establishes

John as a leading arts and cultural figure. This really began with Desperate Living; it was his greatest benefit from the movie—and a priceless one.

The transformation did not happen overnight. New Line had now opened the door to show that they could handle U.S. distribution and international sales of U.S. products. Formerly they distributed foreign films to college film societies and small art movie houses. That did not attract big production money, which is where Bob Shaye wanted to go. He wanted to become a Hollywood mogul. The cheesy shock films of John Waters were not his first choice to get there, but it was the hand he had been dealt, and he played it. He leveraged Desperate Living's small crack in Hollywood's door into the Hollywood movie giant that New Line later became.

With John's new found public profile, our movie date nights became irregular. He travelled frequently, and he was increasingly absent from the Fells Point Friday night bar scene. We met occasionally to vaguely discuss what was happening with Desperate Living, and what might come next—what new countries had picked it up, what cities in the U.S. it had played, and he'd bring me photocopies of reviews.

Money was a popular subject, since John was seeing more of it than ever before, and elevating his tastes. John had never had a credit card, but with flying around, having to rent cars and stay at hotels, it was becoming obvious that he should have one. I'd had a Diner's Club card since college, so I'd had experience with one. In the beginning, John thought credit cards were bourgeois, but when I explained to him that they were essential for travel and keeping track of expenses like business meals and bookstore purchases, he decided to get one.

John took his first trip to Europe, England mainly, and was thoroughly enchanted. He was never a coffee or tea drinker, but after his return when I visited his apartment, he always served tea. It was very good tea in fine China cups with English biscuits, elegant creamer and sugar bowl, and he raved about English culture. This was from a guy who claimed he hated food. It was quite a change.

John also discovered the joy of all-cotton sheets in English hotels. Formerly, his bed linens were whatever he found at a Baltimore thrift shop. Now, they had to be new 300 thread count Egyptian cotton designer sheets that could only be found in the best New York stores, where he was spending more and more of his free time. Instead of shopping exclusively at thrift stores, he was paying more attention to assembling a wardrobe of cutting edge designer clothes from New York's most chic boutiques. The Prince of Puke was going through a life change. It didn't surprise me; I'd been to Europe several times and knew what he meant. It was nice to see John learning that life was not one hideous side show after another.

John was also inching his way toward achieving bona fide fop status, and I was impressed. His shocking movies, writings, and lectures were good attention getters, but his personal lifestyle was becoming more attracted to good restaurants, even more money for books, frequent invites to celebrity parties, and more interviews with the mainstream press.

My one-year contract at Maryland Public Television was up soon after DL was on its merry way, and I was offered another one-year contract there. I had become familiar with Sarah Risher and Bob Shaye at New Line. They were grateful and impressed that I shepherded Desperate Living through without any tragedies. When I mentioned the possibility of one day moving to New York, they hinted that they might need a sharp, low-budget production manager for more movies, which were very much in their future plans.

With this good karma, I decided to go out on my own, and declined the new public TV contract. I had been stuck at UMBC for nearly four years, and didn't want to settle down in another state job at a boring public TV station. I had tasted the big time with Desperate Living. There were no other opportunities in Baltimore for low-budget films. But I had my sound recording equipment, a few years' experience, and recognizable credits, so I could survive as a freelance sound recordist, while prepping to be a movie producer—especially in New York. Time was running out. I had to go for it.

6
Downtown New York City

....

Within days of leaving Maryland Public TV, I was recommended by a cameraman there to a friend in NYC who was breaking into low-budget features. He was starting a film in a few weeks that needed a soundman. The pay was good enough that I could live in a cheap hotel for a month, make some good connections, and still come home to Baltimore with some money. I took the quick train ride to New York, met with them, and they offered me the job. The Fox Affair was being made by a pair of Iranians who had specialized in making expensive propaganda films for the Shah. This was 1977 and with the loosening of censorship in Iran, they discovered that Western films with glitzy locations, glimpses of female nudity, flashy cocktails, and pistol-packing dudes were very attractive to Iranian men looking to escape their restrictive Islamic past. It drove the Mullah fundamentalists crazy, but the Shah seemed to have them under control.

The Iranians set up shop in New York, to crank out low-budget, non-union quickies, dubbed into Persian and shipped to their theatres in Iran. The demand for these films was insatiable, and they promised me an unlimited amount of work, if I would work cheap to get this one off the ground. Sounded great to me.

Since the production office was off Times Square, I looked at several hotels nearby where I could stay for the month of shooting. All were ridiculously cheap, but I decided on the Edison Hotel on 47th Street. At that time, NYC was at its lowest point. Times Square was mostly porno movie houses and convenience stores that sold hot dogs and flea powder to the homeless who squatted in abandoned buildings. The Edison was once an elegant 1930s deco palace in the heart of Times Square, but had become a flop house by the 1970s. The front desk people were appalled that I wanted to stay there for so long. Empty wine bottles lined the hallways. An occasional scream echoed down the hall at night. Dirty handprints covered the walls, and the threadbare carpets were sticky with God knows what. My room was a shoebox and you could barely turn around in the bathroom. It had a shower that turned from barely tepid to a scalding hot gusher when an upper floor toilet flushed. I kept the glass shower door open so I could jump out quickly without shattering it trying to escape getting boiled alive like a lobster. The front desk shrugged when I told them about it. It was cheap, so what could I do? I figured this was just paying my dues like all great artists who moved to New York to make it big.

The cast and crew were non-union people trying to break into the big time too, and I kept in close touch with some of them for years. The exception was an angry filthy-mouthed White Russian émigré, Walter (but everyone pronounced it "Valter" like he did), who was the king of New York low budget film technicians. He owned beat-up movie cameras, a van full of rusty lights, and was angry with me, because I brought my own recording gear, which denied him of renting his to the Iranians. When I told him what I was being paid, he said I was too cheap and ruining the business. At the same time, he said if I had a film in Baltimore, he'd bring down all the equipment and expertise, beat any price, and slip a little something extra under the table for me.

I think most of his work was in the porno industry. Many Russian émigrés who had worked in the Soviet film industry had jobs on the night shift of the big NYC film labs, and he could sneak them film to process for cash—even XXX rated porn that was still illegal.

I travelled through many unfamiliar sections of New York while shooting The Fox Affair. We shot in cheesy discos all over town and staged a nude pool scene at a private gym on Wall Street one Sunday morning. A friend of Valter's arranged it. I spent days shooting soft core sex, drugs, and drinking in flashy stretch limos, which were cheap, easy locations—and driven by Valter's Russian buddies, of course. One day we drove through endless cross-town traffic to a private dump out in Long Island where a car was blown-up—another Valter connection—by an unlicensed special effects person.

We didn't have a film permit, insurance, craft service or a caterer. But the Iranian guys and the rest of the crew were friendly and encouraging, except for Valter who was a certifiable nut and whom everybody ignored. The atmosphere was like a Waters film, where everybody knew they were paying their dues, and trying very hard. We were paid on time without asking, and the producers threw a nice wrap party, promising to call us all again soon for the next film. They urged me to permanently move to New York right away. They planned to shoot twenty more films in the next two years, and said they would call me soon.

Much of the crew stayed in the low-budget groove for many years. The big exception was Skip Lievsay, who was the production manager, but went on to become the main post-production sound guy in the NYC movie scene, doing all the

Coen Brothers films, plus Scorsese, Spike Lee, and Jonathan Demme. I gave him his first feature film sound editor job on Polyester, where he was a savior.

John was proud that I had landed a Job in New York, but could also see that I was likely on my way out of Baltimore, and he might lose a helpful worker bee. But because it was just three hours away, Baltimore was almost a suburb of New York, so even if I did move there permanently, I could still work with him.

Despite the near flop of Desperate Living, John got busy taking notes for his next film, travelling to openings and lectures, and quietly beginning to write his first book, Shock Value, where he could detail his bizarre life story to his expanding fan base. Back in Baltimore, while waiting for more calls from New York, I traveled around the country working as a sound recordist mainly on small informational films and TV commercials for producers in Washington, DC, and Baltimore.

John and I met for updates when both of us were in town, which wasn't regular, especially since his summers were spent in Provincetown. He didn't have money for a new film at this point, but New Line was encouraging him to write another script. They weren't happy with the reception of Desperate Living, and I think were actually ashamed of it. They wanted something more mainstream gore fest, like George Romero's Night of the Living Dead, Tobe Hooper's Texas Chain Saw Massacre, and Wes Craven's The Last House on the Left which were break-through low-budget films that made millions of dollars and marked a profound change in the American movie business. You didn't need big stars, top union crews, or $50 million budgets any more—you just needed buckets of fake blood and sexy teen victims willing to go topless in a few scenes.

John's films were breakthrough, but only with sophisticated big-city art-house audiences. White suburban teens, the people who bought movie tickets by the millions, were not so interested in things like insider gay jokes. Plus, John's obsessive fantasies, and sophisticated urban irony and satire that poked fun at their very lifestyles and core cultural beliefs went way over their heads. After three John Waters movies, it was becoming clearer that he would not propel New Line to the big time, on the level of Romero, Hooper, and Craven.

If New Line were to put big money into John's films, he had to move away from the silly fantasy world of Desperate Living. John had to write something that a mainstream audience could identify with. No gay Wizard of Oz salutes, no clownish cults, or ugly experts. John had to tell a good story that normal people could relate to. It was a simple thing to New Line. But John had a hard head, and a harder road was still ahead.

I kept in touch with the Iranians in New York, hoping they would have another film soon. They were optimistic, but the political situation back in Iran was rapidly unraveling. Islamic fundamentalists were demonstrating by the hundreds of thousands, demanding the ouster of the Western-friendly Shah. They wanted their country to be a strict theocracy with no alcohol, no discos, no sex in the movies (or anywhere else), and no commerce with the United States. In my last call to the Iranian producers, they were horror-struck. Religious mobs had burned their theaters and made bonfires with the prints of their decadent Western movies. A few weeks later, the Shah was kicked out of the country, the ayatollahs took over, and the rest is history. The next time I called, their phone had been disconnected, and I heard the producers with so many big plans had become waiters in a Persian restaurant in Queens. This would not be the first disconnected phone number that would mark a big change in my world of low-budget movies. But it was the first time I experienced that things could go very wrong on the road to fame and fortune.

With all the traveling I was doing, I was away from my home in Fells Point many nights. I was the only urban pioneer in the block, and felt eyes peering out the neighbors' windows wondering about the single guy who was hardly ever there. The older lady next door who had lived her whole life in the neighborhood occasionally said hello, but never much more.

Many people who had moved to Fells Point in the 1970s had been broken into several times or assaulted. My house had been broken into three times in four months. It must have been dumb kids, because they stepped over my $500 microphones and took a $5 clock radio. I called the cops, but they could only suggest putting bars on the windows and doors. I didn't want to live in a prison.

After my last break-in, I drove out to the suburbs and sat in my car outside a gun store for an hour trying to decide if I would buy a pistol to keep under my pillow. Not wanting to deal with the uncertainties of shooting a teenage glue sniffer, or getting shot myself, I resolved instead to leave Fells Point and move permanently to New York at the first opportunity.

I had never upgraded the house beyond Vince and Delores' kitchen redecoration, and the bar scene was changing. When John was in Baltimore, he was becoming more uptown oriented anyway. He became good friends with a wealthy, well-connected lawyer who lived with his wife and precocious children in a mansion in Baltimore's most elegant uptown neighborhood. They were cultural rainmakers and had adopted the Baltimore Film Festival as their pet project and spent hundreds of hours

raising funds, writing grants, and learning the joys of hob-
nobbing with filmmakers and large, enthusiastic audiences.
John's encyclopedic knowledge of art films, as well as his own
growing international reputation was a perfect match. Instead
of 50 cent rum and cokes in Fells Point on Friday night, it was
martinis and caviar at dinner parties with members of the City
Council, the library director, and Baltimore's wealthy Jewish
philanthropists, who were responsible for building most of the
city's world-class cultural institutions.

It gave John the opportunity to strut his stuff in his new
designer wear. No more Baltimore thrift store Hawaiian
shirts in Fells Point bars. He would wear raw silk shirts, un-
constructed linen jackets, and pencil-thin black ties on Friday
nights now.

Surprising everybody, I got married to someone my friends
barely knew, after just a three week courtship. Our wedding
was to be a secret, because we didn't want all sorts of fussy
plans, and thought everyone would be aghast that we married
after hardly knowing each other. The morning of the wedding
day I felt a little sheepish at having absolutely nobody come
to the wedding, so we decided to call our very best friends
to be witnesses. I called John and Charles and asked if they
could meet me downtown on Mt. Vernon Square at noon to
witness a surprise. I didn't say what. They came in jacket and
ties, suspicious that it might be my wedding. John was thrilled
to have been asked to a secret ceremony. He has since married
many people, himself, as a minister in the Church of LSD or
something, but he was the best man at my wedding.

After the ceremony, we drank champagne together at a
little bistro for an hour. Out on the street I asked a bystander
to snap a photo of us. It's the only wedding photo we have.

Robert and Catheryn Maier's 1978 wedding photo snapped by a bystander on the street, Mt. Vernon Square, Baltimore.

l-r Charles Roggero, Robert, Catheryn, John Waters
©Robert Maier

After the champagne we headed to the airport for a honeymoon in France. After a quick stop in London to upgrade our wardrobe on the fashionable Kings Road, we rode a motorcycle through Cannes, visited the famous film festival, which was going on at the time, and gawked at the paparazzi swarming around Farrah Fawcett, the great pin-up girl of the 70s. Waiting for our plane home from the Nice airport, we saw Muhammad Ali, who graciously gave my wife a big smile and an autograph, after she ratcheted up enough courage to ask.

I was ready to leave Fells Point, and my wife didn't take to my dark, sinister house either, so we decided to move uptown— to the apartment building next door to John's. It had a 24-hour desk clerk too and we liked the idea of security, because I still traveled so much for work. The apartment was on a corner of the eighth floor, so it was much brighter than the Fells Point row house, and had wonderful panoramic views of the city. It was also in beautiful shape, with elegant old-world plaster moldings, parquet wooden floors, marble bathrooms, and a formal dining room. It was very similar to John's apartment, and like living on Fifth Avenue, until you went out on the street.

My wife's best girl friend in Baltimore, Sheila, was a budding artist and poet who visited New York regularly and had moved there after several break-ins at her Baltimore apartment. She was in a serious relationship with the famous artist Larry Rivers, who had connections for cheap living space in the rough lower Manhattan loft area that was attracting urban pioneer artists—newly dubbed "SoHo." She urged us to move to New York, too, but we had literally been in the new apartment for a few weeks.

But the new apartment had its downside. It was a very, very bad neighborhood, and the bloom of our elegant apartment wore off quickly. Getting from the parking lot to the apartment building was scary. Many nights we'd hear drunken fights on the street outside our windows. One night, hearing terrible screaming, I opened the bedroom window to see a guy getting beaten on the sidewalk. I started yelling, and then threw an empty water glass, which smashed on the sidewalk next to them. The thug looked up, marked my apartment window, and took off with an "I'll take care of you later" look. It was a bit of a motivation to move—already. We planned that this apartment would be a bus stop for a year at most, mainly to see if John would make another film soon, and nurture our New York possibilities for a while.

Andy Warhol's Cocaine Cowboys

Then the phone rang. It was Joe from the UMBC days asking if I was interested in working the summer on a new feature he was co-producing and shooting—in New York. Actually in Montauk, at the tip of Long Island, nearly as far from Manhattan as Baltimore. An actor/director friend of his, Ulli Lommel, who was a name in German New Wave cinema, had recently come to the U.S. to seek his fortune. Most of the film would be shot on Andy Warhol's isolated beachfront compound of 4-5 buildings near Montauk. The crew would bunk up in the compound's several guest cottages. Others would stay in a cheap nearby motel. The story was of a country/rock band that was writing and rehearsing songs on an isolated estate preparing for tour, but also flying kilos of cocaine from South America using a hidden airstrip nearby. The leader falls for an aloof Danish super-model and the mob is chasing them because of a drug deal gone bad. They had already signed Jack Palance, the great menacing Oscar-nominated star from the 1950s and 60s. Now in his 60s, he would work on any film for $5,000 a week, and so lent his star-power name to many low-budget wonders whose producers hoped that a name would give them a better shot at distribution. Joe said they would pay in cash weekly, and my wife was welcome to come too. I said absolutely; another low budget movie; another interesting fork in the road, and a step closer to New York City.

Faced with the fact that we would be leaving our new apartment in Baltimore to live in New York for about three months and still had boxes to unpack, we thought maybe we should just move there now. We had to make a decision quickly, because the movie started in two weeks. My wife called her friend with the news that we would be living on Andy Warhol's estate and shooting a movie that summer. Could she help us find an apartment in Manhattan? Manhattan was still mired in the economic collapse of the early 1970s, and rents could be as cheap as Baltimore. We jumped on a train the next morning and found a loft building with an elevator for $600 a month that afternoon. It was on the corner of Spring and Wooster Streets, the heart of SoHo, surrounded by wonderful cheap restaurants and funky old neighborhood bars. It was about the price of our Baltimore apartment, but much smaller. Every other person on the street was a working artist. Little Italy, Chinatown, and Greenwich Village were short walks away. Today the rent would probably be $6,000 a month.

When we told the Baltimore landlady that we were moving out, she flipped because they had painted our apartment in an assortment of expensive custom colors because we said we would stay there for several years. We claimed this was a once-in-a-lifetime career opportunity, and just had to leave. It meant breaking the lease, but that didn't mean much to us. We ignored the threatening letters after we left, and they eventually gave up.

Because of the imminent start of the movie, I had to leave my wife to deal with the moving and drove my car with my sound gear and clothes straight to Montauk. She followed five days later, riding shotgun in the moving truck. We timed the moving arrival to match the first day off so I could drive back to SoHo, pick her up and return to Montauk, not bothering to unpack a thing. Meeting my wife in April, getting married in May, honeymooning at the Cannes Film Festival, moving to a new apartment in June, then moving to New York in July began the roller coaster ride where we moved ten times in ten years.

The instigator of the film was Tom Sullivan, a sad victim of the 1970s I-wanna-be-a-rock-star culture. Tom allegedly had made a fortune flying hundreds of small plane loads of cocaine from the Amazon jungle to his base in Texas. He was an ambitious country boy from an Oklahoma oil family who wanted to be rich and famous. He hit a roadblock when his plane went down in a fiery crash in Mexico. The legend was that he crawled several days through the jungle, and survived, but had hideous burn scars all over his body, and a bad limp from a shattered leg. He wore a black leather glove to cover one especially gruesome hand.

He claimed it was the end of his drug career, and had decided to become an international celebrity spending some of his drug money to get there. Tom, as a new kid in town with a million bucks burning a hole in his pocket met the Andy Warhol entourage at Studio 54, and became a mark for hustlers who prowled New York's underground art scene. Learning that the Rolling Stones had rented Warhol's estate to prep a past U.S. tour, he felt that could be his path to stardom too. He would be a famous rock star, modeled on the Rolling Stones' sex, drugs, and rock 'n roll image. Tom hired three country musicians from Oklahoma, complete with walrus mustaches and mullets, and decided to make an art movie of the band and their exploits.

It wasn't clear at the beginning how involved Warhol was. Later, his name was all over the PR material for the film, as if he had produced it, but he never seemed to have much to do with it. He spent a few weekends on the set and had a small cameo snapping incongruous Polaroids in the film. He was approachable, and I spoke with him a few times during waits for camera set-ups. He said he had just rented the estate to the film company, and was doing Tom a favor by appearing briefly in the film. He said he didn't like beach, the sun or isolated Montauk, he just rented it out.

Left-behind paperwork from the Rolling Stones tour made interesting reading during the off time. It included incredibly detailed plans for plane schedules, what kind of backstage food and drink must be ready (at least 120 bottles of Heineken and Perrier, a case of Jack Daniels, platters of specifically named cold cuts and pastries), what kind of vehicles had to be rented, the specific drinks, and even the number of pillows required by each Stone in his bedroom. It was an impressively detailed and massive undertaking.

When I asked Andy if he would ever make another film, he answered, "No, making movies is too much work; I just like taking Polaroids and putting my name on things now."

This appeared true, considering his latest movies had been "Andy Warhol's Frankenstein" and "Andy Warhol's Dracula," on which he did nothing. I bought his biography and proudly showed John that he had autographed it. John sniffed, "Andy signs everything. His stuff is more valuable when it's unsigned."

I doubt that Andy had any money in the film. The movie seemed a little bit of a put-up job. The script consisted of Tom's scribbled notes, and most of the shoot days consisted of Tom, Ulli, Chris, and Joe, the director of photography, arguing about the best way to stage a scene. Some days Tom seemed distracted by other business, and we didn't shoot a foot of film. The rock group never seemed to rehearse. They'd sleep until mid-afternoon, then start drinking Heinekens and try to pick up whatever miscellaneous chicks might be hanging around that day.

Work days began with a leisurely delicious breakfast fixed by the wonderfully cheerful resident cook, a young lady in her early 20s, who was friendly to everybody. We then hung out waiting for someone to tell us what to do. There were no call sheets or shooting schedules. We assumed that this was how German New Wave filmmakers worked, and were happy enough to hang out on the main house's back porch and stare at the ocean. The cook had trained on millionaire yachts in the Caribbean, and a continual flow from her kitchen of marinated melon cubes or fresh-made guacamole helped alleviate the boredom. We were paid in cash every week—not a bad gig at all.

Visitors drifted in, sometimes celebrities, hoping to catch Andy there or to check out the rumored movie. They weren't interested in an unknown band, or a cheap movie with no big names, and usually disappeared quickly. One mysterious fixture was Catherine Guinness, a proper British heiress of the Guinness Brewery family. She wrote for Andy's gossipy Interview magazine, but mostly lounged in corners reading books, not wanting to mix with the odd collection of American riff-raff who appeared to have to work for a living. According to biographers of the Warhol Empire, Catherine had a passionate fling with Tom Sullivan, and fell head over heels for the cocky drug-runner/cowboy. Tom evidently quickly dumped her for the more famous Margaret Trudeau (recently divorced from husband Pierre Trudeau, the dashing young Prime Minister of Canada and an icon of the swinging 60s).

This seems improbable, because Tom was totally wrapped up with Winnie Hollman, the Danish supermodel, who stayed on the estate too, and played the lead model part. Tom never seemed to give Catherine more than a howdy-doo. But these were times of experimental sexual liberation, so maybe all three were getting along fine together. The most grotesque sexual moment—that illustrated the times—was when Chris, the German producer, paraded one of the visiting young ladies into his private office/bedroom off the kitchen. This was right in front of the cook, whom he had been screwing, but otherwise generally ignored. She went berserk, throwing knives and pans around the open kitchen while everybody watched, wondering if she would take one of the knives into the bedroom. Chris stormed out of his room, told her she was nothing to him, and then slammed the door shut. She vented louder. Five minutes later Chris returned, walked up to her and dangled a used condom in her face. She burst into tears and ran out, leaving everyone absolutely pissed off at this idiotic piece of Euro-trash. From then on, he was marked, and no one would have anything to do with him except Tom, his band, and the other two Germans.

One day a few members of the Ramones showed up to hang out. I don't remember their names (their names were fake anyway, so I guess it doesn't really matter). For a lark, they did little cameos for the film, and stayed around for dinner and beers with us. It was a long way back to Manhattan. After dinner, we went to a little bar in the village and continued the party. A local band played Top-40 tunes, and a few people danced. The Ramones fit right in with us and were hysterically funny. Eventually half the club watched their antics more than the performing act. Pretty soon, everyone knew that the Ramones were present, and started chanting "Ramones, Ramones, Ramones," louder and louder. The lead singer in the local pop group finally gave up in the middle of a song and asked over the PA system "OK guys, everybody knows you're here. Would you please come up and play a little for them?"

They looked at each other in a why not sort of way, and ran up on the stage where the other musicians handed over their instruments. They launched into a full-tilt "Rockaway Beach," and the audience went insane. What a dream come true. People danced on the tables. They shouted and whistled.

Tom and a couple band members who had come along watched absolutely stunned. This is what they wanted, and they probably wondered if their pampered life on the estate would get people up and grooving like these scruffy Ramones. The Ramones were magic. The Cocaine Cowboys had money, but maybe that wasn't enough. Did they have what it took to play on endless road trips in third rate clubs? Or were the free Heinekens and a string of ingénues enough for them?

Jack Palance was one of the greater characters. Twenty years earlier, he had been a household name, but now about the only work he could get as an actor was in low budget movies. Jack was not a man of many words, and mostly wanted to be left alone, but we were in awe of him, mainly from his tough guy character in the classic Shane. He was a delightful cynic and ridiculed just about everything but my gentile Southern wife, who he was happy to chat with while sitting on a bench, chomping on a cigar stub and gazing out into the ocean. He made fun of the long-hair 70s pop/drug culture of the band and the film crew, and the intensity of the brooding German artists. He walked through his part, and was more interested in getting back to his isolated farm in northern Pennsylvania than delivering a brilliant performance.

I didn't care. He was the biggest movie star I had ever worked with, and a childhood hero, so for me he walked on water. I would be lucky enough work with him again a few years later. Low budget movies had their own subculture of has-been actors, crew, and vendors that kept turning up on film after film, and he and I were part of it.

One shoot day, we ran into legal trouble. We had set up the camera, a few lights, and sound for a quiet dialogue scene on the broad lawn in back of the main house that faced the beautiful rocky beach. In the middle of a take, a group of strangers walked up. This wasn't a big deal, because groups of visitors regularly appeared out of the blue to check out the scene. They usually stood politely back to watch, but this group walked right into the middle of the scene. Ulli shouted out in his crisp academic English, flavored by a thick German accent, "Excuse me, but ve are chooting a movie here, und you've interrupted a scene."

"Well, you'll have to stop, 'cause we're federal agents, and we're doing an investigation," answered a guy with a walrus mustache and bandana around his head. He looked nothing like a cop. Ulli answered,

"Yes, zis is very funny, but you may have ruined a very good take, zo please, you are velcome to vatch, but step back out of the scene."

"No, this isn't funny," the guy said, and pulled out a wallet with a big gold badge on it. He then pulled out a big black pistol from a holster behind his back and shouted, "We're Drug Enforcement Administration. Everybody sit down where you are, drop everything, and put your hands on the ground."

Thinking this had to be a prank, no one believed a word or moved; it had to be one of Andy's jokes. It was like a scene from the movie. Tom then walked around the corner with another group who were carrying shotguns and shouted,

"It's all right everybody. They are federal agents. Be cool, and do what they say. We didn't do anything wrong. I've called my attorney, and he's flying up from Manhattan. This is all a big misunderstanding."

I sat and didn't budge. I'd never had a gun pointed at me before. Tom said they would search the place, and looking through the house's open doors I saw the front drive filling up with cop cars. I thought, oh great, this movie is all a big front for a drug smuggling operation, and I'll end up going to jail. What about my career then? I knew a couple crew people had a few joints in their rooms and I hoped one hadn't accidently landed in mine.

The agents quickly searched the main house and each cottage, but came up with nothing—that they told us about. Tom's lawyers appeared about two hours later and they assured us that nothing bad would happen. They had found about an ounce of grass, total, and nothing else, except a cash box, and though rattled, we continued shooting the movie for the last few hours of daylight.

That evening, another guy arrived with a case of electronic gear. He was an anti-surveillance expert hired by Tom to check the entire estate for electronic bugs. He went from room to room and cottage to cottage, turned on a little beeper, then went outside to his electronic gear to see if he could pick up the beeper on a receiver. Maybe the feds had dropped some bugs in the rooms, and Tom wanted to be sure to find them. Things were getting creepy. The crew wondered who these Germans really were, and what was Tom Sullivan really up to? He couldn't act, couldn't sing or play music, and paid little attention to his band or the movie. He spent almost no time with his beautiful Danish model girlfriend, and disappeared for hours in his airplane or on a horse.

Suddenly we wanted this job to be over and to get out before we ended up in jail, or more likely screwed out of our last paycheck. It began to dawn on us that the whole operation had an aura of sleaze; the chicks, the booze, the drug talk, the isolation, and the airplanes coming and going. They weren't a very pleasant group of people, and it seemed the film was going nowhere fast. Several of us thought Sullivan might still be smuggling cocaine under cover of the movie, and picked the Warhol estate because it was remote, had a hidden air strip, was close to Manhattan, and was owned by a celebrity who was close to the high-rolling drug culture. Maybe he had hired a group of schlumps to "make a movie," but had no intention of finishing it, because he was smuggling millions of dollars of drugs. The few hundred thousand dollars spent on a film crew was a minor business expense to cover their tracks.

The real story was not so exciting. The reality was that a maid, working in the nearby motel where some cast and crew stayed, had caused the bust. One morning she saw a pile of crudely wrapped packages containing white powder and several handguns on the bed. She told the manager, who called the police, who called the DEA, who thought they would uncover a huge cocaine smuggling ring. But it was the prop master's hotel room, the white powder was sugar, and the guns were cheap plastic toys—just props for the movie. The cops did seize $25,000 in cash from Tom's strong box, but that was not uncommon on low budget movies where producers are rarely trusted and everything is COD. $25,000 covered about two weeks of expenses. We breathed a huge sigh of relief, and the movie was completed in a few more days.

Victor Bockris' book Warhol provides a different and ironic point of view of Tom Sullivan's association with Warhol and his friends and associates.

> "[Tom] Sullivan had blown into town several months earlier with $2 million in cash to have some fun. Young, naive, and uneducated but good-looking and romantic, he was perfect fodder for the New York hustlers who moved in on him like sharks in a feeding frenzy. Soon Sullivan found himself renting three connecting suites at the Westbury Hotel on Madison Avenue.

According to Catherine Guinness, 'We met Tom in Studio 54. We were there one night and he just sort of picked me up and carried me off.'

Andy introduced Tom to Margaret Trudeau, who had recently left her husband to have some fun herself. Swept off her feet by the charismatic Tommy, whose pirate-king image was topped off by pockets overflowing with wads of cash and a black-leather-gloved hand disfigured in a fiery plane crash, Margaret Trudeau soon found herself at the centre of the Factory's night life. Andy felt sorry for Catherine, who continued to see Sullivan on the side..."

Brigid Berlin, who was working as the Factory secretary at the time, rang Bob Colacello to complain about Catherine's behavior:

> "You've got to get back to the office.... It's just going to hell. Catherine's running wild, giving all-day lunches, falling asleep on the couch in the dining room after lunch. And the other day, when I walked into the dining room to help her clean up, you know, she was making out with that boyfriend of hers who wears those gloves to cover up his burned hands. It was really disgusting."

Shortly after renting the Montauk estate, Sullivan was joined by "a team of two German geeks, an actor turned director, Ulli Lommel, and a borderline producer named Christopher Gierke." They proposed to make a film "with Sullivan's bank roll, starring Tommy himself of course and, they eagerly suggested, somebody like Bianca Jagger."

Victor Bockris:

> "Sullivan and Lommel cooked up a story about a drug smuggler who tries to get out of the business by turning himself into a rock star. A band was rounded up and imitating the Rolling Stones, Montauk was used as a

base for their rehearsals. The veteran actor Jack Palance was made a cash-in-advance offer he could not refuse to star as the band's manager and shooting commenced in June."

Albert Goldman (pop culture writer and friend of Warhol) on Tom Sullivan:

"The spring the movie was conceived was the climax of his long career as a drug smuggler. That spring was a disastrous season. First he broke up with Margaret Trudeau in London. Then there was a horrible plane crash in Florida in which his closest friend was incinerated, and then hard on the heels of that a great big shrimp boat full of contraband came in but Tommy cracked up and couldn't handle it. But he owed for the merchandise."

Vincent Fremont (close colleague of Warhol):

"We were never told they were going to make a movie… Mr. Winters [the caretaker] called me and said, 'there are all these cars parked all around.' There were un-marked police cars and the East Hampton police did a high-speed chase and they were arrested for gun pos-session."

Albert Goldman:

"When the police came up to the house, they grabbed $25,000 in cash… but that wasn't anything because the night before the Colombians had shown up and threat-ened to kill him and he gave them a million in cash."

Warhol appeared in a cameo role in *Cocaine Cowboys* for an extra $4,000 on top of the three month Montauk rental. But when Vincent Fremont went to collect Warhol's fee, the film's "ersatz producer" pulled a gun on him.

Life in SoHo

I happily returned to my new life in SoHo when the film's Montauk segments finished, and it suddenly ground to a halt. We got paid, but hob-nobbing with celebrities wasn't all I thought it should be. Another group had apparently taken over shooting the Manhattan segments, and they didn't call me to work on it. Like many low-budget films, the initial backers ran out of money and sold the project for pennies on the dollar to someone who hypes it with a new title or over-blown star credits and a catchy poster or a title that has nothing to do with the original film. It was a formula used for years in the horror/gore genre, but has disappeared as audiences have become more sophisticated and not so gullible about casts of has-beens, phony hype, and misleading poster art.

The final curtain fell for Cocaine Cowboys when Tom became too reckless and got horribly addicted to coke. This snorting cowboy became too much for his Danish model girlfriend, who moved back to Manhattan even before the movie ended. The movie died a quick death, and Tom's dreams of rubbing elbows with the international jet set evaporated along with his drug money. I ran into Tom and Chris a few times in SoHo restaurants. They looked increasingly burned out, and didn't say much about the movie or anything else.

Ulli Lommel has directed more than forty cheapo gore flicks, with names like Killer Nurse and Dungeon Girl—probably for the Asian/Arab DVD market. As a body of work, they have attracted some of the meanest reviews you'll ever read on IMDb (Incompetent directing, disjointed writing, and awful acting are the only consistent elements throughout.).

In a final footnote, High Times magazine reported that Tom died shortly after in a Brooklyn gutter from a heart burned out by coke and deluded ambitions of joining the beautiful people.

7

Polyester

· · · · · · · · · · ·

The first year in SoHo was a blast. I took advantage of a loophole in the tight film union membership rules, where if you had sound credits on three feature films, you could join the union, so I became a union sound recordist. This let me work on lucrative union shoots in New York City. Most of the work was on TV commercials, and I spent many days on New York City's most famous movie stages. It was a dream come true. I zipped out every morning on the subway to a different studio, wearing my headphones around my neck like an Olympic medal. Union commercials had big budgets, and I learned tons watching real pros work. They were shot in 35mm film with cranes, dollies, every kind of light imaginable, and a full union staff including Directors Guild of America, and Teamsters—a first for me. Fussy Art Directors asked for the moon and got it. Masterful food stylists spent hours gluing perfect sesame seeds on Big Mac buns. Celebrities were paid big bucks to shill for whatever was being sold that day. I even worked with George Burns, then in his late nineties, who sang the praises of IBM. Other oldies but goodies from New York's golden age that I worked with included Garson Kanin, Ruth Gordon, and the "King of Swing," Benny Goodman. Only in New York. I also was pleased that you made more money in a day on a union TV commercial than in a week on a low budget movie.

John and I spoke on the phone at least once a week. He came to New York regularly, and we'd meet for an early dinner, usually before some party he'd been invited to, but that I had not. He couldn't believe that I was developing roots in Manhattan, that I had a very cool address, and he was fascinated with my stories of shooting with big budgets on NY sound stages. He said was very happy that I was learning all these new things we could use on his future higher-budget productions. I was also sternly warned not to get too cozy, because he would never have that kind of money.

John had finished most of the script for Polyester, and had given it to New Line. He was struggling with New Line about their delivering on the money they said they'd find. The script was much less violent and shocking than Desperate Living, specifically lampooning middle-class suburbia, and developing the "kids gone bad" theme that began with Female Trouble and would continue in most of his future movies. New Line reacted in the beginning as they had with all John's films I worked on—a tepid response that bordered on cold feet. At the end of the day, Desperate Living was a financial non-starter for them, so they were paranoid. They ultimately hoped to find someone else to finance Polyester's production and save their money for something more of a sure box office hit.

They wanted a gory horror film that would sell tickets all over the world, not another high-concept satire on bourgeois values, filled with insider gay jokes, John's sexual obsessions, and niche appeal characters like Edie the Egg Lady and Mink Stole. They wanted The Baltimore Chain Saw Massacre.

John did brainstorm the Odorama gimmick (and its name) for Polyester, where odors would accompany a few scenes in the movie. He hadn't worked out the details, but New Line thought it could excite the press, and maybe sell more tickets. It was New Line's favorite aspect of the movie, and Sarah Risher threw herself into researching adding odor to a movie. It had been tried before, usually by spraying perfume into the theatre. Smell-o-Vision and Aromarama were the major competing systems that sprayed scents into the theaters in the 1950s. They were flops because of the expense involved in rigging theaters to release and waft the scents through the theater on cue. A bigger problem was that smells lingered and mixed with each other, and the dramatic impact was lost in a confusing jumble of odors, many of them not very accurate anyhow. They also took a while to circulate through the theater, so that by the time the scents made it to the people furthest from the vents, the plot had moved on, and they were mystified by smells that didn't match the picture at all.

An acquaintance of Sara Risher who worked in the printing business suggested printing cards with scratch and sniff stickers attached, giving viewers a tiny personalized whiff that quickly dissipated. If the stickers were numbered, the numbers could flash on the screen at the appropriate moment, and cue the audience to scratch. The 3M Company had invented the secret scratch and sniff process. Only they could print the smell impregnated cards and adhesive stickers that had appeared mostly in magazine perfume ads. They had a menu of existing scents, so there would not be the expense of creating them. John consented to write scratch and sniff scenes into the movie based on 3M's "smell library." Fortunately, the library was quite extensive, but we decided not to tell 3M that "rotten eggs" would be #2 on the scratch and sniff card, and have nothing to do with rotten eggs.

Odorama had to overcome several problems. First, New Line wanted Odorama and non-Odorama versions of the movie, in case the Odorama thing flopped. I suggested super-imposing flashing white numbers in the bottom right hand corner of the frame for the Odorama version. A second printing master would be made without the numbers, for the non-Odorama version. It was very simple. The only expense would be making a second printing master. For technical reasons, the Odorama master with the flashing numbers would be a little more expensive. This was a big issue, because New Line resisted spending money on anything, and always searched for a cheaper way, even if there were expensive consequences down the road for cheaping out in the beginning. But of all the possibilities, it was by far the cheapest.

The second issue was the jaw-dropping cost of printing the Odorama stickers. Like most printing, it is only affordable in huge quantities. 3M required a pre-paid order of hundreds of thousands of scratch and sniff stickers, which cost almost as much as the movie's entire production budget. New Line had to warehouse pallets of the cards, then count, pack and ship them to each theater that showed the film. Odorama suddenly became a big burden. Nobody could guess how many cards should be sent to a theater. If they didn't send enough, the movie goers would be angry. If they sent 2,500, but sold only 1,000 tickets, the theater had to return the rest. This cost money. Sometimes theaters claimed they lost the cards, or threw them away by accident. Sometimes they were lost in shipping, or sent to the wrong address. The financial losses were impressive, and uncontrollable.

Luckily for John, these problems didn't become apparent until after the funds were raised and we were well into editing. As we prepared for distribution New Line began to realize the immense hassle of weighing down their shipping department with Odorama card tracking. When they tried to get theaters to pay for the cards, the owners balked. They didn't want the hassle either. So, New Line faced an expensive extra that was driving their accounting department insane and would sour their relationship with John for years.

Though New Line had been encouraging John (before the Odorama reality sunk in) with the idea of their funding Polyester, they didn't have the cash in the bank. They set the production budget at $300,000—a huge jump from Desperate Living's $65,000. But for this, John needed at least one real name star. He also had to have Divine. It had to have an R rating, not an X like his previous films. He had to have an original music score, and truly professional production values (mainly shot in 35mm, and John would not be allowed to operate the camera). Finally, it had to reserve a large chunk of money for Odorama development and manufacture.

This meant a laughably tight budget for the actual day-to-day production costs. One crew member was paid $15 a day. Production assistants worked sixty hours a week and received nothing. A big issue was the Screen Actors' Guild, because of the requirement to hire a recognizable box office name. Agents and actors turned New Line down flat when they heard it would be a non-union film. New Line could afford a big name, but there was no way to make the film, and pay every actor and extra SAG wages. SAG contracts require that if one actor was in SAG, then all must be. It would have added $250,000 to the budget and New Line refused to take that kind of risk with what was still considered an underground movie.

New Line continued dragging its feet until Britain's top off-beat producer, Michael White, expressed an interest. Michael produced the wildly successful Rocky Horror Picture Show, the hit all-nude off-Broadway Musical Oh, Calcutta, and dozens of other cutting edge London plays. Michael was flush with cash from his successes, and decided he would partner with New Line to make the film. Michael was real, and the money was real, and suddenly John called to say we were finally going ahead, even with all New Line's restrictions. I asked John, considering the financial issues, if it would be possible to get more production money. He said he didn't dare because the deal was so fragile already. After the production was underway, it would be too late to turn back, and the investors would have little choice but to keep funding it. This is the dirty underbelly most low-budget producers face. You cross your fingers, promise the investors you can do it for the budget, then come back begging for more when the money starts running thin.

The demands were daunting: make the movie in Baltimore, work with executive producers in New York and London, hire a name actor who will work non-SAG, make a deal with Divine (whose new agent had come to see him as an expensive box office name too). We had to shoot in 35mm (which required that all equipment and lab work come from New York). We were also required to purchase a full production insurance package, including $300,000 life insurance policies John and Divine. This would prove to be an unexpected hurdle.

Out of the $300,000, I had to deduct $35,000 for Odorama, $10,000 for New Line's "overhead," $10,000 for John, $10,000 for the name star's one week of shooting, and $15,000 for Divine's two months. If I had known anything, I would have said it was impossible, but I said yes, I would see that it was done for $300,000. The below-the-line budget was closer to $175,000. My fee was a flat $5,000 for almost a year's work. My bonus from John at the end was a silver cigarette lighter from Tiffany's. It was actually quite fitting, but was sadly stolen in a New York bar a few months later.

John had a few doubts too, because he was about to undergo a sea change in how his movies were produced. His first worry was that I was in New York. How could I produce a film in Baltimore? Having had over a year in the New York film business, I said the reality of shooting a 35mm movie with New York executive producers made it a New York production on a Baltimore location. Much of the pre-production and most of the post-production would be done in New York. This realization shocked him, because it meant a loss of control. When he asked if I could save money by doing sound and production managing like I did in Desperate Living, I laughed and said,

"Look at the script: night-time car chases, bullet hits, underage actors, trained animals, fake thunderstorms, helicopter shots, video scenes, a dozen locations—all on a ridiculously low budget."

I would have to work 80 hours a week just managing the production. I would be constantly on the phone juggling dozens of issues, or the movie would collapse. The production manager/line producer could not do sound on a movie like this. It wasn't a documentary on monkey life in the Amazon.

Worried about the complexities too, John finally accepted, but was concerned that Pat, his dearest soul mate and muse who had always had the production manager credit would not want to give it up. When I suggested she be credited with the more appropriate Casting Director and Associate Producer titles, John felt that might be demeaning and could cause trouble. Pat however seemed satisfied with the assistant director credit. She spent most of her time with casting and extras management, which was a plateful. Pat later became an Emmy award winning casting director working on several HBO series made in Baltimore in the 1990s. IMDb lists me as both Line Producer and Production Manager, which are essentially different titles for the same job. I would have liked to have the Line Producer screen credit at the time, and probably deserved it, but I didn't want to push things too far and create friction.

Polyester didn't have an on-set first assistant director or a continuity person. John didn't see the need. Most of the crew knew each other well, so John felt he could run the set and plan his shots, just like he'd done on his five other movies. To find competent people for those jobs would require bringing in experienced pros from New York. Script supervisors and assistant directors did not exist in Baltimore, and anyway John wouldn't consider spending one extra penny for something that didn't appear on the screen. No one went to movies looking for good continuity or superior assistant direction (the Ed Wood philosophy).

The next big issue was that John did not want to give up operating the camera. In the two years since Desperate Living, I had been wearing John down on this issue. In that time, a revolutionary new technology, video assist, had been developed. It allowed a black and white video feed from film cameras to be played back on a video monitor, and be recorded on small VHS recorders. John could therefore watch everything the camera was recording, and even check it with instant replay. I invited him to a TV commercial shoot to see how it worked, and he fell in love with it. This decision immediately ratcheted up his production quality. A skilled professional operating the camera meant no more soft focus shots, wobbly zooms, or other telltale amateur errors.

With Michael White's major financial participation, New Line's position as Executive Producer was confirmed. A long contract with John was drawn up, which made him very nervous, because of its many restrictions and warnings. New Line could remove him from the film if it went over budget, the technical quality was not up to standard, if he changed the script, or even if he acted immorally (ha, ha). This required him to trust me even more.

I had nearly daily meetings in New York with New Line going over things like insurance policies, whether or not to sign with Screen Actors Guild, equipment rental sources, creating an official production company for the film (named Juno Pix, Inc., after Bob Shaye's daughter, to avoid any liability for New Line), Odorama, lab contracts, and sound editing. New Line had a deal with a small lab that struck all their prints, but used other labs' machinery around town to process original negative. It was a little under-the-counter, in a New York City kind of way, and awkward, because I never knew who was processing the film. But their prices were great, and New Line had a great credit line with them.

New Line combed through the budget line by line, suspicious that someone might be trying to steal money or maybe because they could save a few pennies here and there—or just to learn more about the process. Shaye and his colleagues, Sara Risher and Michael Harpster, plus their attorney and finance VP, knew next to nothing about filmmaking. They didn't have deep financial resources, but it was the heyday of non-theatrical distribution, and they kept a staff of about twelve persons very busy shipping their catalog of about 150 mostly foreign and art films to colleges and small art theaters around the country. Business was good, and they wanted very much to become producers as well as theatrical distributors.

They were happy to have me around, for my experience with John and the other movies I'd worked on. They gave me a little desk in a windowless office where I could make phone calls and go from meeting to meeting with each executive in turn, explaining how the movie was being organized.

I phoned John several times a day, reporting the details of every meeting, and he finally admitted he was very grateful that I was in New York and could handle all the administrative dealings with New Line. This freed him to concentrate on casting, art direction, rehearsals, and tweaking the script at home in Baltimore. He didn't like New Line's pushy macho business culture and executives who didn't really get his humor.

John tried to deal mostly with Sarah, who was sensitive, appreciative, and enthusiastic, in contrast to the growling alpha males above her. Poor Sarah had a crush on John, so she was a good inside advocate for him. However, she was steam-rolled and frequently under-appreciated. Many times I'd enter her office and see tears in her eyes, after a screaming meeting with Shaye. "He's such an asshole," was as much as she'd say; sensibly never sharing details.

Polyester's Early Issues

Divine was a big issue. With the very mediocre response to Desperate Living, both John and New Line knew that Divine had to be in Polyester. However, Divine had been experiencing success with his live stage performances and was making a passable living, getting good press, and making good celebrity connections. On the other hand, he was always broke, and needed a solid gig that would put him on a hundred screens simultaneously and create thousands of column inches of press across the world. He also needed an advance that would put a big wad of cash in his pocket. Besides, Divine wanted to be in the movie and continue this streak with John he'd enjoyed since high school. It had been six years since Female Trouble, and it was time for a reunion.

An unexpected bump in the road was Bernard Jay, a dapper gay theatrical producer with a bespoke British accent (he was from South Africa), who had recently moved to New York, and bought the rights to the off-off Broadway play, Neon Woman, in which Divine appeared. Divine zeroed in on Bernard as a sharp businessman and cajoled him into being his agent. Repping an overweight drag act who threw dead fish at the audience was not exactly gentile Bernard's cup of tea, but he had come to America and, though he'd rather have produced at the Public Theater, Divine fell on his plate first. Bernard dreamed Divine would become a legitimate actor, beyond the one dimensional Clarabelle the clown-homicidal maniac of Pink Flamingos and Female Trouble. Bernard did not think eating dog doo, having sex with a rosary, or serial rape were funny in the least, or a recipe for broad success. He did see a place for Divine as a serious, sensitive multi-faceted male actor.

Bernard was the only agent John or New Line had to deal with, and they were unprepared for it. The other original Dreamlanders accepted John's first offer—which wasn't much. We originally budgeted $5,000 for Divine, thinking he would jump at it. He probably would have, except for Bernard, who insisted it was impossibly low. John and New Line had to come back with something better when Bernard insisted on a much higher number, plus a percentage of the profits. Bernard knew fellow Brit, Michael White, from his London days, and smelled big money behind both him and New Line. He also knew that the script was based around Divine, and that Michael White's participation required Divine to be the star. Negotiations dragged to within two weeks of the start date, and John began freaking out, calling New Line nearly every day, begging them to make the deal with Divine. New Line finally caved, and I added Divine's fee of $15,000 plus another $5,000 in expenses to the budget. Everyone was overjoyed, except perhaps Bob Shaye, who did not like losing battles, especially financial ones, especially to a bunch of fruitcakes.

The next battle was Tab Hunter, the California-handsome 1950-60s heart throb actor-pop singer John had convinced to be the big name on the movie. Tab would be a crossover to the suburban shopping mall theater circuit. Blonde and square-jawed, Tab was the American girls' dreamboat; the handsome and rugged Marine and cowboy who'd ride off into the sunset with you. The real irony was that Tab was gay, but firmly in the closet and though Hollywood knew plenty, in the 1950s no one dared discuss such things.

Tab had been out of movies for fifteen years, but was a big draw in the dinner theater circuit where the middle-aged women's audience thought he was still a hunk. John had tracked him down and presented Polyester to him. Since it was the 80s, and Tab was more comfortable with his gayness, he thought it would be a hoot to co-star with Divine, and work with the most openly gay filmmaker in show business. The fee of $10,000 for ten days in Baltimore wasn't too bad either. Everyone was surprised that he took the role because of his goody-goody reputation, but it was a good omen for the movie, and everyone was ecstatic—except me, the production manager.

The big question was the union issue. If Tab was a member of the Screen Actors' Guild, he couldn't act in Polyester, unless it was a union film. That would add hundreds of thousands of dollars to the budget not just for actors, but unions snitched to each other about potential new films, so the IATSE (International Association of Theatrical Stage Employees) film worker union, the Teamsters, and the rest would ring my phone off the hook and demand expensive contracts too, or they would throw up picket lines which the union actors would refuse to cross. The unions had it all figured out. What a mess.

If Tab was a member of SAG and insisted that we sign their contract, it would be impossible to use him. Since I was the only person who had experience with unions, I had to broach the subject with Tab. I reached him on the phone at a dinner theater in Omaha. The gist of the conversation was this:

"Tab, you know John's films are very low budget, and we've worked very hard to get together your fee, which you deserve, but we're worried about the Screen Actors Guild. Are you still a member?" I asked.

"Gee, I don't think so; it's been ten years since I've been in a movie. I don't think I pay dues anymore," he said.

"Well, we can't afford a SAG contract, because all the other actors would have to be paid union rates, and this is a tiny budget. Maybe next time we'll go union, but not on this one."

"Oh yeah, that must be tough. I don't see I have much future in the movies anyway. I love doing dinner theaters, and thought it would be fun to be in a John Waters movie with Divine. I absolutely love the part."

"And everybody wants you to do it too. But can you do it without a union contract?" I pressed.

"I don't see why not. What are they gonna do, kick me out? You think they'll find out?"

"Tab, you can't exactly do this under an assumed name. It's kind of the point. They will find out. You are the star, and it will be all over the media around the world."

"Well, screw 'em. I'm not doing any more movies after this one, and if I do, I'll worry about it then. I really want to do this."

"OK, great then, I'll let everybody know, and we'll get a contract to you in the next day or so."

I immediately called John to tell him the good news. It was a huge relief. We had jumped the second big cast hurdle. Just in case, I urged that we keep Tab's name out of the press until shooting was over. The union would definitely pressure him if it found out. Though getting a big name star to work non-union was a low-budget dream come true, it came back to bite us later. An important lesson: actors are always acting.

It was now time for serious pre-production. We opened a bank account for Juno Pix in Baltimore. John had to sign all the checks, not me, underscoring his personal responsibilities in the deal and compounding his day-to-day worries. He was signing big checks, and he had little idea of where the money was going. After every one, he gave me a look that said, "Please watch out for this money. I'm trusting you, and my whole life is riding on this."

Part of this new high-budget world was the cast insurance policy. If John, Divine, or one of the other principals died, or couldn't finish the movie because of health problems, the insurance company would pay back all the money spent, so the film could be either abandoned or re-shot. It was a big ticket item that required the insured principals to have thorough physical exams. Not terribly surprisingly, Divine failed his physical—for being morbidly obese.

When I called John to tell him, he was shocked. OK, Divine was fat, but he was still in his 30s, swam nearly every day, and did strenuous stage shows, so he had to be fit enough for the movie. But the insurance police only compared weight against height, and in that measurement, Divine failed. John demanded that I not tell anyone, because it would throw Divine into a depression. There was no possibility of halting the production or replacing Divine. However, the insurance company offered to cover him for an additional $10,000 premium. New Line and Michael White went for that. It gobbled a big chunk of our $35,000 contingency—before one foot of film rolled through the camera. New Line said I'd "have to make it up somewhere else." It was to become their favorite line—New Line's line—in this and the other movies I did with them.

Without saying a word, John and I revisited some of the worst moments of Desperate Living—the flood, the cold, the 18 hour days, the broken down extras buses, the bad food, and thought, oh Christ, here we go again, what are we thinking? No matter how well you planned, shit happened, and usually because you didn't have enough money to prevent it happening in the first place. It was a big, big gamble.

Getting the 35mm camera package out of New York City was another union problem. From my other low-budget projects in New York, I had met an up and coming native New Yorker, Mike Spera, who ran his father's business of renting film editing rooms in the film production buildings around Times Square. To grow the business, Mike acquired several hugely expensive 35 mm movie cameras, mainly to serve New York's emerging low-budget movie business. Not only did he undercut the rates of big rental houses, but he operated under the radar of the unions, so non-union shoots could rent his gear without being accosted by teamsters who hung out on the loading docks of the bigger houses. I got a bargain-basement deal on the camera with my promise, as an up and coming low-budget production manager, that I would bring him more business. Which I did, and helped him grow his company. Mike was a big part of New York's blossoming low budget film industry, which had been choked by the unions until then.

In Baltimore

It was finally time for me to leave the New York meetings behind, and get my boots on the ground in Baltimore for final pre-production. Vince had found a perfect ranch house in a midscale suburban community that bordered a golf course. Everybody's lawn was perfect, there were large trees, big, shiny cars, and the right amount of kitschy suburban touches like negro jockey boy mailbox holders and robin's egg blue vinyl siding. It was in a cul-de-sac, which also helped us logistically, because we would be fairly free from the prying eyes of traffic on a through street.

The street was ironically named Heavitree Hill, and the house had been on the market for a while and was empty. The owners, who had moved to Florida, jumped at renting it for a thousand dollars a month. It had a big garage, driveway, full basement, spacious rooms, and four bedrooms. It was decided I would live in the only bedroom that was too small to shoot in—saving the cost of a motel room and not requiring an overnight security guard. I was to be night guard once again. The basement and garage were production offices and staging areas. It was still tiny, but better than the mud pits of Mortville.

I brought down a couple low-budget buddies from New York to be the sound recording team, and put them up in a sleazy motel a few miles away. They hated it, but loved hanging out at the trashy bars where they found the local girls to be very easy. One Saturday night during the production, they stumbled into the house around 2:00 a.m., girls in arms, waking me up after a very hard week of shooting. I asked the soundman what's up, and he answered,

"We met these girls and told them we were making a movie here, and they wanted to come see it... and meet you" (wink, wink).

The rooms were full of lights, cables, delicate props, and camera gear. It was not for drunken partiers. Even worse, I didn't want them blabbing to all their bar friends about the cool movie being made right around the corner. John would kill me.

"You what?" I said, pulling him into the next room. "Get them out of here. Take them somewhere and get them so drunk they don't remember this place at all. And if you ever breathe a word about his movie, or bring anyone here, or come here again yourselves when we're not shooting, I will kick your asses back to New York in a New York second."

He looked at me sheepishly and said, "You want me to leave one of the girls with you?"

"You fucking idiot. Get out now! And be quiet, for God's sake, what will the neighbors think?" It felt like a scene from the movie.

Blending into the quiet suburban neighborhood wasn't easy for a John Waters' movie. I could have been a bit more officious to the neighbors, but assumed like most people in the movie business, that the whole world wanted to be a part of the movies, and would bend over backwards to accommodate a movie crew, if their neighborhood were fortunate enough to be selected for such a blessed event, even a John Waters movie.

This attitude, called "cinematic immunity" spreads far and wide in the movie-making world. Cinematic immunity is the concept that movie making is so important to our culture that normal rules do not apply to people making movies. Examples from my career include things like blocking off the best parking spaces at a sporting event, blocking the view at concerts, blocking precious traffic lanes during rush hour, getting "blue light" police escorts across Washington, DC, just to get from one location to another more quickly, shooting noisy scenes at night in quiet communities, and giving out ear plugs to complainers, and telling construction workers they are making too much noise and must stop working for several hours until our toilet paper commercial was finished.

Cinematic immunity works for a while, because no one knows really how long it takes to shoot a movie scene, and how disruptive it can be. Neighbors can't park, can't mow their grass, can't get deliveries, can't leave their home without permission, and can't let their kids out to play without being yelled at by a production assistant with a walkie-talkie, just so the movie people can get their scene shot. Because details like lighting, costumes, make-up, sound, camera moves, and actors getting their lines right is a complex ballet, a one minute scene can take all day to accomplish. To the uninvolved observer, it can be like watching paint dry. Rather quickly the novelty for the neighbors wears off, and having a movie in the neighborhood becomes a real inconvenience, rather like having a gang of gypsies camp on your front lawn and take every inch of parking space for two blocks with their equipment trucks, portable dressing rooms, catering vans, and spot-a-pots (also known in the trade as "honeywagons").

This level of repeated disruption has caused many "hot" neighborhoods around the country to ban filmmaking completely. This includes Georgetown in Washington, DC, and Greenwich Village in New York. Being the nation's movie capital, Los Angeles is more forgiving, because so many residents work in the "biz," but even there, some of the more popular neighborhoods are off-limits. Many cities want to attract movie production because they perceive them to be good publicity and money-generators, but the more popular they become, the more irate the neighbors become. The situation reaches a tipping point, and the movie makers tend to move on to new places where their cinematic immunity is still effective.

With the Polyester location I initially printed a polite, understated letter of introduction and put it in the door of each home. It explained that we were a movie crew from Baltimore making a teen comedy. The shooting would take about five weeks. Only one or two loud scenes would be filmed outside, and most of the time would be spent in the house. The movie would be rated PG-13, and neighbors could watch outside or visit the set for a quick tour, if they were interested. I included the phone number and asked them to call with any questions. I didn't hear from anyone and assumed they were delighted with their new neighbors—little did I know. My hands were full with other issues, so I moved quickly on. This was before I had learned the essential value of becoming friends with location neighbors.

Our first un-neighborly event occurred before principal photography. Polyester's title sequence is a long, smooth helicopter shot, establishing the suburban location, and then a birds-eye view slow zoom into our house at the end of the cul-de-sac with it's neat yard, trimmed bushes, and hideous robin's egg blue vinyl siding. A quick dissolve takes us to the front door, where a transition to a Steadicam shot glides through several tackily decorated rooms, then up the grand stairway to Divine's bedroom, where he is trimming his toenails. It would be an expensive, complicated opening shot that would establish this as not your usual down and dirty John Waters film.

We were shooting in early fall, and needed to get the helicopter shot done before the trees changed colors, so it was a big rush. Also the house interior didn't need to be dressed for the helicopter part, and no cast was involved, so it was Scene 1, Take 1.

I rented a helicopter with a special aerial camera mount flown in from Florida. Dave, the cinematographer, and Art, the assistant cameraman rode in the chopper. I talked to them from the ground on a walkie-talkie, making sure no one walked into the shot. I thought it would be a brief thing, and didn't bother notifying the police or neighbors. There was no permit process at the time anyway, and if I had asked, would probably have been refused. I decided to follow one of my regular rules: better to apologize later than be told no up front.

The shot required the helicopter to approach and descend slowly, then hover 10-20 feet above the 30 ft. high oak trees in full leaf. Dave would creep-zoom into the front door, after the helicopter slowly glided in sideways, then hovered. When we described the shot, the pilot, who had flown hundreds of combat missions in Viet Nam, twitched a little and said it was about the hardest thing you could do in a helicopter. Flying sideways was tough. A dead hover was tougher. Helicopters were much healthier places to be when moving forward at about 50 miles an hour. While hovering, a wind gust or prop wash could drop them into the trees. We were a little nervous, but he was game to try it, and assured us that he was the last person who wanted to go down. He promised he wouldn't do anything to risk a crash. Art and Dave were a little doubtful, but were willing—the cinematic immunity thing. I was glad to be on the ground.

While they made final preparations to take off, I raced back to the house to be sure the coast was clear. One of the neighbors was out front with a little dog. I ran over, walkie-talkie in hand and said a helicopter would be hovering over the houses in a few minutes, so she should take her dog inside where it might be "safer." Bad choice of words. She panicked, scooped up the dog, and flew into her house, expecting God knows what. Seconds later, I heard the roar of the chopper, and hid under a tree to stay out of the shot. The pilot circled several times over the houses, scoping out the scene. The jet engine had an ear-splitting scream, and the rotor wash bent the treetops like a tornado, ripping leaves off and scattering them across the lawns. It was so loud that the walkie-talkies I brought were useless.

The thing thwop-thwop-thwopped 50 feet over my head, and I about pissed myself. The chopper then glided off and it was quiet and calm again. Art came on the radio, and said that was just a test. They would roll on the next pass. He asked me to make sure the shot was clear. No worry about that. Not a soul had looked out their windows. I was sure they were hiding in their basements, petrified. The chopper roared back again, and this time hovered perfectly still. The crazy pilot kissed the tree tops with the chopper's skids. The noise and tree sway was like the end of the world. I thought branches would be ripped off the trees and smash into the parked cars. The helicopter lifted gently and scooted off, but returned a few seconds later, flying sideways in a beautiful tracking shot. This take ended quicker, because the pilot lifted, jerked left and headed off, brushing the treetops. Art's voice crackled over the walkie-talkie.

"We're going down. Emergency landing!"

"What do you mean going down, what emergency, where?" I shouted into the walkie-talkie.

"We landed on the golf course across the street. The pilot and Dave are running away."

"Holy shit, what now?" I thought, jumped in my car, and raced the 200 yards to the golf course. The helicopter sat in the middle of the fairway right next to a green, its rotor still spinning. Groups of golfers stood around staring at it. Art and Dave stood well away from the chopper waving frantically.

"Get away, it might blow," they yelled.

And take my movie career with it, I thought.

I went over and they explained that on the second hover, an emergency light started flashing, and the pilot said he had to set down immediately, and looked for a clear spot away from trees. The closest was the golf course. He said when they hit the ground, to get out, leave everything, and run. The engine was too hot and might seize and explode. The maneuver had evidently taxed the engine to the max, which the pilot later told me was scheduled for an overhaul the next week. This was to be its last flight. When they hit the ground, Dave and the pilot jumped out, but dutiful Arthur stayed long enough to pull the film magazine off the camera, hoping the film would be usable. The pilot was really shaken and said he was going to find the clubhouse and have a few drinks. In all his years of flying, including Viet Nam, he told them this was the closest call he'd ever had.

I rushed the film to the lab in New York, and miracle of miracles, the first take was good enough to use, and is what you see when the film opens. It was an expensive opening shot indeed, especially counting a $200,000 helicopter transmission. The next day, I called the helicopter rental company and complained that we weren't satisfied with the service received, because we only got two takes done. They had sent us a crummy helicopter, that almost killed two people, and we would not pay for it. They were not happy, and for two years John kept getting invoices from them, which he and New Line refused to pay.

To keep things going on the film, I needed production assistants, which again John questioned. What would I do if I had PAs running around doing everything for me? Already, I wasn't doing sound. Was this a holiday for me? I stood my ground knowing that PAs do a thousand essential behind the scenes jobs—like cleaning the toilets in the house. There wasn't a budget for PAs, so they had to be volunteers. The job was six or seven days a week and involved stuff like running to the store ten times a day, setting out lunches, making coffee, keeping traffic gawkers away from the house, cleaning up at the end of the shooting day, carrying equipment up and down stairs, chauffeuring cast members to their hotel rooms, running to a photocopier—all the glamorous work.

The key production assistant turned out to be Rachel. She was a recent graduate of Yale University with a math degree and her father was an MD and professor at Johns Hopkins Medical School. She was a brain who could have been a rocket scientist, but she was movie crazy. Her only experience with film at the time was on the program committee of the Yale Film Society, but she wanted to work in the movies. Rachel lived with her parents in a ritzy part of Baltimore and drove her mother's hand-me-down Volvo station wagon, a real bonus to the production.

In the beginning, I didn't think she'd stick it out. She was nervous, quiet, and docile, and so was given all the worst jobs: unclogging drains, cleaning up after lunch, driving back and forth from the location to Baltimore city to pick up a key costume part an actor had left at their hotel. To make things worse, people thought she was an Ivy League egghead—not at all like the hardscrabble "hillbilly rip-offs" that stereotyped most Dreamlanders, so she was the butt of constant joking and Baltimore-style sexual harassment. Her hair was cut short, and she was thin and wiry, and moved around kind of boyishly. The gays accused her of being gay "but she didn't know it yet." Chris Mason, the unabashed and hysterically funny lesbian hairdresser would grab Rachel and goose her, ask her to come shower with her, or go on a date to one of Baltimore's lezzie bars.

Rachel, with utmost earnestness, tried to convince everyone that she was straight, which doubled the taunting. But Rachel was tough, and shrugged it off. She stayed to help me well into the evening, after everyone else left, scrubbing floors, washing windows, and carrying tons of leaking trash bags to the closest nearby dumpster in her Volvo wagon. I'd explain all the production paperwork to her; show her my production book, crew contracts and how to track money. She found it fascinating. A few times, it was so late that she asked to spend the night on the couch. That could lead to rumors. There's no keeping secret about such things in a movie company, and John would kill me if I had been even suspected of violating one of the principal production rules. Off she went into the night, to return less than six hours later, day after day without complaint, and not paid a penny.

Rachel and I did become good working colleagues, and I mentored her on several other low-budget movies. I got her a job as a production accountant with New Line in New York, but she soon moved to Hollywood and used her math skills and other knowledge she rapidly absorbed in Roger Corman's accounting and production department. She became New Line's line producer—replacing me when New Line decided to produce movies only in LA, and not New York. After my difficulties with her Hollywood crew on Crybaby, I lost touch with her. Her career since then has been mostly directing episodes for U.S. TV series shot in Canada. It's weird to see her long list of director's credits on IMDb. When she first started, she couldn't even take a still photo and never wrote anything more entertaining than a shopping list for crafts service. Though she produced Crybaby for Universal, at some point Rachel soured John and Pat, because she never worked on his movies after that. Such is the moving wheel of show biz.

Money was always a hair-raising problem on Polyester. To afford the high salaries and costs of Divine, Tab, and Odorama many areas were severely under-budgeted. The line for accounting services was $500 (because that was part of my job). The total props and sets budget was $12,000. The budget for office rental, supplies, and phone for the entire film was $2,000. The meals budget allowed $113/day for breakfast and lunch for 25 people.

Procuring food for the movie company was a comedy in and of itself. Product placement was a new big thing, and food product manufacturers, including soft drinks, beer, bakeries, and cereal companies tripped over themselves to provide free stuff to movie companies. For example, it was so easy to call Pepsi's marketing office, tell them you were making a movie and wanted to feature their product. I could ask for fifty cases, and they arrived the next day at our location. The sky was the limit. Cases of Tuborg beer, Pepsi, and cartons of Oreo cookies and Snickers arrived by the carload. The crew put in custom requests for their favorite snacks. Local Baltimore companies like Utz Potato Chips, Cloverland Dairy, and Berger's Bakery made free weekly deliveries of their stuff. Pepto-Bismol sent a hundred bottles, hoping to appear in a shot.

The beer promo was especially funny, because in the story Divine turns into a hopeless alcoholic. Her floors are littered with crushed Tuborg beer cans. Tuborg, which was brewed in Baltimore, assumed that their product would be seen in a nice suburban backyard bar-b-que, with healthy, well-adjusted people playing catch and taking responsible sips with their burgers, not Divine puking their beer into his handbag. Our promo product started filling up the two-car garage, so I got the idea of having a yard sale of candy bars and other stuff to get sorely needed cash. It was a big hit with the neighborhood kids. I found a Fells Point bar that would buy as many cases of Tuborg at half price that I could supply. That was so illegal, but it was for art, and there was always cinematic immunity, so that was OK. The big insult was when I took the cash to buy Heinekens for the wrap party, because the crew was so tired of the cheap Tuborg.

Breakfast was exclusively promo coffee, milk, cereals, granola bars, and pastries, set out by Rachel or the other PAs who were required to come an hour early every morning to get the 50-cup coffee brewer going. We always paid cash for lunch, because I figured the absolute cheapest way to feed 25 was to make deals with carry-out restaurants in the area. We'd rotate daily between Italian, Chinese, pizza, and Greek picked up by the PAs and set out on tables. For the $113/day food budget, we ate pretty well, and maybe saved money. However, since we worked many fourteen hour days, most of the savings went to buy pizza for second meals.

Sodas, always promo Pepsi products, were free and unlimited. Ironically, Pepsi's big placement moment in the film comes when Divine, hellishly hung over after a night of guzzling, stumbles to the refrigerator, and sucks down a two-liter bottle of Pepsi. He is at his absolute worst in the film, and there is a lingering close-up of the Pepsi label and Divine's smeared makeup, wrecked hair, and parched, cracked lips. John and I wondered for years if Pepsi would sue us for that one. They never did—no product company ever complained—no such thing as bad publicity.

Location shoots in public were a hoot. We selected a nearby cheapo motel, The White Gables for the scenes where Divine's husband Elmer was banging his secretary. This recent on-line review of the motel, which still exists, says it all:

> "The room was disgusting, dirty, dank, smelled awful. The employee on duty was absolutely the rudest man ever. I was afraid to sit on the furniture. I would rather sleep in my car than to ever stay in this motel ever again!"

I made a reservation with the Pakistani front desk clerk to rent a room for one day. I said we would be filming a small movie in it. He didn't understand me very well, and I didn't want to press the point. I only rented one room because I thought the cast could get wardrobe and make-up done at the house, and then take a five-minute ride to the motel. As always, when the crew arrived, our presence expanded. Most of the furniture was moved into the parking lot to make room for the lights and camera. Pat insisted that the cast couldn't just stand around being gawked at in the parking lot, so I went back to the front desk and asked if I could also rent the room next door. He noticed the commotion outside and jacked up the price from $25 to $85 for the second room. Then John said he needed a place to watch the action on the video assist, and the camera crew needed a place to layout their gear. So I went back to the clerk and rented a third room.

This time the clerk got suspicious.

"What you doing with so many room?"

"Oh nothing, just taking a few pictures. We'll be finished in an hour."

"Pictures, what kind pictures?" He said, and for the first time left the counter and walked out into the parking lot. He groaned when he saw the dozen cars, two trucks, movie lights on tall stands, ten crew people rushing around, and his crappy furniture from three rooms piled in the middle of the parking lot. A grip had already jimmied open the third room door with his credit card, and the crew was moving their gear in. The clerk flipped.

"What you doing my motel? I call police. You can do this here!"

"Wait, wait, wait. We won't hurt anything. We'll leave it better than we found it. Don't worry."

He stared like an alien space ship had landed in his parking lot.

"Look," I said, "we're renting three rooms, and won't even spend the night. It's a good deal; you're making a lot of money."

"No, no, you blocking all rooms on this side I can rent to nobody."

He was right, the crew had laid cables and set up chairs and crafts services along the whole right wing. Light stands blocked at least five other rooms, and the commotion spread out like a hungry amoeba.

"OK, ok, I'll rent ten rooms, and we won't use half of them. No cleaning bathrooms, no fresh towels, no making beds; it's a good deal. I'll pay cash too, let's go settle up. We'll be finished in an hour." I tried to lead him back to his office before he could get any more ideas. He seemed satisfied, but mumbled something to himself in Urdu. I pulled out my personal credit card and put $300 on it to quickly seal the deal.

Back at the set, John, having seen the ruckus came up to me.

"What was that all about?"

"Well, I just rented ten rooms for $300."

"Why?" said John, his eyes bulging.

"Look, how much we've spread out. I didn't write the script."

John rolled his eyes in desperation. "Where's that money coming from?"

"Hey, it's a legit location fee; the guy was about to call the cops; we'll make it up somewhere else."

The shooting went fine, but took much longer than planned. After everyone wrapped and left, I idiot-checked the rooms, and was shocked to see that all ten rooms had been more or less trashed. Furniture had been moved, beds stripped, every towel and toilet used, and soap bars opened and left on the counters. Several of the cast had taken showers, each in a different room. So much for not using the rooms. Grateful that I hadn't left a business card with the clerk, I quickly snuck off hoping he wouldn't see me.

On the positive side, we made the White Gables Motel in Millersville, Maryland famous by including a close-up of its sign—which for some reason always gets a big laugh. It's still there. Be sure to visit on your next trip to Baltimore. Ask for Room 27. And have fun.

Dealing with a New York film lab was a logistical challenge. I had originally planned to ship the exposed film twice a week by FEDEX. Thinking more about it, shipping the equivalent of $20,000 in production money, unattended, to New York was almost a crazy idea. We had three free PAs, and the four-hour train ride to New York cost about as much as FEDEX. I asked Alan Treadwell, a sharp, friendly volunteer PA, if he'd like to take a few all-expenses paid trips to New York City to do an extremely important job on the film. He was enthusiastic, but not ecstatic, because it meant 8 hours on the train at least twice a week. Sadly, his NYC sight-seeing consisted of a ten block subway ride to Times Square, where he'd drop the negative at the lab and pick up the printed dailies.

He'd have a half-hour to grab a Nathan's hot dog for lunch, with the $5 expense money I gave him, and then scoot back on the subway to catch the next train south. Most of the time, it was a ten to twelve hour travel day, and the novelty wore off quickly. Alan survived it because he was quite the avid reader.

As the production progressed, the number of trips increased, because we had to get quicker reports from the lab. Many set-ups were complicated, and we didn't want to tear down sets or return props that we might need for a re-shoot, because there was a problem with the film. Also, Tab and other actors were with us for very short periods, and we didn't want them to leave, and then have to pay for them to return for a re-shoot.

Alan was the absent crew member. He didn't learn much about filming, but never complained, never made a mistake, and he didn't quit. After about 40 one-way trips to NYC (8,000 miles) in twenty-five days, he was totally over the train, subway, and bad neighborhoods that bordered Amtrak's line between Baltimore and New York. Alan followed me to New York and worked as an excellent production assistant on a few movies, but he disappeared—maybe to California—and I lost touch with him. He was truly the unsung hero of Polyester.

The neighbors were calm in the first weeks of shooting, but there were a few irritations. Sometimes we had lights on the front lawn, and we usually got started early in the morning. I made sure people didn't hang out front, so you wouldn't know that a movie was being filmed there. Several scenes required us to be on the front lawn, and they were something to stare at, especially the scene when punk rocker Stiv Bators in his punked out wardrobe and hot car laid a long rubber patch in his grand exit. On another day, a noisy anti-porn demonstration-turned riot was staged on the front lawn, but went off without complaint. Most neighbors thought it was hilarious. Parking was the biggest problem, because there wasn't much space in the cul-de-sac, and if a driveway was blocked, I quickly had the car moved and the peace was kept. The PAs did little helpful chores like return neighbors' trash cans to their back yards, and cut their grass when the power mower noise wouldn't interrupt filming.

The lack of complaints lulled me into thinking everything was fine. A more experienced production manager might have hob-knobbed with the neighbors more regularly, bought Girl Scout cookies from them, and maybe visited their church on Sunday morning. My hands were filled with putting out fires, juggling the shooting schedule, and squeezing pennies from the budget.

Then, in the middle of a hectic shooting day, the postman delivered a registered letter. It was from an attorney hired by one of the neighbors, which said they would sue in county court to shut down the filming as a public nuisance that violated neighborhood covenants and local laws. That was a shock. We ran the letter over to John's attorney. It contained a catalog of our minor indiscretions and a few others that were simply made up. It claimed that our parked cars would impede emergency vehicles, that there was excessive late night/ early morning noise, cars that squealed dangerously in front of the house, that mountains of trash were piled at the curb, that helicopters buzzed the neighborhood dangerously low, that too many unrelated people were occupying the residence. Above all, it claimed we were conducting a commercial operation in a residence, which violated the local zoning laws—and oh, for good measure, naked people were running across the lawn. This never happened, but since it was a John Waters film who would believe that?

I asked one neighbor, who had been friendly and encouraging, what they thought, and they said the complaint was instigated by an older couple a few houses down, and that no one else had a problem with us. We waited to hear from John's attorney about what to do. This was about as big a problem as I could imagine.

Since the complaint was officially filed in county court, the Baltimore Sun newspaper picked up on it, and a reporter called the house. Not having much experience with the press, I chatted with the seemingly friendly reporter who thought the suit was a hoot. I inadvertently gave him a few good quotes when I said the suit was filed by one "cranky neighbor" and that the movie was small, and "just a bunch of freelancers." The story ran the next day with these damning quotes and other misquotes and misinformation. I thought the reporter would write a supportive story about young artists from Baltimore taking a big risk making a low-budget movie, but instead he attacked us as a pack of devils who were plaguing a neighborhood of innocent retirees and must be stopped. I wanted to wring the reporter's his neck, and ever since, have stress attacks when called by the press.

John's lawyer called to say he had spoken to the lawyer who filed the papers (the neighbor's brother, of course), who said the couple were lonely, and wanted attention. If someone went over to talk to them, apologize, and be friendly, they would probably drop the suit. That someone would be me, and I had to prepare. Van trimmed my hair, nice and straight, I put on my only shirt and tie, and for good measure got Tab to sign a headshot photo. That evening I walked over to their house and knocked on the door. Mr. X, a stern-looking man in his 70s looked down on me as I said, "Hello, I'm Robert Maier, and I work with the company filming next door, and I wonder if you'd have a few minutes to talk about it." Acting like he expected it, but without an ounce of warmth he said, "You may come in," then called over his shoulder to his wife, "honey it's a man from the movie next door."

His wife came into the room smiling and excited. They invited me to sit down. I was as apologetic as I could possibly be—though scared to death. I made a personal pitch. This movie was my big break; I had grown up in Baltimore, and just moved to New York. They were surprisingly sympathetic, so I added, looking at the Mrs., "I just got married a year ago, and my wife is expecting a baby, and I can't wait to get back home with her." It was a kind of a fib, my wife wasn't pregnant, but she was expecting a baby, in a couple years anyway. But it seemed to work well. The Mrs. brought in coffee and cookies, and they began asking all sorts of questions about what it's like to make a movie. It was as if the lawsuit didn't exist. They just wanted someone to entertain for the evening.

At the end, Mr. X said he wanted to teach me a lesson, to respect people's property and not barge into a neighborhood and ignore the residents. I didn't mention the flyer I had put in their door nearly a month ago, asking them to call me anytime with concerns or complaints. He promised to call the attorney in the morning and withdraw the suit, which was all I needed to hear. I left them Tab's signed photo, which they said they'd

The huge camera rented for one day to shoot scenes from the TV in Divine's bedroom in Polyester ©Robert Maier

give to their daughter, who was more his generation. It was a good lesson in location management: coddle the neighbors. I left with smiles and handshakes, and assured them I would alert them about any future outdoor activity, to see if they had any problems with it. I returned to my little cubby next door, popped a Tuborg, and quietly celebrated by myself before calling John. A few weeks later, John handed me a hefty statement from his attorney, to be paid from the production budget. I'd just have to make up for it somewhere else.

More money stories: When making travel arrangements for Tab, he said he only flew first class, and we had to fly him from Los Angeles. I thought he lived in Connecticut, a much cheaper flight. He did, but he was in LA working on a dinner theater show, and we had to fly him from there. That was thousands of dollars, again, not in the budget. John and New Line groaned loudly, but what could they do? I suggested they use a local actor and forget about the name, I guess being a little snarkey.

When New Line told me to try to negotiate him down—like flying coach, John pushed back, saying he didn't want Tab upset and delivering bad performances or attitude. Tab had explained that when he used to fly coach, he was miserable with a line of people that formed in the aisle demanding autographs and making him pose for pictures the whole flight—very understandable.

When I offered to call Tab again, John lit into Bob Shaye saying he was wrecking the film by being so cheap with important stuff, and all the investment would go down the drain. We were already under enough pressure, and didn't need an angry star. Besides, Tab would donate many hours promoting the film with interviews when it was released. This was the issue I'd frequently confront in the two other films I did with Shaye. He would generally concede to a logical argument, but stressed out everyone until he did. He was the original Mr. Champagne on a beer budget.

Some notable events were unrelated to money. One Sunday morning, we staged a car wreck in front of an empty lot on a nearby highway. It was a big scene for John. We had lights on tall stands, a generator truck, camera package, grip truck, vans, make-up table, sound crew, and crafts service. We even had a permit from the county and a couple cops to direct traffic. Two horribly wrecked cars had been towed to the spot, and splashed with fake blood. A prop ambulance flashed its lights. In one set-up, a real ambulance tech—hired as an extra—picks up a bloody severed head. He shrugs his shoulders and tosses it into the woods, like "he won't need this anymore."

Drivers, thinking it was a real accident, slowed down to gawk. Plus, Sunday morning traffic was backed up going into a church parking lot across the street. I chatted with the ambulance tech as traffic crept by, while he held the bloody prop head in his hands, remarking how realistic it was. One lady, in a car right next to us, caught a glimpse of it, and began screaming. It freaked me out, and smelling trouble, I had the head put away, since the shot was over. Other props included shrouded bodies lying around so the gawkers—most of them headed to the church—got an eyeful. Shortly afterward, a man came up and with shocked concern and said, "I'm a minister at the church across the street. Could you use the services of a pastor?"

I told him we were making a movie, pointed out the camera, lights, sound crew, and said everything was fake.

"Oh, I thought you were a TV news crew."

He walked away mortified that we had staged such a horrible movie scene on a Sunday morning right in front of his church. It was not the brightest scheduling or location decision, and I hoped he wouldn't complain to County officials. We skated on thin ice with every location, and needed government cooperation to control traffic, secure parking, and allow us to film in places like courtrooms, jails, schools, etc. And no matter how much you prepare, location movie shooting is bound to piss off somebody.

I hurried everyone out of there. Lucky for me a real TV news crew hadn't shown up—they would have loved that story. As usual, I was the last person to leave, and was getting into my car when a sober-looking couple from the church walked over and asked me to relay to the victims' families that the church congregation was praying for them. I froze like a cat in headlights, then answered,

"Why, that's very nice of them. I'll surely tell them, and I know it will be appreciated. Thank you for telling me."

I didn't dare go into the movie thing. Evidently the pastor hadn't mentioned that either.

Editing of Polyester was done in John's spacious apartment. We rented a 35mm editing machine from a supplier in Washington, DC, and Charles drove downtown to John's apartment during the shooting to prepare and organize everything. He worked there alone for more than a month. He didn't like the commute to a bad part of the city, but he had no choice.

Having an editing studio in his apartment was a little intrusive for John's personal life. Charles had a key, and one morning let himself in, as usual. While rummaging around the apartment getting things ready, a nude guy appeared in the hallway on his way to the bathroom. Charles is in no way anti-gay or a sexual prude, but he was an organized methodical guy, and felt his private office/studio had been violated. He started to worry, would it become a haven for orgies, with nude men walking around all day? He didn't say anything to John, but came to me and asked if I would ask John to be a bit discreet during working hours. I wasn't sure how to handle it either, but I had spent many hours with John and knew he preferred to keep his personal sex activities well out of sight of friends, certainly with me. I figured it was just an accident. When I told

John that Charles was concerned, he was terribly embarrassed. He had just overslept, and was not yet used to this new work routine, and then swore it would never happen again. It didn't.

The month of shooting wrapped. No one was injured, the budget wasn't in such bad shape, and the film looked great. John worshipped the video playback on this new camera, and ended a confident, happy man. New Line and Michael White had gotten a great deal. The worst was over, and for the next few months, John edited quietly in Baltimore with Charles.

8

New York Beat

. . . .

I returned to New York City with great relief from the suburban home that I never left for nearly eight weeks. I got to shop at Dean & DeLuca right around the corner, the Italian bakery every morning, have my pick of cheap Chinese, Indian, Japanese, or Italian restaurants every night, and eased into the cool life that was SoHo in the early '80s. I started visiting New Line every day to deal with the accounting, approve late-arriving invoices, and make an updated post-production budget. It grew to be such a large job, they actually threw me a little more money.

Manhattan at the end of the 1970s could be a pretty grim place. Bums were everywhere trying to wash motorists' windows for a dime. The country was in a recession, and NYC's infrastructure was collapsing in a series of blackouts, sanitation worker strikes, and water shortages as it skirted bankruptcy. It had acres of empty crumbling buildings. But it was fertile ground for artists from around the world. The abandoned lofts of lower Manhattan were incubators for theaters, filmmakers, musicians, recording studios, art studios, galleries, writers, and journalists. Dance troupes, experimental restaurants, clothing designers, and edgy night clubs made stabs at fame and fortune. It was cheap. Artists could live in an abandoned loft and eat and party for free at art openings every night. They found galleries to show their work, critics to write about it, and people to discuss it into the wee hours in Alphabet City's cheap Indian restaurants.

While working part time with New Line, I was contacted by a friend who was production managing a low budget movie, and wanted me to be the sound recordist. It was being paid for by Rizzoli, the respected Italian art book publisher that wanted to get into producing cheap art films. Originally titled New York Beat, it explored the punky new downtown New York art and music scene. This scene included Andy Warhol worshippers, people who dressed every day entirely in black, and pierced and tattooed their bodies to the sound of bands like Blondie, The Ramones, and the experimental art band, Tuxedomoon. It introduced graffiti as art, the first rap DJs, and Szechuan restaurants. It popularized cheap brands of beer like Pabst Blue Ribbon in East Village incubators like the Mudd Club and CBGBs. We would shoot live performances by a dozen experimental bands, and a soundtrack album of that music would be produced.

Re-titled Downtown 81, it wasn't released until 2005, because much of the original footage and sound had disappeared after a disagreement between the producers and creative team. The film was conceived by a young Swiss fashion photographer, Edo Bertollio, and the edgy downtown New York culture writer, Glenn O'Brien. Edo was part of NYC's punk-era "Euro-trash" invasion. He wanted to be in the scene, and had the money to do so (his father, a Swiss engineer, invented the ball point pen). Naturally, he hooked up with punk scene expert Glenn, who wrote a rambling arts column for Andy Warhol's Interview Magazine, called Glenn O'Brien's Beat.

The story was of a young graffiti artist, Jean-Michel Basquait trying to make it big in the no-wave music scene. Basquait was totally un-famous at that time. Warhol, who was the octopus of the NYC art world, had recognized Basquait, through his ubiquitous SAMO graffiti tag, as someone with commercial possibilities, so encouraged Glenn to make Basquait the star of the movie. Neither Glenn nor Edo had worked on a movie before. Rizzoli executives in Milan, knowing nothing about movies either, but concerned about the several hundred thousand dollars they were putting into the project, insisted on hiring an executive producer in New York. Unfortunately, he had no movie production experience either, except working at a stock footage house that specialized in preserving historic films. Not exactly good training for a hit and run documentary/drama shooting on NYC's mean streets.

Glenn and Edo were impressed that I had just finished line producing Polyester, and had worked with Tom Sullivan and Warhol on Cocaine Cowboys. They thought I fit in well because they wanted their crew to fit the edgy-arty atmosphere of downtown NY. They did not like Patrick, the producer hired by Rizzoli, who was an upper west-side, Central Park jogger kind of guy who didn't get graffiti art, punk rock music, or SoHo's grimy streets and clubs. They said they wished I could be the line producer, and they tried to push Patrick out. It sounded nice, but as things progressed, or, rather unraveled, I was happily detached from the Euro cluster-fuck that ensued.

Basquait, son of Haitian immigrants, was a smart kid who wanted to be famous, but did not spin with the world. He began by tagging structures across Manhattan with stick drawings and inscrutable snippets of freeform poetry, always signed SAMO. Everyone in New York City knew the name, because it was emblazoned on hundreds of bridges, subway cars, and boarded up buildings. No one except a few downtowners knew it was Basquait. But graffiti was getting accepted as a new art form, and it charmed the art world's chatteratti even if city officials considered it vandalism.

New York Beat was shot between Thanksgiving and Christmas. It was snowy, blowy, and stinging cold. The crew was as tiny as the budget, so once again there were no niceties like snacks or hot coffee. To get a warm drink, we'd duck into one of the Greek coffee shops for a "regular," bring it outside, and stamp our feet on the cold sidewalk waiting for someone to figure out what to do. Because I had no production manager responsibilities, it was very fun.

One day we went to a sketchy neighborhood in the South Bronx to shoot a new kind of music called rap. It originated in the summers when kids brought their records and record players out to the street to dance where it was a little cooler. These kids couldn't afford musical instruments or lessons, so they learned to "play" vinyl records instead. They cleverly took instrumental chunks from hit records, and then recited their own rhythmic poetry over the music.

Chris Stein and Debbie Harry of Blondie were music consultants on the movie and very into the new rap music. They arranged for us to film the pioneer rapper, Fab 5 Freddy, who had his turntables set up on the street when the film crew arrived. The neighborhood went wild because only news crews responding to big fires ever paid them any attention, and here was a group of white film people making a special trip to check out their music. Soon after, when Blondie's AutoAmerican album was released, they included a rap in the song Rapture, mentioning Fab 5 Freddy in the lyrics. Rapture flew to #1 on the charts and stayed there for weeks. It was the big push rap needed, and it never looked back. Ironic that it was introduced by a white blonde chick, but on the other hand, Debbie and Chris were the ultimate cool couple, so why not?

On New York Beat, we had no wardrobe, make-up, or continuity. Maripol, Edo's Italian girlfriend was the Art Director, but didn't do much more than kick a few piles of trash into the background, and chat with whatever downtown celebrities might be visiting. Actors wore whatever they showed up in. For Basquait, it was difficult, because the concept of personal responsibility was completely foreign to him. On the second filming day he showed up shivering in the icy wind because he had left his established wardrobe coat wherever he had gotten high the night before. Maripol went around the corner to buy him a heavy brown coat that would be his permanent wardrobe for the movie. At the end of the day, the production manager demanded that he give back the coat for safe keeping until the next shoot day. Basquait whined that it was his only coat, and he'd freeze without it. After a fifteen minute harangue, Edo said Basquait could keep the coat if he promised not to lose it.

The next day he showed up without it. Amazingly Maripol found a close match, so we didn't have to reshoot the previous day's scenes. This time at the end of the day, when the production manager asked for it back, Basquait said nothing. Next morning, he showed up wrapped in a blanket, which he must have pulled off his bed. The blanket was his off-screen winter coat for the rest of the filming.

Chris and Debbie were near the peak of their success, growing from a downtown New York art rock band to a global mainstream pop group. They had bought a few of Basquait's paintings, more or less keeping him alive, and hoping that other NYC scene makers would jump on the bandwagon. Chris regularly came to the shoots, but Debbie kept a low profile. She was such a big sex symbol she couldn't walk ten feet down the street without starting a riot.

Glenn's script was an outline, not a script, and Edo didn't have a clue how to direct. Edo simply asked the person next to him how they thought a scene should be blocked and shot. Most of the time was spent chatting and waiting around for downtown scenesters who had parts, but rarely showed. Basquait didn't bother to show half the time. Many days the production manager had to go to his loft and drag him to the set, still high from the night before. He slept in a corner until we were ready to roll the film, then Edo and Glenn would wake him up, give him a few lines to mumble, and he'd go back to sleep until the next. Basquait quit the movie several times, and it was considered that maybe he should be written out of the film—run over by a car maybe. The frustrated production manager volunteered for that duty. Why, everyone wondered, was this nobody loser being allowed to run the film into the ground? Little did we know.

I became friendly with Basquait—not that he was a person of many words, but he was desperate for money because of a tragic drug addiction. Towards the end of the film, I finally accepted one of his many invitations to visit his loft, see his paintings, and buy one. To me, his art was mostly badly drawn figures on an elementary school level. My wife and I didn't want to spend any money buying weird primitive art, but in the corner I noticed the 3x3 foot painting he had carried in many scenes in the movie. It was a rough collage of crumpled pieces of paper, colorful oil slashes, and a primitive face brushed on an old wooden packing crate top he'd found in the street. I thought it was a great souvenir of the film, at the very least. He didn't want to sell it, but when it was clear I only wanted that one, and would pay $100 cash, he said OK. It didn't have his signature on the front, and I asked him to sign it. He didn't like that idea, because it was a finished work. I said it was probably worth less unsigned, so we compromised and he signed it on the back in broad black strokes.

Dozens of primitive line crayon drawings were scattered across the floor, which he begged me to buy for just $5 each. I knew he would just spend the money on heroin, and thought his art would go nowhere, so I didn't feel good about buying more. He was disappointed, but followed me out the door rushing to his dealer ready to blow his hundred bucks. I walked the ten blocks to my loft carrying the bizarre painting, hoping no one would think I had done it, or worse, actually paid something for it.

Boy was I dumb. A few months later, after a big hype from the Warhol and Blondie crowds, Basquait had a sell-out SoHo art show, and was hailed by art critics as the big new thing. He moved into Warhol's building to churn out more work, leaving the New York Beat film crew completely bewildered. After his big show, I ran into him outside the SoHo art supplies store across the street from my loft. He looked very healthy and trim, wearing new jogging shorts and a T-shirt. I congratulated him on his show and skyrocketing career, and he asked if I still had the painting I had bought for $100—its value now was over $4,000. He said that painting meant a lot to him personally, and he would trade any of his new works for it; much larger ones that would sell for more.

I refused. The painting had a back story that I didn't want to give up, just for a more expensive painting. He finally shrugged his shoulders and walked off. It was the last time I ever saw him, but the painting has a continuing story.

New York Beat stopped suddenly when Rizzoli became sketchy about continuing its financing. Edo had thousands of feet of film, and an editor trying to make sense of it in a midtown loft editing room. There wasn't much yet to show Rizzoli,

Snapshot of part of the painting I bought from '80s artist Jean-Michel Basquait for $100 and sold six years later for $10,000 in a Sotheby's auction to pay down my huge credit card debts. I wonder where it is now. ©Robert Maier

and they just stopped sending money. Fed up with Rizzoli and their man Patrick, Edo and Glenn hatched a plan to sneak into the editing room one night and take all the film to secret place where they could control their work. It was a felony, but they knew the Italians lacked the organizational skills to track them down or do anything about it. Who knew how clean the money was anyway, this being another "cash only" production?

I visited the editing room a few times, but the editor worked very slowly, because she wasn't being paid and she had several other jobs. The film made little sense, but its edgy/punky look was a valuable artifact of the time. My 24-year old son, Philip, is a big fan of the movie and its music, and swears there's a big underground cult with the same opinion. The wrap party held at a private loft was a real downtown New York bash. Loud bands and rappers played, but I don't have much memory of it after Edo shoved a huge pill into my mouth, and insisted I swallow it with a shot of tequila. He said it was a "speedball," a mixture of heroin and speed. I remember the disco lights melting the walls, and nothing more until I woke up in my bed 24 hours later—resolving to just say no, forever more.

Continuing with Polyester

With New York Beat behind me, I immediately started back with Polyester, visiting New Line's office and talking to John almost daily on the phone. The editing in Baltimore was nearly finished, so I had to deal with the final lab work, the optical effects, Odorama, sound track music, and sound editing and mixing, all of which had to be done in New York. The biggest question was who would do the music sound track. New Line had worked with Michael Kamen, a young up-and-coming composer/arranger who had collaborated with Pink Floyd and other British rock groups on huge projects. Sarah knew he wanted to make more of a splash as a film composer, and would bend over backwards for a breakthrough movie. I had to make a deal with him, offering just $10,000 for a movie score that normally cost $75,000 or more. Sara complimented me highly about how I had made Polyester on such a low budget, and assured me I could talk Kamen into it.

Before I called Kamen, I met with the New York Beat crew in their secret editing room. Chris Stein was there, and I got the brilliant idea to ask him if he was interested in doing movie scores—like maybe Polyester. To my surprise, he said, "Hell yeah!" His goal was to do movies, because the rock star thing never lasted long. Glenn and Edo were encouraging, because Waters was probably the hippest American filmmaker at the time, and Chris was their good friend. I explained there was very little money, but Chris said money wasn't an issue. In fact they had just bought a million dollar house uptown and were building a studio in the basement where the score could be recorded. Debbie was the real valuable name in Blondie, so I asked if she could sing the title song. Chris said she'd probably love to. So, when could they start? Right away, I answered. I had to confirm with John and New Line, and would call in a day or so.

I went to see Sarah at New Line. I told her I had been working with Chris and Debbie, and they wanted to do the music for Polyester. At first blush, she was gaga. Her favorite song was the Blondie hit, Heart of Glass. They had three hit albums, and their newest album, was shooting up the charts. They would be—by far—the biggest name ever attached to a New Line project—and they would work basically for free. It was like a $250,000 investment in Polyester. Sarah ran to Bob Shaye's office to tell him, and they both quickly returned. Initially they were delighted, but then started questioning. Had Chris done a movie before? No. How well did I know him? Not that well. We had just met on the movie. Would he really do it, or get distracted and walk away to something better? I couldn't guarantee anything, except that they were super stars who said they saw this as a great career opportunity.

Michael Kamen was another issue. He had virtually been promised the Polyester music contract. He was a proven entity who'd scored several movies and New Line wanted to cultivate a relationship with him for their production future. Shaye, not wanting to give up the box office potential of a Blondie soundtrack asked if we could have dual composers, with Kamen taking the organizational lead. Then, if the unproven components, Chris and Debbie, had a rock-star flameout, they would be covered.

New Line asked me to gently present that possibility to both, after all, both were doing it mainly for the credit, and they might not want that diluted. I reminded New Line that Waters had to approve it too. Shaye blew that off with a "Don't worry about him, we need the names." Sarah said she would call their investor partner, Michael White, in London to get his opinion. I loved the idea of Chris and Debbie doing the score, but John could be unpredictable.

First, I felt I should clarify things a little bit more with Chris, and set a meeting the next morning in New York Beat's Chelsea editing room. When I asked how committed he would be to the project, he said 100%, and gave me a little lesson in the pop music cycle. His goal was to move into composing film scores—where the money and consistent work was. Blondie had taken nearly eight years to get to where they were, and now that they were near the top, probably wouldn't last more than another year. They argued constantly. They were tired of touring, tired of recording, and tired of each other. It was time to move on, and this was a great opportunity to move to another step. I thought it was remarkably level-headed for a rock star.

I asked again about Debbie's involvement. Specifically, would she sing a title song and could there be a Blondie soundtrack album? Chris hesitated and said it would be probably be impossible. She was locked into a bad deal with the record company that paid a great advance, but forbid her to sing on anything but its recordings. They would want $100,000 of which she'd get almost nothing. When they were struggling, the record company offered them what seemed to be a great deal, lots of cash, a recording contract, and promotional support, but it was an exclusive deal for Debbie. Everyone else was just back-up. She was the big ticket item, and her voice was owned by the record company. Being young and inexperienced, Chris and Debbie went for it, and now were beginning to regret it.

Debbie would help write the songs, and probably sneak in singing anonymous back-up, but that would be it. With Debbie's big name out of the picture, I felt more comfortable about bringing up Michael Kamen's involvement. Chris was surprisingly amenable. It was his first movie job, and he would love to work with a pro. He would write and produce several songs for the movie, play all the guitar parts in the score, and work with Michael as needed. He still wouldn't charge a penny for it.

I went to New Line after the meeting, discouraged about not having Debbie sing or use her name. Sarah and Bob were too, but they still saw an advantage. Any name attached to a movie is like a straw to a drowning man. Debbie could hype the movie, and Chris' name and Blondie were still huge. Kamen would still be a friend of New Line, and probably would like the idea of partnering with America's #1 rock group. With one big step taken, I would call John and Kamen for the next. I couldn't know it at the time, but Michael went on to win several Grammy awards and two Oscar nominations, and was one of the most respected film composers of the 20th century, before dying tragically young of a heart attack at age 55.

I phoned Michael, introduced myself, and told him that the good news was we definitely wanted him to write and produce Polyester's score, and that we could start right away. The bad news was the entire budget was just $10,000. There was a long silence.

Finally, he said, "That won't even cover the recording studio and tape costs. What about musicians? Do I pay my own cab fare?"

I apologized about the budget, but said it was locked tight, and I was lucky to have that much.

"Well, OK, but we'll have to do it fast, and at night. I'll have to work on other projects to pay my bills too," he said.

I took a deep breath and then continued,

"Michael, one other thing, I know Chris Stein and Debbie Harry of Blondie, and they want to work on it too. New Line and Michael White in London like the idea of having them associated with it. Chris wants a co-composer credit, but he would work for free, and Debbie would help write and sing backup. And Chris knows great musicians who would work for free too," I said hopefully. After another long silence, Michael, being a true professional who knew how the music business worked, said OK. He would arrange for studio time and we would begin as soon as I got him a video copy of the movie's final cut. It worked out better than I expected, so I called John in Baltimore.

John was a different story. Although he would later change his tune, he did not like the idea of a Top-40 rock band horning in on his work of art. We already had Tab Hunter and punk-rock star Stiv Bators as names. He didn't want a "disco group" that his audience would hate. I explained I had been working with Chris and Debbie for months and gotten to know many of the NY art hipsters, and that Blondie was a huge influence in the underground punk rock music and art scene—his audience. John liked the anarchy of punk rock, and started to come around. Maybe it would help. Could he meet Chris and Debbie to check them out? It was Thursday afternoon. He was coming to New York that weekend, but was booked with continual meetings. It had to be Sunday morning at 9:00 a.m.

I called Chris, who always had his answering machine on and never returned calls, but he picked up this time. I said John would like to meet him and Debbie Sunday morning at 9:00 a.m. Was that too early? He said sure, come by their loft; they didn't usually get up until after 1:00 p.m., so they would definitely be there. He gave me directions and said if there was no answer, just keep ringing the doorbell, and they would eventually wake up. I was heading into the last lap.

Sunday morning, John and I met at a coffee shop around the corner from Carnegie Hall, which was near Chris and Debbie's place. We agreed it was a little weird meeting rock stars at 9:00 a.m. on a Sunday morning. I said it was a sign of their wanting to do the project. Chris had given me the address and said to ring the button labeled Huffnagle. Like he said, it took a few minutes, but finally a sleepy voice crackled over the intercom, "Yeah?"

John and I looked at each other. "It's Bob Maier and John Waters to see Chris."

"Take the elevator to the Penthouse," the intercom crackled back, and the door lock buzzed, letting us in.

The elevator opened to reveal Chris in a CBGB's t-shirt and jogging shorts, looking a mess. His hair all tousled, and deep circles puffed under his eyes, he seemed still half asleep and turned saying, "Follow me."

John and I glanced at each other as we walked through a small sparsely furnished living room and kitchen to the bedroom of this small penthouse apartment. The bedroom was strewn two-feet deep with clothes, record album covers, magazines, and a guitar in the corner. A king-size bed covered in thick down comforters filled the room. Chris jumped into the bed and under the covers, and started poking a lump beside him.

"Debbie, wake up, John Waters is here to talk about his movie."

John and I looked around nervously for a place to sit, but there were no chairs.

"Just get on the bed," said Chris, and he started shaking the lump beside him. "Come on Debbie wake up. We have people here."

John and I, unfamiliar with rock star protocols sat uncomfortably on the edge of the bed. We needn't worry about getting too close, because it was a giant bed and Chris and Debbie were both small people. Chris propped himself up with a few pillows, then reached over to an ashtray to poke through the remains of several joints obviously left over from the night before. As Chris lit one, the lump next to him began to stir on its own, and Debbie revealed her sleepy face with a big smile. She was stunning.

"Hello."

"Hello, Debbie, I'm John Waters, I'm very happy to meet you. This is quite an informal first meeting, I must say," he chuckled.

She smiled back, "Oh well, it is pretty early for us, but we wanted to meet you. Thanks for coming."

Chris said, "This is a temporary place, we bought a house across town, but there's some tax problems, and we might have to sell it. When you sign with a record company you get a big chunk of money up front. We never had money before, and didn't understand the tax thing, so we owe a lot," he volunteered. Many rock stars of the period had similar problems.

Chris was very humble, and let John know he was totally in the driver's seat with the movie, and he was very happy for the chance to work on it. Chris had the joint burning quite well and offered it to us, but we waved it off, knowing our full day's work ahead. I hadn't smoked pot for years anyway. Debbie said she supported Chris' desire to go into movie scoring, and would do everything she could to help, but was sorry she couldn't sing. Well, she could, but couldn't legally use her own name, so what good would that be? The meeting was rather short and sweet. Chris talked about odd-ball musical styles and groups John had never heard of, and would usually set him off, but in the magnetic presence of these two rock stars, instead of making snarky comments, he just nodded his head and smiled politely. It was uncomfortable with the four of us on the bed, so John and I were happy to bring the meeting to an end. I said I'd bring by a contract from New Line next week for Chris to sign. Debbie said they were always there during the day and to just drop by.

When we left, John smiled with relief. "I really like them. I'm glad they'll be involved. I'm glad you introduced them to me. I just hope I like the music."

"I'm sure you will, and Michael Kamen's an experienced composer. You've got the best of both worlds and on budget too, for once."

He didn't think that was so funny, but I thought, thank God I don't have to argue with him about this. It was the right thing. Over the years, John grew close to Debbie, gave her a big part in Hairspray, and is still good friends with her.

As promised, I returned to their penthouse three days later with a hastily drawn contract from New Line. Debbie answered the intercom this time, and buzzed me up. She opened the door at the top, dressed in a mousy brown overcoat, and wore a black scarf that hid her famously blond hair. Huge black sunglasses covered her face. She shouted over her shoulder in her New Jersey accent.

"Chris, it's Bob Maier!" Chris walked in from the bedroom carrying a guitar and asked if everything was going well.

"Oh yes, it's great. I have the contract right here."

"Oh," Debbie said, returning to me, "You're just in time. Would you mind walking me to the pharmacy and back? I hate to go by myself. If people recognize me, it's hell. It's just around the corner. Would you please?"

With her so covered up, people might stare, but not much chance of her being recognized. And of course I'd be ecstatic to walk down the street with Debbie Harry.

She dropped the contract on a table and yelled "Chris, sign these, we'll be back in a minute." Chris nodded, as the elevator door closed behind us. Out on the street, not a soul recognized her. What a terrible disappointment. Here I was escorting one of America's hottest women down 49th Street in broad daylight and no one knew it. Why did she have to wear those damn sunglasses and head scarf?

On the other hand, I knew how it was for celebrities in public. People have no problem coming up to your face, demanding autographs, asking personal questions, critiquing your work, calling out, "Look everybody, it's...!" like they've discovered free money lying on the street. When John and I would go to the movies or a restaurant in Baltimore, sometimes people would recognize him and stare unblinkingly, like we were dogs that just started talking.

From the outside, the attention and worshipful stares seem glamorous, but it's not. People don't see you as a human being, but as a play toy. Some celebrities like it, for others like Debbie, it's a burden, and it's what drives celebrities to live in gated communities, fly on private planes, and vacation at island villas. It wouldn't be my last celebrity escort job—and despite sympathizing with Debbie, to me it was still a treat.

The recording sessions began two weeks later. True to Michael's promise, they were night work, and went from 10:00 p.m. to 3:00 a.m. John insisted that I attend every session to report on how it was going—not that I didn't want to be there, but it doubled my work schedule. Kamen was a great choice and a genius. From the beginning he took the reins. It was more of a learning experience for Chris, who got the message that he wasn't needed so much and came to only about half the sessions. Michael was kind enough to include him as much as possible in the process, but Chris had many other commitments too. A big one was promoting Blondie's new album, and especially the single from it, Tide is High, that was racing up the Billboard Hot 100 chart.

One evening when he was at the studio laying down guitar tracks, a message was delivered by courier: Tide is High had just been named #1 song on the Billboard chart, Blondie's first. Everybody in the studio cheered, and the usually mellow Chris sported a huge grin. Here I was in a recording studio with the #1 rock group in the world, working for free on a movie that I was producing. Couldn't get much better than that—but it did.

Chris and Debbie were friends with Bill Murray, who was a huge star on Saturday Night Live, and had just finished the hit movie, Caddyshack. Murray wanted to be involved in Polyester too, and Chris suggested that having him sing the title song would make up for Debbie's not being able to. I told Chris I would check with New Line, and they went gaga again over it—especially since Murray wouldn't charge, and they could freely use his name. Adding yet another big name to Polyester's credits made me the golden boy in New Line's eyes. They offered to start paying me a few hundred dollars a week to keep me guiding Polyester through its increasingly complicated post-production process.

I called John with the good news, but he was livid. He hated Bill Murray. He hated Saturday Night Live. He hated Caddyshack. This might seem strange, because they were young, edgy, and irreverent artists, and it would seem they would be John's people. But Murray was a mass-audience TV phenomenon, while John was an underground and dangerous artist. John bragged at every opportunity that he never even watched TV. John's humor was not doofusy like Bill Murray's. John's was angry, gay, and shocking, and he didn't want it diluted. SNL's founding writer, Michael O'Donohue's infamous "comedy," Mr. Mike's Mondo Video, which shocked America's sensibilities because it featured cats being thrown in a swimming pool was more John's cup of tea.

John was pissed-off that there was so much meddling with his work in New York, while he was in Baltimore. But New Line prevailed, because the brass ring in movie sales is big names. John never thanked Bill, and pouted a little that he had been unfairly compromised about it. In the long run, it probably didn't add much to the movie, but it was fun for me to work with another big star. Murray showed up at a session, late one night in a baseball cap and T-shirt. He sang two takes, often off key and then took off. I didn't know whether he was singing off key for the humor, mimicking a lousy suburban lounge singer, or he just couldn't sing. But I didn't want to rock the boat.

In the end it was a funny and very appropriate song for Polyester's opening title sequence, and you can clearly hear Debbie's "ooo, my daddy, daddy," back-up vocals. Because of the back story, with the scary helicopter shot, Chris' song, Kamen's arranging, and Murray's lead, not to mention Vince's superb art direction, and Divine's wonderful reveal, it is my most favorite scene in all the Waters movies.

The pressure to finish the movie was relentless, because New Line had to firmly book theaters for the first run in New York City months ahead of time. I worked all day with the sound editing crew, the optical house, and meetings at New Line, then all night with Michael Kamen in the recording studio. If I didn't spend two hours a day updating John, he would flip out.

One day the Polyester Association of America, a trade group of fabric producers, had seen some pre-publicity for the movie, and called Sarah at New Line to inquire if they could help promote the film. Fearing they would sue after seeing the movie, New Line panicked until their lawyer discovered "polyester" was a non-trademarked name. Sarah never called them back, figuring they might not appreciate the plug when they saw the movie, but at least we could stop worrying about copyright infringement.

Odorama had continuing problems. The ultra-conservative 3M Company, the only company able to make the scratch and sniff stickers wanted to pull out several times because they were suspicious about how their precious product was being used. "Fart" was not listed in their smell library. They did have "rotten eggs," and if New Line ordered a million of those, stored safely in a warehouse, it didn't matter what 3M thought.

Kamen had the same 24-hour schedule as I. But to keep himself and his engineer going in the wee hours, there was a steady stream of the popular creative fuel, cocaine. It was so common in recording studios of the time that mixing consoles had mirrors built in to accommodate snorting lines.

Coke dealers had regular night delivery routes for New York's recording studios, and the crews looked forward to their visits. Watching the volume of coke going up noses made me nervous that we wouldn't complete the project before a drug burnout. I never told John, because he would totally flip out.

But Kamen was a master, and put together an amazing score for next to nothing. At the end of each session, around 3:00 a.m., I'd walk the fifteen blocks to my loft, down Fifth Avenue, through Washington Square Park, and into SoHo to clear my head. The streets were deserted, and New York City was all mine. I never thought about getting mugged, and never had a problem, but one night a cop car pulled up and asked where I was going. I said I had just finished a recording session and was walking home to Spring and Wooster. I guess I looked pretty harmless so he said, jump in; I'll give you a lift. That's the New York City I miss.

Polyester was finally finished and opened in several NY Theaters. Critics noticed the increased production values and John's move to a more mainstream plot and characters. Many praised it as an entertaining, different, developing piece. Odorama was nearly unmanageable, and though it sounded good on paper, never drew the audiences New Line and John had hoped for. Tab Hunter, as a box office draw was a disappointment. He was too much of a has-been—his audience was in their sixties and didn't go to underground movies. The addition of Blondie and Bill Murray to the soundtrack didn't generate much as much buzz as hoped for either. In the end, with all the distribution costs, Polyester probably did not make a profit, but in the movie business, you never know for sure. On the positive side, it generated great press and exposed John to a much wider, more mainstream audience. It was a sensation at the Cannes Film Festival, because the French love anything

John (l) Bob(r) at opening night party for Polyester in New York City, looking serious and wondering what the next step will be. It would be five years before John made another film.

that pokes fun at American suburbia, so it heightened John's recognition with the international glitterati.

Bob Shaye, suspicious of John and the project from the very start, had asked to see the rough cut before we went into full post-production. Charles brought it to his elegant apartment on the upper west side, and they watched it alone. At the end, Shaye stood up and groaned, "Another stupid John Waters movie." He had taken big financial risks on Female Trouble and Desperate Living, without much profit. John's cult art movies were not what he wanted to produce, and if Polyester didn't click at the box office, it would be his last John Waters movie.

Bob was not overly impressed with the extensive press attention. He wanted extensive money in the bank. But having had a taste of movie-making, he set himself a clear goal of making a movie that he controlled completely, from script to director to cast to distribution; even the financing. Only then could he produce the box office hit he craved.

9

Alone in the Dark

$\cdot$ $\cdot$ $\cdot$ $\cdot$ $\cdot$ $\cdot$ $\cdot$ $\cdot$ $\cdot$ $\cdot$ $\cdot$ $\cdot$ $\cdot$ $\cdot$ $\cdot$ $\cdot$ $\cdot$ $\cdot$ $\cdot$ $\cdot$

A lone in the Dark was to be that movie. It began pre-production about a year later. It would be New Line's can't-fail horror/slasher flick; a dream money-maker by a savvy distributor who knew what the audience wanted: a scary story, gory special effects, a cast with a couple big names, and a good dose of topless teen love scenes. They would pick a budget-conscious writer/director they could control so it wouldn't become an artsy-fartsy personal statement.

What they got was a snarky statement by a first-time director, a psycho special effects crew who couldn't deliver anything on time, a passive-aggressive cast of seasoned names who knew their way around a low-budget set more than the producers or director, and perhaps cinema's most embarrassing-to-watch-ever love scene.

Jack Sholder, the director, was an erudite intellectual who had studied in Europe and had a degree in Literature from the notoriously experimental Antioch College. Unlike Waters, his hero was Jean Renoir, not William Castle. Jack's main work had been making American trailers for New Line's foreign imports, which kept him busy and in constant touch with Shaye. He was an odd choice for a low-budget horror flick, but Shaye felt that he could bully him into making a profitable teen movie. Bob and Jack regularly visited Upper West Side wine and cheese bars to discuss Cinema and they were quite close, so Shaye felt he could hold him on a tight leash.

Because I'd come up through the Waters school, Shaye wasn't sure if I had earned an important place in Alone in The Dark. Having worked closely with New Line through dozens of thorny production problems on Female Trouble, Desperate Living, and Polyester, I felt I was the obvious choice for production manager, but Shaye resisted. A friend of his wife, another erudite wine and cheese buddy, Benni Korzen was first choice. I was told he would be the production manager, and I would assist him for the time being. Benni had come from Denmark and most of his movie credits were as an importer of explicit Danish sex videos that made it through U.S. customs because they were classified as "medical instructional films for use by psychotherapists only." It was a good market, he assured me, but he was tight-lipped about the details.

I started working in New Line's office immediately, without any title, hoping to be the assistant production manager or something. Benni had partially broken down the script, but then gave it to me to finish. This set the pattern. Benni would begin a project, get distracted, and then turn it over to me to finish. I asked him if I could run through my production manager's checklist—hiring crew, securing an equipment deal, lab deal, editing studio, office supplies, film permits, SAG contracts, production office setup, all the little things normally done in early pre-production. He said he had it all under control, and said he would give me the information needed "at the right time."

Though I went to my New Line office every day, there was no firm commitment or start date for the project. Jack visited regularly, anxious to begin casting—and get onto the payroll. Shaye and Benni had long, closed-door meetings about who knows what, then Benni would come to me with a few disconnected scribbled notes like "get Tom Savini's phone number" (Savini, who started with George Romero on Night of the Living Dead, was the top gore special effects guy in low budget movies). It was a surprisingly disorganized beginning, and made Waters and me look like a finely tuned machine. No one knew if Shaye was serious about moving ahead. The big problem seemed to be the lack of outside investors. New Line never wanted to use its own money or credit line, and would only do so as an absolute last resort.

As the weeks wore on, what was originally planned as a comfortable fall shoot was looking like a mid-winter New York freeze fest, like my previous winter's New York Beat. Then suddenly, after hours of secret pow-wows between Benni, Shaye, and Sholder, Benni came into my office.

"OK Bob, you have been asking for more to do, and this is your big moment," he said in his sing-song Danish accent. "I have been selected to be the Executive Producer of Alone in the Dark, and you will be the production manager. Bob Shaye is just too busy to give the film his full attention, and he has asked me to take it over. We have cast Martin Landau, Donald Pleasance, and Jack Palance in the lead roles. And we begin in four weeks."

"Four weeks?" I gasped. "Do you have the budget, the scene break down, the shooting schedule, the crew?"

"I have nothing," Benni answered. "You will have to do it all. I don't know how much money we have, but it has to be done very cheap—and I understand you are the expert in that. So it's up to you."

Oh my God, here we go again, I thought. Here I was sitting around for a month, and now in four weeks I had to hire fifty people, find a dozen locations, get union contracts, set-up a functional production New York City production office, and do it "cheap." The budget was a work in progress, but I couldn't go over it—whatever "it" was, when Benni said "it's up to you." So much for a smooth start to New Line's perfect low budget money-maker. We were now officially a 100 car freight train heading down from the top of the mountain, and the brakes just failed.

Benni did have a list of people he preferred to work with, but due to the low budget, many turned the job down, and most of the people eventually hired worked in a job they had almost no experience with. They were doing it to expand their resumé. I include myself, because I had never managed a full production in New York City. I came into Alone in the Dark wanting to be assistant production manager and learn from an expert. Then again, Sholder had never directed a movie, Benni had never executive produced a movie, Shaye had never produced a movie, and so it went. A freight train comin' down the mountain.

I charged ahead and worked sixteen hours a day. But it was like walking in mud. There were constant hurdles, not the least of which was money, as usual. Every time I'd present a bid to Benni, like camera rental, he'd say,

"Cut it in half, you can do better than that."

As a result I had to make deals with the sleaziest, junkiest, most unreliable equipment suppliers in New York—generally people who supplied the porn industry. For example, I rented an unshelved truck for the lighting equipment, which totally pissed-off the lighting crew, who dumped all the gear in a pile, allowed it to slide around, which cost way more in damaged equipment and overtime than a proper truck that secured the equipment.

Unions were a big issue. Besides SAG for the actors, no other film unions could be used. But since unions share information, I began receiving daily calls from New York's half-dozen film worker unions, like camera, lighting, editors, and art directors, asking us to sign their contracts too. They saw us as a union-busting film, and did not want us to succeed. Initially, I dodged their phone calls, but the Teamsters (truck drivers) were especially persistent. One day I got a call from our insurance agent, a tough New Yorker who carried a pistol on his belt, saying he'd heard from a friend in the Teamsters that I wasn't returning phone calls and that could mean real trouble. It was not healthy to ignore the Teamsters, he said. They knew all about the production, the trucks and cars we had rented, and where they were parked. If I didn't at least show the courtesy of returning their calls, they might smash the windshields and headlights, flatten the tires, and bust off the radio antennas–as a start. I could personally be in danger. Some of these guys didn't fool around, and I needed to contact them, pronto.

More than a little scared I immediately called the union rep, first apologizing for being so rude. He was very nice on the phone. He said he understood our situation and wanted to work with us, not shut us down. To prove it, he offered a special deal.

Normally, a NYC movie required 12-18 teamsters. They would drive each truck, pick up and return all the stars in hired cars, and chauffer production assistants on their errands around town. If it had a steering wheel, a Teamster drove it, and they were on the set the exact same hours as the crew, including overtime, whether driving was required or not.

The rep said that in the spirit low budget cooperation, they would require that we hire just three stand-by Teamsters, who would hang out in the union hall. We could drive our own trucks, but they'd come and help if needed. They wouldn't do overtime, no matter how long the crew worked, so we could be confident of a fixed price. Not a bad job, just hang out for the day and make $350. The rep said they were supporting the idea of a low budget film industry in New York, to keep them from running off to some other state. I guess it could be called a bribe, but everything's negotiable in New York, and it was better to compromise than take a hard line. It was a good lesson.

Shaye didn't see it that way, and with every expense I brought for approval, railed against the greedy over-paid movie people who were driving him to ruin. I was under strict orders to shave every penny possible, and not give in to anybody. Here were the general rules of low budget movie spending:

- Get everything on credit.

- Don't pay anyone until they threaten to sue.

- Promise anything but prompt payment.

- Focus on a future relationship when they would make real money, but only if you got a great deal now.

- Get product placement donations for everything to preserve cash.

It was relentless, and Shaye lorded over his fiefdom like a tyrant. Everybody feared going into his office—which I had to do a lot. In one period, he had a curious affectation of keeping an open bottle of tequila on his desk, and swigging from it regularly during meetings, like a rock star on stage. He offered everyone in the room a snort from the bottle, and I was torn between accepting his hospitality or not accepting to show I was conscientiously managing his movie. I never knew if he was serious or just testing me. Then there were the meetings with Michael Harpster, his partner, who was a tea-totaling health nut. On his desk sat a fuzzy metallic globe at the end of a long metal rod that connected to a base that plugged into a wall socket. I thought it was an artsy desk lamp, but he said it was an "ozone generator." It supposedly created a healthy atmosphere around his desk. Every once in a while it buzzed and sparked like a mosquito catcher. It unnerved me and I hated sitting in the room with it.

Due to the penny pinching, we had to play catch-up from day-one and change direction to do what we should have been doing in the first place. When disasters occurred, money always appeared to fix them. The initial crew was too small, so the shooting schedule fell behind on the first day. The cheap lighting equipment was bent and broken, and took a long time to get functional. We never had enough cars to run errands, and the art department shoppers disappeared for hours using slow-moving city transit busses.

The big-name cast members, Donald Pleasence, Martin Landau, and Jack Palance, drove Shaye insane. Pleasence was a low-budget movie "maniac" character staple, but in real life was a savvy sophisticated guy who had been a name for 30 years, and took shit from no one. At this point in his career, he'd do any movie for a big paycheck, and happily signed on to Alone in the Dark, sensing Shaye's greenness as a producer. On his arrival, Pleasance kicked some dirt in Shaye's direction, and refused to stay in the cheap hotel we had arranged for him. When Shaye told me to lay down the line, and tell Pleasance the hotel would not be changed, he told me to book him a flight on the next plane to London; he was out of there. Now, that's balls, I thought. Shaye immediately relented and Pleasance moved to a nice East Side hotel, where he promptly ran up monstrous room service bills for his favorite daily snack, champagne and oysters on the half-shell.

Shaye had me call the hotel to stop room service, but Pleasance called back in minutes, screaming that he'd never been treated so rudely, and would not leave the hotel room for any shooting until his room service privileges were restored. Facing only two more weeks to get through shooting, Shaye realized it wasn't worth alienating the star of his million dollar movie for a few hundred dollars worth of champagne and oysters.

One day I visited the set and Martin Landau, the great actor from Mission Impossible and an Oscar winner, cornered me. He had not received his per diem checks, as required by his contract, even though he'd been asking for a week. His contract hadn't been signed either, though he had worked every day.

"I wanna know one thing from you," he shouted, "why is Bob Shaye trying to fuck me?"

Startled and embarrassed, all I could think of was how much I'd loved Mission Impossible when I was growing up, and working with Martin Landau was a huge honor. Here he was cussing me out in front of twenty people.

I tried to burble an answer but couldn't get a word between all the "fuckins." His final words were, "You go back to Bob Shaye and tell him to stop fuckin' me." He turned on his heels and stalked off, leaving all the witnesses, including Jack Sholder, aghast.

Mellow, erudite Jack sidled up to me and calmly whispered, "You've got to tell Bob to stop upsetting the actors, it's hurting their performances."

Right, first I would quote Landau, and then, oh, by the way, Jack said you should stop upsetting the actors. Shaye would have thrown me right out his tenth story office window. Instead I went to New Line's chief financial officer down the hall and said he would probably lose Landau if he didn't get the contract and money to him —today. He rolled his eyes, said he would handle things with Bob later, and then wrote a check and signed the contract. I drove back to the location and handed it to Mr. Landau personally, feeling like a total worm.

Jack Palance sort of remembered me from Cocaine Cowboys two years earlier, but was not any friendlier because of it. He was in Alone in the Dark for the money, just like the others. The less time and effort it took the better. He commuted to the set in an old pick-up truck from his farm in northern Pennsylvania about two hours away, and would be livid when the shooting schedule changed, and he had to spend an extra night away from home. Unfortunately the shooting schedule changed 5-6 times a day, so I spoke to Mr. Palance regularly, and he was usually quite perturbed when I informed him of yet another change that interfered with his personal life.

Benni, Jack, Shaye, and the 1st AD meticulously scheduled the scenes that were to be shot each day, but generally fewer than half were completed. Set ups took forever. Rehearsals of indulgent, complicated shots took forever. This meant the number of shooting days would double, essentially doubling the budget—a true disaster in the making.

I met with the executives on Sunday mornings to plan the week's schedule, and Jack swore he could get the scenes done. Then sure enough by the end of the day Monday, we'd be a day behind. Same thing with every other day. Jack was an inexperienced director, and more interested in getting good performances from the actors and gorgeous shots than being on schedule or on budget. But many other factors contributed to the slow production pace; winter weather, inadequate equipment, small crew size, traffic jams. More than once Palance's truck got stuck in a snow storm in the Pennsylvania mountains and he didn't show. Shaye was livid that his low budget dream money-maker was spiraling out of control.

One Sunday, Shaye called a special morning pow-wow at his apartment to discuss the situation. The first assistant director, Benni, and the director of photography were there, but Sholder was notably absent. Around plates of exotic salami and expensive cheeses, Shaye said he was seriously considering replacing Jack to stem the money gusher caused by falling so far behind. In his mind, Sholder was just so disorganized he could not manage the complexity of a shooting day.

We looked at several possibilities: having Benni direct, or the DP, or bringing in another director, and sending Jack to the editing room where he was most talented. In the end, it was decided that Jack should stay, but Benni would stand by his side every minute hurrying him along and figuring out how to simplify things. From this point, Benni became a glorified assistant director, and I moved from production manager to producer—without a producer credit or producer paycheck. It didn't solve anything, because, I suspected, Benni secretly had no problem with adding a big film to his resume. The film was looking great. It wasn't Benni's money, so if it took longer and more money, it only made him look better. Shaye was doomed by the egos he had hired. Ultimately Jack proved to be a talented director and the film won several awards, but the money vs. art conflict was bloody.

I had plenty of ideas how to save money from my experience on low budget films, which was greater than Shaye, Benni, and Sholder combined. But they were brutal things like: cut scenes from the script—it was too long anyway, and why shoot things that would never make the final cut; simplify the stunts and special effects. We could find closer locations that weren't so pretty, but would save hours of travel time. Kill off one of the stars early and cut their contract in half. Tell Jack to use simple zooms instead of time-consuming dolly shots. We could fire Benni, because his hurrying of Jack on the set didn't seem to improve the situation. We could hire a seasoned low budget hack TV director who knew how to make a short shooting schedule work. My ideas were all rejected, as I knew they would be, because they would hurt the "production value." So I started worrying less and less about money too, since Shaye was all talk and no action, and would never abandon his two buddies, Jack and Benni. I became a convenient whipping boy when it came to complaining about money.

In one meeting, Bob laid the blame squarely on me for going over budget in the special effects area, I reminded them that I had warned him specifically against his choice of crew.

"Yes you did," he replied, "but you didn't warn me loud enough."

I put that down in my notebook, but wondered how to measure "warning me loud enough."

The problems rolled on. One Sunday morning around dawn, I received a call from the grip that they had just wrapped a location, but the 24 ft. truck with all the lights wouldn't start, so they left it there. I had to go pick it up—an hour's drive outside Manhattan. I called a production assistant to go with me, and I would drive the truck back to its mid-town parking spot. It had been a long time since I'd driven a 24 ft. truck, and I'd never driven one in Manhattan. I arrived at the location, an historic mansion in New Jersey, and saw that our big yellow rental truck blocked its front entrance. I knocked on the mansion door and finally a guy opened it. I said I was with the movie company and had come to take the truck back. He went off like a rocket.

"You must have the stupidest people in the universe working for your movie. I want to know the name of the person in charge here last night. Are they idiots? Certified idiots?"

Uh-oh, not again, I thought.

"Get in here and look what they've done."

He walked me to a huge ball room that had been the location. It was spectacular, with floor-to-ceiling wood paneling, ornate trim and a broad wooden parquet floor.

"This is a national historic site. Everything here is irreplaceable," he hissed.

It looked fine to me. I expected leaking garbage bags, splintered furniture, and smashed windows, but then he ran up to a grand piano in the corner. Pointing to where the legs met the floor, I saw two-inch wide streaks gouged into the parquet floor boards because the piano had been dragged across them.

"This floor is priceless. And now it's ruined. They had to push it the entire length of the room. They couldn't use a dolly? Or furniture pads? Are they morons?"

"We have insurance for this, and I'm sure they'll take care of it," I said. "I'll call them first thing tomorrow morning."

"Insurance? This floor is a national treasure and can never be replaced."

Speechless, I finally just walked out to deal with the truck, listening to his raving echo through the mansion. I got back to Manhattan six hours later after waiting for a replacement battery. Not a nice day off. When I called the key grip, he said he barely remembered moving the piano. They had worked a

20 hour day, and a fresh wrap crew should have been called to make sure there were no problems. It was a production problem, not his. The day had been scheduled for eight hours, but true to form went twenty.

I shouldn't blame the grips. He was right. Another low-budget hell boondoggle. A wrap crew would have cost $1,000. The floor repair would be ten times that.

In another episode, a group had to drive three hours north of the city to shoot in an abandoned diner. It belonged to a friend of the Art Director, and there would be no location fee. I begged them to pay a fee and shoot closer to Manhattan, but this was a "perfect" diner, and both Jack and the Art Director convinced Shaye and Benni to let them shoot there.

On the scheduled night, the crew drove upstate into a blizzard. They arrived several hours late, and when they entered, found the water pipes had burst and water had frozen in huge sheets. The owner had forgotten both to check the water and ask for the electricity to be turned on. So it was a bust, and another huge waste of money, especially with having to scramble for a motel where the cast and crew could lay low until the weather straightened out. I rented an empty diner just outside Manhattan to shoot in next week.

As for the vaunted special effects, we had hired a low-bid gore effects guy who was late on every piece he was assigned, requiring additional surprise re-schedules. He was an arrogant artiste, and would not be pushed around either. His greatest work for the movie would be a life-like severed head, but the shooting date for it was getting closer and closer, and he refused to show anything. I finally barged into his studio and demanded to see the head. He showed an off the shelf Styrofoam model's head that looked like ketchup had been squirted on it.

"For this you're charging $5,000?" I said.

"Bob Shaye's only paid me $1,000. I said $5,000, and all up front."

"Bob's an honest guy, he'll pay you when it's done," I said.

"Tell Bob Shaye he's a schwazoole. And you're a fuckin' fool for working for him." Another kind message to deliver to Bob. And what the heck was a schwazoole?

Back in Shaye's office, I told him the efx guy hadn't done a thing, and said I'd call Tom Savini, the guy I wanted to hire in the first place, who was more expensive, but might still bail us out. Savini was a great guy. He was renowned for his work on George Romero's and other gore films, and had wanted to do Alone in the Dark in the beginning, but his bid was too high. Fortunately he had a few days and agreed to put a great severed head together in his Pittsburgh workshop, fly with it to New York in a carry-on bag on the shoot day, do the final touches on the set, then leave. The scene was shot on schedule without incident. Fortunately they didn't check carry-on baggage back then.

I passed these stories along to John when I spoke with him, which was still several times a week. He was so happy he wasn't involved with New Line, and hoped he wouldn't have to be on another production. I was ready for it to be over and take a nice, long break. John said that both he and New Line were distressed with how quickly Polyester had disappeared from the scene, and how little it was returning to the investors mainly because of Odorama expenses. This surely contributed to Shaye's unhappiness. John could tell that Shaye was in no mood to discuss backing another John Waters film. He was only interested in a guaranteed low-budget money maker, and given John's track record after Pink Flamingos, that would probably not be him.

John had no other reasonable choice beside New Line. Sarah was a big cheerleader, but New Line had decided not produce any movies in the U.S. in the foreseeable future. Instead, they would invest in a cheap science fiction movie called Xtro, which would be shot by an experienced production company in the UK. There would be no work for me on it. Who knew when they would produce another again? I should stay in touch though. Do lunch one day, etc. As Alone in the Dark wrapped, this could be the end of my road with New Line.

John, hoping it really wouldn't be the end of his road, felt that the safest path would be to reprise his big hit with Pink Flamingos II, but probably not with New Line. He was already writing it, and asked if I would help him with the budget—for free. I said, of course. Compared with Alone in the Dark, Polyester had been a blast, and I hoped that John would find money outside of New Line and be able to continue to make movies.

10

House on Sorority Row

. . . .

Istayed in New York, working mostly on day jobs as a
sound recordist. They were quirky odd-ball things, like a
particularly memorable instructional video about child care.
On that one, the director began coaching one of his child
actors with,

"OK Johnny, f-f-f-fuck, sh-sh-sh-shit, I want you to walk
through that f-f-f-f-fuckin' door, sh-sh-sh-shit and p-p-p-pick
up the f-f-f-f-fuckin' p-p-p-paper."

Wide-eyed, I asked the cameraman what was going on.
He had worked with the director before and explained that he
had Tourette's syndrome, which made him cuss and stutter
unconsciously. I'd never heard of such a thing. What a curse
when working with children. I could not keep a straight face.
This infected the cameraman, and our giggling took an hour
to get under control. Oh I wish I had kept a copy of that tape.

I met a guy who needed a sound recordist for a documentary
about the murderous FARK revolutionary group in Columbia.
I thought that sounded like real fun, but when he learned
I didn't speak Spanish, he said that if I got separated in the
jungle, I'd certainly be tortured and killed as a spy. I said that
wouldn't bother me, and in a last ditch plea, said hopefully,
"Well, I do speak French," but no dice.

I had many sound gigs for a TV commercial producer who shot mostly food close-ups, which didn't need sound, but who liked to put on a big show with a big crew for the ad agency and its clients. One day I recorded the sound of ice cream melting for a Pet ice cream commercial. For me, it was a fascinating education in food styling that I put to use later when I produced similar spots.

A producer from the BBC hired me to do sound on a documentary of a huge Beach Boys concert in Central Park. I was stationed with the main camera on a short platform in the center of the audience. It pissed off the people behind us, because we blocked their view, and we were showered with empty beer cans and half-eaten food for the first hour until they ran out of ammunition.

I was getting tired of the sound thing, and wanted to get back to movies. Having now production managed three movies, I had a track record, and got little nibbles around New York, but it was still a difficult business in a difficult economic time. I hung out with Amos Poe, the downtown art-filmmaker who had made a splash a few years earlier, with his inscrutable film, Subway. I hoped he had a source for funding his next movie from the New York art crowd, and he hoped I had an in with New Line for money, but neither panned out. After Polyester's high point, things were a little discouraging. For the first time in several years, I did not jump from one great project to another. Little did I know this would be the pattern for the next ten years.

Finally, I got a call from Baltimore from a group planning a low budget horror film, initially titled Seven Sisters. They needed an experienced low budget production manager who knew the Baltimore film scene.

I took the train down to meet them, and stayed with John in his apartment for a few days. He had changed dramatically, becoming an amazingly gracious host. He was now cooking food, and proudly made me a simple, but delicious dinner of pork chops, mashed potatoes, and a salad. He was proud of the all-cotton sheets he had bought for his newly re-decorated guest bedroom. We stayed up late talking about next moves. His book, Shock Value was a success, and he was working on another titled Crackpot. It was much easier than making a movie, especially since he could pad it with many photos and interviews.

The next night was Friday night, and he gave me a tour of the new gay sex club culture that had sprouted in Baltimore. Upstairs, it was pretty normal with the guys drinking and chatting like any bar, but downstairs, it was wide-open sex. It was a first for me, and after a few minutes I said I'd seen enough and wanted to leave. He was embarrassed and we quickly left. He thought it was a good field trip for me, but I had grave doubts, and, though this was before AIDS, I seriously worried about all my gay friends' health because of the number of partners they had. And with this visit to the bar, I confirmed it with my own eyes. I had an uncle who contracted syphilis after screwing around too much at a young age. It rotted his brain and he became an imbecile who had to be kept hidden away in an insane asylum. His tragic story was a major aspect of my parental sex education.

My meeting with the horror film group went well. I had now worked on five feature films, so I had the chops. This was yet another extremely low-budget film, funded by a local guy who owned a string of successful a/v equipment rental companies. He thought for a few hundred thousand dollars, he could expand into the "highly profitable" horror movie business. The first-time director/screenwriter was the son of a successful Los Angeles dentist and had just graduated from film school. He worked for free, and his father was in a position to put more money in, if needed, to help move his son's career along.

Initially it was an ideal low-budget film concept. It was a contemporary story, set in one location, with a small cast of beautiful young women, and almost no extras. The mansion we shot in was large enough that the cast and most of the crew could live in it. The large kitchen could be used for all meals, and it had plenty of rooms for shooting scenes, most of which consisted of groping around in the dark. With this scenario, very little would need to be spent on sets, wardrobe, or lighting. The writer/director purposefully conceived it to be as cheap as possible, and it seemed to be a sure thing for its $300,000 budget.

We cast seven young non-union actresses from New York and LA, several of whom went on to become soap opera stars. I brought down several of my seasoned low-budget crew people from New York, who were hungry for movie credits and for whom a month on a rural Maryland estate was a vacation. The cinematographer, Tim Suhrsted, was a talented, hard-working Baltimore native who had worked with me at Maryland Public Television. He had just moved to LA, but was having a difficult time breaking in the movie biz. He happily returned to Baltimore to stay with his family for a month and get a real movie under his belt, charging us only his travel and minimal living expenses. It worked, because Tim went back to Hollywood to shoot more than eighty big movies and major TV series episodes.

The beautiful cast from the slasher movie House on Sorority Row, posing with the guy who paid them to take their clothes off. Several later became soap opera stars and one is a noted children's book author.

As with most low-budget movies, the best laid plans began to crumble from the first day. The crew had had much more experience than Mark, the director, and as with most inexperienced directors, Mark fumbled. He was a quiet, brooding person. The outgoing actresses didn't understand what he wanted. The crew was frustrated at his lack of shot planning or understanding of coverage, when they had to go back and re-light the same set-ups three or four times. Mark's personally selected assistant director was an old friend who had never been on a movie set, and the critical aspect of scheduling cast, props, wardrobe, special effects, etc., became a mess. From day one, we fell behind.

Early on, the cook proved herself to be totally incompetent in preparing food for twenty people, and the food budget hemorrhaged because she had to buy carryout or we would have starved. Fortunately my wife, who had come with me and hoped for a small part, had grown up in the south and knew how to plan meals and cook. She took over the kitchen, ordered wholesale food delivered every other day, prepared hearty meals like roast turkey, ham, and pot roast very well, not to mention chocolate cake and pecan pie, and won over all hearts.

The hair and makeup person, Diana Mona, was a successful Baltimore TV commercial stylist with great skills and a winning personality whose good looks brought her regular acting and modeling jobs too. I had worked with her on many projects and she always told me to call her if a movie job came along. I tracked her down in Los Angeles and she was delighted to work on this little horror movie for next to nothing. To me, it was a dream come true to have such a polished pro aboard.

Diana's side story was that she had done some fill-in make-up work on Barry Levinson's very popular first movie, Diner, which was shot in Baltimore, Levinson's home town. Levinson, like Waters, had grown up in Baltimore, but on the Jewish side of town, which was very different from the Protestant and Irish Catholic neighborhoods where John and I had grown up. Levinson loved Baltimore and had returned to his roots, as he did with many other productions like Avalon and the long-running NBC series Homicide: Life on the Street.

He fell for Diana, and a solid relationship grew. She even spent time with him in Los Angeles, but Diana announced to him that she was returning to Baltimore to work on a low-budget slasher movie for almost no money. Barry was a very successful Hollywood writer who had partnered with Mel Brooks on many projects including High Anxiety and Silent Movie. He was a top writer on the wildly popular TV series

The Carol Burnette Show, and had been tagged as one of Hollywood's most up-and-coming writer/producers.

I had worked with Diana for several years, and asked her why in the world would she leave Barry Levinson to work for a couple hundred dollars a week on a grueling low-budget horror flick? The answer was that she was forcing Barry to make a decision. She didn't want to be a live-in Hollywood chick that lasted a few months until she was replaced by the next make-up girl. She wanted to get married and have a stable life. Barry quietly visited the set one day, and he must have been appalled at the messy crew and living conditions. I knew he had just made Diner, but didn't realize the depth of his Hollywood TV credentials. Naturally my hands were full so I didn't have time to spend with him, and he wasn't interested in anything but talking to Diana anyway.

A few days later, Diana told me Barry had proposed to her, and she was moving back to Hollywood to marry him. She promised to finish the Sorority Row shoot, which she did, and then pretty much disappeared from movie production. Sorority Row is her only movie credit, but she has four children, and has remained married, which is a pretty respectable run on its own.

A big plot element was a large swimming pool, which as the story progressed, turned from clear and inviting to an algae-clogged cesspool hiding the dead bodies of the gradually disappearing co-eds. Managing the transformation was a major headache. Pool "experts" said just stop the chlorine, and it would turn green in a few days. Our shooting schedule depended on this, but after shooting all the clear water shots, and stopping the chlorine, the pool remained clear. Another expert said to add a five-gallon jug of water from a nearby pond and it would turn overnight. The next morning the pond had a green tint, and we shot several scenes. We woke up the next morning to find the pool a sickly opaque green. It was impossible for shooting. Our pool expert said no problem, we could "shock it" and coagulate the dead algae, which would sink to the bottom, and then we could vacuum it up from the bottom. It didn't work. We thought we could filter it, but it clogged the filter. When we tried to pump it empty and start all over again, it clogged the pump we rented. Nothing worked. It became a malevolent character with a life of its own and added days, and many dollars to the shooting schedule.

On top of the pool troubles, things weren't going so well with the a/v rental business, and our funds trickled to a halt. Initially, money showed up a few days late, and I made a few urgent purchases from my own pocket. We missed a weekly payroll date, and several vendors reported angrily that their checks had bounced. I called the funder, and he assured me it was a temporary cash flow squeeze, and he would personally bring $5,000 cash that afternoon to make the payroll. When he arrived, as promised, I called the anxious crew together. The funder explained to everyone that he was experiencing a very temporary cash squeeze, but his company was solvent, was worth several million dollars, and everyone would get paid. He handed me an envelope of cash. He thanked the crew for their hard work and patience, and this would be just the first of many films they would produce. To seal the promise, he passed out a stack of canary-yellow golf shirts with his company logo on the back. They were the exact opposite of what this angry crew wanted.

He quickly left, promising to return soon. I looked into the envelope to find about $800 in cash. My heart sunk. That little bastard. Not knowing what to do, I headed back to the production office. The crew was right behind me, ready to collect their late pay. I had no choice but tell them he gave me $800, not the $5,000 needed to cover the payroll. The $800 would buy gas for the cars, food, and pay the electric bill so we could keep shooting. The pay would have to wait. We were in a pinch, but not in a disaster. We had food, film, all the equipment needed, and a roof over our heads. There was no choice but be patient and keep shooting. I was friends with all the crew, they'd surely understand.

Everyone bought this, except Bud, the gaffer, who was notoriously aggressive, but worked cheap and had a truck full of lighting equipment, so he was a favorite of low-budget producers. He jumped up and said, "This is bullshit. I'm out of here, and taking my truck with me."

Worst case scenario. You can't shoot a horror movie at night without lights. Thankfully, most of the crew was doing this more for a resume credit than the pathetic pay anyway. Tim Suhrstedt, the cinematographer, had a lot at stake, and didn't want three weeks of hard, unpaid work to go to waste. He followed Bud out of the room, and the camera/lighting crew had a pow-wow. They would give it two more days. They weren't throwing in the towel yet, but they were pissed off.

As if by a miracle, $10,000 appeared in the production bank account, which I had opened at a little rural bank down the street. The a/v company, who had heard about the mutiny from their producer had panicked. I ran to the bank, took out $5,000 cash, and returned to dole out the money to the crew. I had a thousand dollars operating cash left, and money still in the bank. We were getting close to the end so barring a catastrophe we just might make it. But then that evening I had two meetings, both about spending money we didn't have.

The first was with the assistant director who wanted to speak with me confidentially. One of the actresses had been feeling ill, especially in the mornings, and it was getting worse. I guessed what would come next, and he confirmed that she was pregnant. It had happened before the movie began, and she did not have a relationship with anyone on the movie team. Baloney, everyone knew they were hooking up. She was too sick to come to set and we were halfway through the movie, so it was indeed a problem. Hard-hearted guy that I was, I suggested we change the script, kill her off earlier than planned, and send her back to LA. Surely she wasn't too sick to play dead for a few minutes.

But she didn't want to leave the movie, and neither did the assistant director or his good friend the director. They all thought an abortion would be the best option, but didn't have the money. It would cost $950, and the production would have to pay for it. There went 20% of my remaining money. I counted out ten crisp new hundred dollar bills from my stash.

"Bring back the change, and um... get a receipt," I said sheepishly, like he was going out for late night pizza.

That pleasant meeting over, the assistant cameraman told me we were down to our last four rolls of 35mm movie film; enough for three days. We needed about 10,000 feet to finish the movie. We had shot just over 100,000, which isn't much for a movie, but the new stock would cost nearly $5,000, and we were on a COD basis with Fuji, the Japanese film manufacturer. I called Fuji in New York, where I had spent about $25,000 cash, so I had a good relationship. The courier to our New York lab would make his regular run, but I would give him a $5,000 check to pick up ten rolls of fresh film from Fuji, and bring it back that afternoon. I told Fuji there wasn't time to get cash from our bank, but Fuji said based on my good payment history they'd trust me on this one, and accept the check.

Next call was to our executive producer at the a/v company, who had said when I needed more cash to call and he would wire it overnight. Payroll was due in two days, and I didn't want the same hassle with the crew I had two weeks ago. He said, no problem, the money would be in the bank next morning.

When I called the next morning, no wire had been received. I called the a/v office to ask what happened. They said they's check into it, and get right back. Two hours later, my anxiety increasing, I called him back. He still hadn't tracked down the problem, but agreed to bring a check personally to the set that afternoon. He didn't show, and didn't answer my many phone calls. It was panic time.

Meanwhile, our lab courier called to say he had picked up the film from Fuji and would be back late that evening. At least we would have film to finish the movie, but what good was it if the crew walked out? The next morning I called the bank to see if by some miracle, the wire had been received. They said there was a balance of $5,000.00, but no wires or deposits received. Evidently Fuji had not yet deposited the check I had sent to New York, and I had to make the payroll that day. I made a quick decision that I didn't realize was a felony and could have landed me in jail for twenty years. I called the bank.

"You know, I wrote a check for $5,000 yesterday to buy some film in New York, but we don't need it, and I have to cancel it. Can I do that?"

"Yes, it's not certified so it won't be paid if you stop payment."

"That's not a problem. Thank-you, I'll tell them not to deposit it, but put a stop payment on it, just in case. And if I came to the bank right now, do you have $5,000 in cash I could pick up? I have a payroll due this afternoon."

The bank clerk answered "yes, but it would leave you with a balance of just $17.83."

"That's OK," I answered, "a wire's coming in today or first thing in the morning. I'll be there in a few minutes."

It was lunch break, and the crew was lined up outside the production office for their pay. I opened the door and said the payroll was a little late. I said I was just leaving for the bank to pick up the cash.

"Bull fucking shit," snarled Bud, grabbing me by my belt, "you're taking a little swim." He had been drinking and blown his fuses. "It's all over for you, Piggy."

Piggy was his favorite nick name for me, maybe because he thought I was a greedy, squinty-eyed, pigheaded weasel. Bud thought that about every production manager he'd ever worked with, so I didn't take it personally.

This time it was a little more nerve-wracking. He had made up a noose, tightened it around my neck, and pulled me outside to the edge of the algae-filled pool. A crowd had gathered, and no one thought he would really do anything, but the noose was tight. Finally, my faithful assistant cameraman, Art Eng, a short, tough, level-headed Chinese-American grabbed Bud, threw him to the ground and told him to leave me alone.

"I want my money, and I know sure as shit this won't get it," Art said.

"If we let him go, we'll never see him again," said Bud.

"Look, both of you can drive to the bank with me, the money's there," I said.

That calmed him down. We went to the bank and I cashed a $5,000 check under the very suspicious eye of the manager, who sensed there might be a problem. In the car when I showed

Meeting with Art Director Vince Peranio (l) on the set of House on Sorority Row; a friend of director Mark Rosman shows his approval. Vince has been the art director on all the John Waters films. ©Robert Maier

Bud the envelope of twenties, he threw his arms around me and kissed me on the cheek.

"I knew you could do it, Piggy," he said.

I made a mental note to never, ever hire Bud on one of my films again, a vow I broke on the very next one, when I needed a good cheap gaffer with a truck full of lights. Ah showbiz.

A few days later, my rep from Fuji called almost in tears.

"Why did you stop payment on the check?"

I explained it was a terrible decision, but I was in a bind, and had to make a choice to pay them or my crew, and I had to get the film completed. Surely he understood. Fuji wouldn't collapse having to wait a few days for their money, but my crew would. The guy was livid, and said I would hear from them again soon—and by the way, I should never even think about buying film from Fuji again. This was worse than it sounded because Fuji film cost about 25% less than Kodak, and as such was the choice of many low-budget filmmakers. It could cause me problems down the road. But the bill did get paid a few days later, so everything worked out.

Nevertheless, suddenly making low budget movies didn't seem so much fun anymore. How nice it would be to work on big studio movies with union crews, honest backers, real budgets, and real money in the bank. If even a sure thing like House on Sorority Row collapsed, was there any hope for low budget filmmaking?

Things wound down further as the shooting came to bumpy end. The a/v company completely cut all ties, even after spending $200,000. Fortunately the director got his father to send enough money to pay people for the last week of work. Many debts were unpaid, including the food wholesaler, phone company, rent on the mansion, and the electric bill. I was out a few hundred dollars in petty cash I'd advanced. Originally scheduled to edit at the a/v company's office in Virginia, the director instead drove all the processed film back and negative to Los Angeles in his car.

The last day, as I packed up the last of my stuff from the office, the original producer from the a/v company walked in. I hadn't seen him since the money completely stopped. He apologized and earnestly said he would make good on everything. He had a new set of investors interested in the film, and other projects were about to come through, blah, blah, blah.

"I'm sorry it didn't work out so well this time, but I'll call you on the next one." His last words.

"Yeah right," were my last words to him.

11

Out of New York

. . . .

Before leaving Baltimore, I had lunch with John at a Korean restaurant to listen to his woes. Polyester was still in the hole thanks to Odorama, but probably due more to the fact that it was still a niche film, and American moviegoers did not rate foot fetishes and fat transvestites high on their list of preferred entertainments. As a result, John and New Line were not getting along so well. New Line was emphatically not interested in backing Pink Flamingos II, so John was beating the bushes for someone willing and able to invest a couple hundred thousand dollars in it. With only one out of his last four movies making a profit, the search had been difficult.

After the difficulties with my five non-union, low-budget films, I decided that it was time for me to move up to the big time. I had now production managed enough released feature films that I could be accepted into the Director's Guild of America. This was the ticket to working on New York's big union movies. Now, I would at least have a chance at working with Woody Allen, Martin Scorsese, Brian DePalma, Sidney Lumet, network TV series like Kojak, and one of the many PBS shows coming out of New York. I could get out of low-budget hell which apparently led nowhere.

I applied for the job of studio manager at the prestigious EUE Screen Gems Studio complex in mid-town Manhattan. I had several interviews and at the last one was asked the classic question, "What do you think is your weak spot?" Trying to be cleverly honest, I said my organizational skills weren't the greatest, but I compensated by keeping detailed lists of everything in three-ring binders. I could put my finger on anything that had happened over the past five years—names, phone numbers, directions, costs—anything. All they heard was "bad organization skills," and the interview and any possibility of my working there was over. I've since learned that the answer to this question is "gee, I can't think of anything— except if you count wanting to work weekends for no pay as a weakness."

Next bump in the road was an interview with a producer of ABC-TV's After School Specials. This series of one-hour dramas was produced with low, but decent, union budgets. They kept many New York film workers employed and were the jumping-off point for big movies. The interview was scheduled for 5:00 p.m. Friday afternoon at the producer's apartment in Greenwich Village. Coincidently, John was in town, staying with friends in the village and asked me to drop by.

The NYC contingent of Dreamland was there, Divine, Mink, and Van. It was great to see everyone again. They were making margaritas, a "new" drink, and gave me one to try. It was two hours before my meeting around the corner, so I thought a small one might loosen me up. It was delicious. This led to a second, and before I knew it, three. I felt fine, but got up near the time for my interview, and nearly fell back down. I never drank during the day, and was shocked that I could barely walk, and had to be at an important job interview in ten minutes.

I tried to hide the effects of the tequila, but the interview was a bust. Slurring my words, the producer could tell I was three sheets to the wind. We spoke a few minutes, she thanked me for coming by, and said she'd be in touch. It was about the stupidest thing I'd ever done in ten years of very careful maneuvering through the film business. I hoped I could survive this one youthful indiscretion, but I kicked myself for months.

Being a techie, the new world of personal computers, and how they could smooth the paperwork side of film production fascinated me. The Apple II was taking California by storm, and everyone was wild about how word processors, scheduling, and accounting programs would revolutionize the film industry. I had kept in touch with Rachel, the Polyester intern who was now in California doing accounting for Roger Corman's studio. Using computers one person could track exactly how much money had been spent, pinpoint budget problems as they occurred, and instantly project cash flow. Normally that was the work of three or four people.

I had managed to borrow a tiny Sinclair computer that I plugged into my TV set, and messed around with it for hours. It had no real software and the only thing I could do was automatically re-type my name on the screen 5,000 times. I couldn't afford the $2,500 price of an Apple II, yet.

Then one day my phone rang. It was a producer who had heard I specialized in low budget films, and I was in the Director's Guild of America. Her company had produced several Mark Twain adaptations for PBS, and had one more in its contract. They were looking for a sharp production manager with solid low-budget experience to get them through. I met with her in her upper Eastside office the next morning—sober as a judge, I might add.

My credentials impressed her, and she liked the idea of cost savings with one of the Apples (PCs weren't around yet). It was critical that this film not go over budget. It was the last in the series and they wanted to take a well-deserved, but deferred profit from it. The previous films had all gone over budget—an easy thing because they were period films with big costume and set expenses, trained animals, big music scores, and lots of shooting on the water. They liked working with top people too. Their director was a multi-award winning Brit, the director of photography was an Oscar-winning Brit, and the Art Director was on his way to the top rung of Hollywood films. Everyone else was from union A-lists with champagne tastes, and little experience with restricted budgets. The producer said the unlimited budget mindset had to change, and hopefully I was the expert who could do that.

Even further, their normally lavish budget had already been cut by PBS, and they still wanted to make their series profit. I offered to work a month pre-production, at less than half the DGA rate as a "researcher." They sent me to Los Angeles for a week where I bought a computer and took a crash course in the same movie accounting program Rachel was using with Roger Corman.

The movie would be filmed in the restored historic town of Harper's Ferry, West Virginia, which would help reduce the set construction budget. In the beginning, things were wonderful. The budget was about $1.2 million, of which they wanted to keep about $250,000 for themselves. My first budget run-through showed that would be easy.

And it might have been, if I had been able to do it in my low-budget style. However, the producers wanted to do everything on this film just like the ones that had gone so far over budget. I wanted to hire my low-budget crew friends from New York and Baltimore, who would cut me great deals and cut me some slack if things got rough.

The producers insisted on their award-winners, at least in the key positions of DP, art, sound, wardrobe, and editing. I could hire the seconds. But these key people insisted on hiring their key people for the crew, or they wouldn't work on the show. There were plenty of early dust-ups on this issue, of which I lost every one. When the dust cleared, I was only able to hire two props assistants from Baltimore. I didn't know anybody on the crew, so I wouldn't have much leverage with them. They had all had worked on the previous films, and were used to the Santa Claus mindset of the producers.

Rachel initially had said she would come back east to do the production accounting and run the new computer program, but backed out after a better offer in Hollywood. I was hoping she would pay me back for getting her started in the business. She worked with me at New Line and on House on Sorority Row, and was doing well in LA. Despite really good pay and the potential for paying back a mentor, she refused. She had gone Hollywood.

I hired a local accountant in Harpers Ferry who had worked with Apples, but problems popped up. The biggest was that the primitive disc drives crashed sometimes after several hours of calculations, and it took forever to get out my vaunted cost reports.

No surprise, the biggest battle was about money. The only place I had leverage was with the art department, which in a period film is the major part of the budget. They were used to unlimited spending, and I questioned nearly every purchase, which irritated the art director to no end. Some things were outrageous for a low budget film. The art director insisted on custom made wall paper that more closely matched the period rather than the close-enough wallpaper of a main location. It would be made by Scalamandre in New York and cost about

10 times normal wall paper. To make it more ridiculous, the owners thought the choice was too "loud" for them, and the art director promised that after the shooting, he would strip off the new and old wallpaper, and then repaper the room in the original pattern. This was Hollywood insanity to a low-budget production manager. Ultimately the art director had his way with the executive producer, and when I asked her about her directive to save money, she recited my old familiar and favorite line, "You'll have to make it up somewhere else."

Every art expenditure had a catch or ten. We needed a dozen horse-drawn carriages for period flavor. No problem, they were in the budget. They had to be stored near the town. No problem, we rented an empty lot. Then they needed security at night. I hired a security guard. He needed a spot-a-pot. Then he needed a trailer to keep out of the rain.

It was the same thing with animals. The horses needed 24-hour attention in their field, so they wouldn't run off or be stolen, so a guard, and of course a trailer for him to live in was needed. A few sets were scattered around the area in remote locations. Each needed their own security guard. Before long, I had eight guards watching six locations, and the budget was bleeding. The art department had become one of Harpers Ferry's major industries.

The only place I could control the art department was limiting prop purchases. The props people rented a very large truck and emptied every antique store within 25 miles, literally filling up a warehouse. After getting the hair-raising bill, I told the art director he had way overspent the budget, and he could not make one more prop purchase. Of course he called a meeting with the executive producer to discuss my outrageous accusation. Fortunately the computer was working, and I brought a neatly printed report detailing every purchase. It showed that as of two weeks earlier, the art budget had been exhausted. I actually won that one, and he was forbidden by the executive producer to buy more props. He gave me an "I'll get you" look and stalked out fuming. Cutting off an art director's funds is like cutting off his you know what.

A few days later, the executive producer and art director stormed into my office.

"Thanks to you we've lost an entire day of shooting," shrieked the producer.

"What do you mean?"

"The art department did not have a critical prop, because you refused to allow them to buy it!"

"What was it?"

"It was the pair of cast iron Pekinese door stops."

"They already bought a dozen door stops, why not use one of the others?"

"The script calls for Pekinese cast iron door stops! Didn't you read the script? Isn't that part of your job?"

"I thought we agreed not to purchase more props."

"But we must have the props required by the script!"

"Then why didn't he buy the Pekinese ones instead of five that weren't in the script? We're $50,000 over the budget on props and sets. He approved the initial budget and contingency, and you said no more art department purchases."

"But it's your job to see everyone has what they need to progress with the filming!"

"Well if you're going to buy everything everyone claims they 'absolutely need' for the filming, then you can forget about the budget. You cannot have it both ways."

She stalked out of the room. It was the end of our good relationship, and the beginning of a long down-hill slide. I'd gotten used to this. Every producer thinks the production manager's job is to print money in the basement, spoil their precious artist crew rotten, and make sure the producer gets all the credit. The art director left me with a "gotcha" look, and I began to contemplate moving my career in yet another direction. Maybe union films were not the answer to low-budget hell after all.

The budget bleeding became a gusher. Again, the best laid plans of a tightly run production were being scuttled by a "the film will be a disaster if I don't get more money" crew clawing more money from the executive producer to build their empires, hire their friends, and win awards. I provided nearly daily cost reports, but the bad news only numbed the executive producers. It was easy to show that the overages were due to their approval of silly expenditures like the $10,000 wallpaper job, renting a herd of cattle and wranglers to give the street scenes more "flavor," and flying in and putting up two union assistant editors from Los Angeles. None of these were budgeted, but suddenly were "absolute necessities."

The job had become yet another grim death march. I worked 14-hour days, six and a half days a week. A few crew members liked my valiant fight against out-of-control expenditures, but confided that this was really how it worked. I was fighting an impossible system and should stop worrying and get with the plan.

Halfway through the film, my wife visited with our son, Evan, who was about a year old. They stayed in my room with visions of calm family time in the evenings. Unfortunately, most nights I didn't get in until after 11:00 p.m., when they were both asleep, and I had to pick my way through piles of dirty room service dishes. They left after a few days, when they tired of the serial emergency phone calls in the middle of the night: cows had broken loose and were wandering on the highway, a security guard hadn't shown up, the National Park Service, which administered Harper's Ferry as a national historic site, said our props blocked a street and had to be moved, now. One night a torrential rain storm flooded a nearby river and washed away an entire set. It was shades of Desperate Living, but this time it was the mighty Potomac River that jumped its banks and washed ever splinter of the set and every prop down past Washington, DC.

I hired a local young woman to be an office production assistant. She loved the work and dutifully stayed late into the evenings. Everyone loved her, and she made it clear she wanted to get out of West Virginia and see the world. One evening, her unemployed redneck husband visited, drunk as a skunk. He accused me of having an affair with his wife, which is why she was coming home so late. He said he wanted to kill me right then and there. He lunged for me, but another PA, Clai Lashley, a big local guy, wrestled him down, and then took him home in the back of his pickup. The guy's wife moved in with her parents, and bravely stuck with the job. A year later she called to say she had gotten a job with the FBI in Washington, DC, and thanked me for hiring her so she could see another side of life.

The worst moment came when a young actor had a heart attack, and died on set in the middle of a scene. He was in great shape, but had an unknown congenital heart problem. The scene required that he walk up a long set of steps, and on the third take he collapsed. A Park Ranger assigned to the crew was trained in emergencies and tried valiantly to save him as the crew watched helplessly, but the actor died before the ambulance arrived. This paralyzing reality jolted the little 19th century fantasy world we had built. I made a dreaded call to his wife in New York, and of course she was hysterical. Everyone in the production office was in tears. The producer OK'd spending $5,000 to fly his body back to New York, and it was torture making those arrangements. They were both poor actors, with no insurance, and their life abruptly hit a wall. It was a time for soul searching. Life could be very short. Did I really want this career? Did I want to spend my life in third-rate motel rooms, working seven days a week in the middle of nowhere, gobbling rushed late dinners while watching the grips get sloshed at the bar every night?

Towards the end on Sunday mornings, my only time off, I drove to the nearby Antietam Civil War battlefield to watch the fog drift through the gullies where 23,000 people had been killed or wounded in one day. I was alone with the ghosts, away from the phones, the fights, and the egos. I gratefully breathed in the absolute silence and couldn't wait to get home.

I was soon back in New York, bruised, but not defeated. The downtown art scene was fading. The rent on our SoHo loft had tripled, and all Manhattan rents were skyrocketing. Downtown Manhattan was suddenly becoming a place for rich people only, and we knew we couldn't afford it any more. Artists fled downtown's gentrification to cheap suburbs like Hoboken, and Long Island City. Just before our son was born, we moved to the tiny village of Piermont, 25 miles north of Manhattan on the shore of the Hudson River. It was cheaper and a calm place to raise a kid.

I still worked in Manhattan, and commuted to work on a bus that stopped in front of our house and dropped me off at 125th Street. From there I took an express subway to mid-town or downtown. I didn't mind it. I got to read The New York

Times thoroughly every day for the first time in my life. On the return trip home, there was always a half-hour to kill with a beer or two in the station's grimy bar. When the bartenders saw me come in the door they'd pull a frosty Heineken from the cooler and set it on the bar.

Despite the poor showing of John's films, things were looking up for New Line, and they moved into spiffy new loft offices off Times Square. They still wanted to produce low-budget movies, so they gave me a desk in a cubicle piled with scripts I would read and roughly budget. I only came in a day a week, and needed to find something that brought in more money.

Investigating any opportunity for a more stable job than low-budget movies, I applied for several non-movie full-time jobs. The Muscular Dystrophy Association, the huge non-profit behind the Jerry Lewis telethons was looking for an executive producer. I had several interviews, but ultimately "didn't have the skill set they were looking for at the moment, but they would keep my resume on file."

I interviewed a few times with the Executive Producer of the brand new CBS Cable channel, which was planned as an arts cable network airing concerts, plays, art films, literary discussions, and more. Unfortunately, the bean counters at CBS decided the audience for an arts cable network was too small and pulled the plug. The concept was squeezed out by the likes of MTV and ESPN, whose programs were better bets for American cable system operators than operas.

Then my phone rang. It was Dave Insley, the Baltimore cameraman I had known since UMBC days, who had shot several of John's films. He had been working steadily as a cameraman for several Baltimore TV commercial production companies and was getting well known. An ad agency had asked him if he could produce a commercial and thereby side-step contracting an expensive production company. He didn't know anything about producing, and thought I would help, which included arranging for camera, lab, and post-production work in New York City. The money was great, and for less than a week's work I made more than a month on a low-budget feature. There was plenty of money to pay for everything, and finally everybody on the crew was satisfied and appreciative. Returning from Baltimore, sipping a Martini while riding first class on the Metroliner, I thought—this is the way it's supposed to be.

Dave's commercial was at this point a one-shot deal, and I still needed to make a living. A friend of my underground filmmaker Amos Poe called me to discuss a big documentary she was planning to shoot in Saudi Arabia. She was a smart ex-model who had attracted a Saudi Prince with her idea of making a film about solar energy in the Arabian deserts. It made sense. The prince figured one day their oil would run out, and wouldn't it be grand if they had a huge solar energy industry ready to take its place. The prince had earmarked $2 million for the project. We'd shoot in Saudi Arabia for a month and include visits to Europe and North America presenting the budding solar panel industry to the world with Saudi Arabia as the industry leader.

The planning dragged on and on. At one point, we were poised to depart on a location scouting trip. I even had an appointment to get my visa, but the plug was pulled at the last minute. Jealous squabbling among the Saudi Princes put the project on hold for months, and after a while, the producer stopped returning my calls. Message received. Another one bites the dust.

But then the phone rang again. This time it was a call from a bright young couple who had received a small grant to produce a promo for a dramatic film about Coney Island's new Russian immigrant community. They were both idealistic writers who had never produced anything, and were earnestly seeking someone to guide them through this promo so they could raise enough money to make the feature-length film. They had one of New York's leading agents, who had already sold an option on one of their scripts to a big Hollywood studio. Very promising. We got along great, and I thought this would be an interesting and good ground-floor opportunity with these emerging artists. Right.

The money was ridiculous, but once again I pulled out my low-budget production manager stops. I borrowed office space from a writer friend in a cheap downtown industrial building. I hired a cameraman friend who owned his own gear. He had a buddy with a van full of lights, and off we went. The actors were terrible, because the young couple wanted real people. They tried to co-direct, but their long philosophical discussions extended every setup trying everyone's patience. The dailies were horrible from bad acting and miserable coverage, but they picked on every production decision that was not theirs. Finally the money ran out, and we just stopped shooting. The young couple felt betrayed that people wouldn't work without getting paid, which was grating, because they both came from wealthy families. The crew barely scraped by from job to job, but the young couple had a nice big apartment in Brooklyn where they chose to spend their trust fund money in places besides the crew's paychecks. Another one bites the dust.

Violated

Then my phone rang again. A strange fellow said he had heard about me around town, and asked me to lunch to discuss a movie he wanted to make. Rocky was barely thirty and claimed to have made millions on Wall Street, but wanted to get into the movie business. Could I help? He had a script; a simple contemporary story, based in New York City about a girl who had been raped and wanted revenge. It was called Violated. He had $400,000, knew nothing about movies, except he loved actor John Heard, wanted it to star a certain young actress, and it had to have several topless scenes to attract a distributor. Piece of cake. The writer would direct, but I could hire every other person, and pay myself whatever I could squeeze from the budget. He would be very hands-off and let the professionals do their job. How refreshing!

We based it out of a friend's loft/production office in Chelsea. I hired my favorite crew buddies, equipment suppliers, editors, and lab. The shoot would be 21 days, with no travel, no unions, no animals, no shooting on water, no special effects, and no stars. The most difficult problem would be to find young actresses willing to go topless. In New York City, in 1985, that was not a problem.

We were small enough to dodge the unions, but the gaffer was concerned about the Teamsters, who had smashed his headlights on his last non-union film. I called my Teamster contact from Alone in the Dark, told him the budget, and offered to pay one "standby" Teamster for two weeks for them to leave us alone. Not a problem. I was part of the family now, because I had called them first and was willing to play the game. Perhaps as I moved up, I'd return the favors. I loved New York.

The director had no idea how to make a movie, but thought his script was brilliant. Pretty soon the DP took over blocking the shots and getting necessary coverage, while the director toyed with the actors. When the DP was ready, he simply rolled and called action, and all the director had to do was jump out of the shot. Otherwise, we'd be there all day.

After refusing several times, John Heard appeared when I promised him $2,000 cash to be on the set for an hour in a two-minute scene with a few lines of dialog. He was union, and the film wasn't, but he was in a slow period and could use the cash. He wore a baseball cap hoping to cover his eyes so he wouldn't be recognized. I didn't tell him it wouldn't matter because the movie press material would scream "starring John Heard."

Rocky's hands-off policy changed as the shooting progressed. I started to notice that he had a real thing for his star actress, and the film started to revolve around her. In the last shoot week Rocky announced that he had re-written the script, and there was now a scene in an indoor swimming pool where all the girls were topless, and that he would direct that one. It was creepy, but we were just in it for the money, and whatever the money man wanted was fine.

It turned out that the director was working for free, and stalked off the set when Rocky not only took the director position, but re-wrote his precious script. Rocky told me that watching the shoots, he had learned that directing was no big deal and he could direct the rest of the film himself. No matter, the direction couldn't have gotten worse.

When I told the film editor that Rocky would be the new director, he was livid. The editor had trashed the direction all along (every editor does) but claimed he could save the film, if we let him direct for the last week of shooting. It didn't happen. Rocky was firmly in the driver's seat.

Rocky wrote in a nude swimming pool scene that was to be shot at a gigantic nouveau riche New Jersey mansion that had a large swimming pool in the living room. The owners were thrilled to have their stunning house in a movie, but we decided not to mention the nudity, and convinced them be out the house while we filmed.

When it came to disrobing, Rocky's star balked. He had not told her that she would even be in the scene, much less naked. But he was persuasive, and after sending all non-essential crew away, and swearing she would only be seen from the neck up, she consented. It was a beautiful pool with a diving board. He waved me and the DP over to the camera and whispered, "Shoot everything that happens now." Rocky told the girls to relax and play in the water while he worked out the scene, which they did, splashing each other, jumping off the sides, and diving off the board. Ten minutes later after the reel of film finished, Rocky told his star to get in the water up to her neck so he could get his shot. She did, and he called a wrap. No dialogue, no acting. She thought it was fishy, but what did she know about directing?

The next day, as usual, she and her agent showed up at the lab's dailies screening. Suddenly the pool scenes shone clear and bright on the big screen. And there she was, totally topless diving off the board. She broke into tears, shrieking that it would be the end of her acting career. Fleeing the screening room with her agent, she yelled that she was finished with the film, and Rocky should never call her again. Rocky sat there unmoved. He knew money fixed everything, and he had gotten his shot.

Then a familiar problem occurred. Money for payroll was a week late, and I told Rocky we had to get cash before the next shoot. He was becoming so unbalanced that I said I needed $25,000, so I could cover payroll and other expenses to the end. I didn't want any more House on Sorority Row attacks on the production manager. He actually agreed and met me at his midtown Chase Manhattan Bank branch. The bank required a stack of paperwork to be completed because a newly passed money laundering law required cash withdrawals exceeding $9,999.99 to have a detailed paper trail.

After counting 250 $100 bills, Rocky handed them to me in a brown envelope. I was surprised what a small package it was—less than two inches thick. I put the bills in my front pants pocket. As a well-trained cheapskate, I took a downtown local subway home, thinking what a payday a mugger would have if he chose me of all the people to rob on the subway that day. I was amazed Rocky trusted me, but it wasn't a big deal to him. Plans for his star occupied his thoughts. I was relieved to give most of the cash the next morning to the crew for their previous two week's pay, and they were happy.

Violated's principal photography wrapped quietly, and it was now up to the editor, Michael, to make sense of it. I was still under contract and took a bus every morning to the Times Square editing suite we had rented on the fifth floor of the famous Brill Building, which reeked of show business history. It had housed song writers, theatrical agents, and film producers for decades. It was built in the early 1900s with high ceilings, marble stairs, and fanciful beaux arts details. The antique elevators required an operator who was frequently difficult to find.

Opening the editing suite door one morning, regular coffee and toasted buttered bagel in hand, I saw two figures wrapped in blankets, asleep on the floor.

"Hello," I said loudly to wake them.

"Hi," one mumbled, "Michael said we could crash here last night."

Michael (the editor) walked in behind me.

"Sorry," he said. "I was hoping to get in before you did. These are two friends of mine, Joel and Ethan Coen. They're finishing their first movie, but their money's running low, and I said they could use our equipment at night, when I left. Since Rocky already paid for it, I thought it wouldn't hurt anything."

Joel and Ethan looked like scraggly teenagers from the street.

"Interesting," I said.

"They're friends of Skip Lievsay. He's doing their sound editing," said Michael.

I first met Skip on The Fox Affair and he had saved my butt on Polyester, guiding me through the New York post-production process, for almost nothing. Enough said. This was payback time.

"Yeah, sure, where are you living?"

"Right now we don't have a place. We just crashed here last night," said Joel.

"Looks pretty uncomfortable; get much sleep?"

"We just quit an hour ago, so not much."

"Hmm... we have three empty offices here. You can camp out in one of them, sleep during the day, and use the machines at night. A bathroom's in the hall, but no shower. I'm not sure how legal it is, but I'll cover for you if there's a problem."

They were so relieved, and swore they'd stay out of the way. We'd never know they were there. I sympathized, mostly thinking back to the endless days, cold rain, and mud of Desperate Living. The editing suite would be a little Mortville, sheltering an up and coming new generation of crazy filmmakers.

"What's the name of your movie?" I asked.

"Blood Simple," said Joel.

"A horror movie?" I said

"Not really," said Ethan, "but something like that."

New York City crawled with low-budget horror movie makers at the time, and I thought yeah, here's another, lotsa luck.

"OK, I look forward to seeing it. Make yourselves at home." Six months later, see it I did, and it knocked me out. I've seen every one of the Coen Brothers' films, and they are my favorite. Whenever I see them on TV, I think back to their padding sleepily down the marble hall of the Brill Building to the men's room, toothbrushes in hand, getting ready for their all-night editing session, as I was heading out the door.

I met with Rocky a few days later at the Jewish deli around the corner. I remember he ordered pastrami on white bread with mayonnaise, and the clerk almost choked. After viewing the rough cut several times, Rocky had decided the movie needed a love scene. He would play the male part, and his star, the woman he was so smitten with, would play his lover. We would do it cheap and fast, just me and the DP as crew. We could shoot it in a hotel room in an hour. Watching Rocky's love sickness grow over the past month, I was not surprised, and I tried hard not to smirk. This new scene had nothing to do with the script, but this is what the movie was all about. It was a $400,000 date, meant to get Rocky in bed with his fantasy girl.

I rented a suite at the elegant Mayflower Hotel on Columbus Circle, at the special movie rate of $1,000 for the night—which allowed us to bring in the camera gear. It needed no art direction. The DP and I set up everything. There was no sound, because there was no dialogue.

It was a silly, tame love scene. Rocky and the actress were topless, and the wildest act was her kissing his hairless chest, but I guess it gave him fuel for his fantasies for months. When we wrapped, since the suite was paid for, Rocky generously suggested I should call my wife to come down and spend the night with me there, as a little vacation. It was nice of him, but my wife was home with our 6 month-old baby, and would not want to schlep the baby and all his stuff into the city. I took the subway to the 125th Street bus terminal and had my ritual beer in the bar. When the bartender asked if I had an interesting day, I said yes, but didn't want to talk about it. He'd never believe me anyway.

Violated finished up properly. A lush music score was written and performed on one of the first "Synclavier" computers by one of the musicians from the Four Seasons who did it cheap, because he too was trying to break into movie music. Rocky dedicated himself to finding a distributor, and actually got Violated released by Vestron Video, the biggest name in early VHS home video. I still occasionally see copies of it in thrift store video sections.

Rocky said it had been interesting, but he was officially out of the movie business, and we didn't stay in touch much—another dead end after another bizarre low-budget movie.

Several months later he called to ask if I would work with him on a financial deal. It involved an off-shore stock brokerage in the Cayman Islands. I would be the official CEO based in the U.S. I would have no duties, but would be paid $100,000 a year simply to sign papers in the U.S. I really wanted to do it, but finally declined smelling trouble. Reminiscing a few years ago, I Googled Rocky, and found he'd been sentenced to twenty years in prison for securities fraud. I could count at least one good decision in my life.

12

Hairspray

. . . .

Dave Insley called occasionally asking me to come help him produce a TV commercial in Baltimore. It was always a low-pressure, welcome paycheck. I had sold my sound gear, so I was fully committed to the production end of things, and maybe I could start freelance producing commercials in New York. Being in the Directors' Guild of America union was a plus, and with well-paying commercials, I could be choosier about the low budget movies that came my way.

On one of my trips to Baltimore, I had lunch with John at Baltimore's only Szechuan restaurant, where he adored the impossibly hot Chicken with Peanuts, because smoking had so dulled his taste buds, it was one of the few foods he could taste.

He was passing around his Flamingos Forever/Pink Flamingos II script hoping to find backers. I had budgeted it at just under $600,000, which followed John's pattern of doubling the cost of each movie. In their quest for the mainstream, New Line couldn't justify that kind of money on another "stupid" John Waters film. Polyester had premiered in 1981. John finished the Flamingos Forever script in 1983. Two years later he was no closer to making it. He had met with many money people, but none would pull the trigger.

One of his big hopes was with the guys who started Polk Audio, mainly Matt Polk. They graduated from John Hopkins University's engineering department around 1975 and invented a high-end line of speaker systems that they produced in a funky old mansion in Baltimore. They were young, original, creative, and had money. They shared John's commitment to Baltimore entrepreneurship. Listening intently to John's pitch and in several follow-up meetings, they came close to backing Flamingos Forever, but with their speaker business taking off, they must have felt it would be too great a risk and distraction. They passed, with regret. John was visibly shaken. It had been five years since John had even began a film, and now here he was starting from scratch. Maybe his career was over. It was a sad thought.

I suggested he try writing for Saturday Night Live, but he hated the idea of working for hire, especially for television, which he never watched. He just wanted to make his own movies. I was exiting the low-budget world and focusing on TV commercials as a more sustainable way of life. John's inability to raise money these past several years reinforced that feeling. Even after nearly seven years of busting my ass for him, I had little to show for it. I faced big gaps between movies that were underfunded by dreamers without a clue. I'd been down that road too many times, and I thought it might really be over for him. He was still hopeful and determined, but we were heading down different paths. I told him to call me, and I'd be happy to help if I could do anything for him, but at that point there was nothing I could do, except try to survive until the next one.

Despite my disappointment with low budget movies, I still visited New Line for a few hours a month, to look over scripts they were considering. It felt good to be in their busier office off Times Square, and I felt something had to break. Bob Shaye called me into his office one day and excitedly said he had just bought an option on a new script and wanted me to do a full breakdown and budget for a New York shoot. The script was by the respected horror filmmaker, Wes Craven, and titled Nightmare on Elm Street. When I started reading it later at home, I never put it down—scared to death. I gave it to my wife saying, "You've got to read this." She couldn't put it down either. Before we went to bed that night we double checked the locks on the doors and windows of our apartment, brought the baby into our bedroom with us, and went to bed shivering. It was that good.

Shaye wanted union and non-union budget versions, because he wasn't sure how much money he could raise. Shooting non-union in New York was its own nightmare, which Shaye well knew, but the story was set in the suburbs, so maybe it could keep off the unions' radar if it was shot there. The budget was done in two weeks. The non-union price was about $1.5 million. The union was well over $2 million. Shaye wanted to spend around $1.2 million.

We knocked around the numbers, and I unhappily squeezed it down to Bob's figure, but wasn't confident with it. We considered the perils of shooting non-union in NYC. If the unions went after you, the budget went out the window. The production manager would be blamed. I wished I could sit down with the unions, show them the script, say look, we have $1.2 million; show me how you would make the budget work with a union crew. Otherwise we can go to Canada, Poland, Mexico, or even Baltimore to make it work. I ran it by several union heads. The Teamsters were always ready to deal. SAG was sympathetic, and working on a low budget agreement, but the others claimed New York was worth the extra money, and refused to deal. "Get more money, or get out of New York," was their answer.

When I presented the final numbers to Shaye, he told me he had hired a Hollywood production manager to budget Nightmare as a LA production and if it was much cheaper, they might make it there. I wasn't scared. I thought unions were much stronger in Los Angeles, and New Line was a New York company—how could they run away from New York City? We were building a low-budget industry here, and New Line was a part of it. Besides, I was the king of low budget, and had shaved the budget so low no one could beat it.

But someone did. The LA production manager beat my budget by almost $300,000, to under $1 million dollars. Shaye said he claimed shooting with non-union crews in LA was not a problem. Union crews worked under assumed names on non-union shoots all the time. Everybody knew it, and no one cared. Ten non-union movies were shooting right then. The industry was much larger in LA so the crew and cast choices were vast, and competition with prices for everything from cameras to costumes beat New York hands down. New York could not compete on price, unless it was a true New York setting. Never had, never will.

Sarah Risher, who had been promoted to New Line's production head called me in for a meeting about their decision. It was grim. Not only would they shoot Nightmare in Los Angeles, but they were opening a full-blown production company in Hollywood, keeping only their distribution operation in New York.

"What does that mean for me?" I asked.

"Well you could move to Los Angeles, but you're really a New York production manager, and we'd prefer to hire an

LA production manager who has the contacts and experience there."

Gulp.

"We might find something for you, but you know our budgets. It wouldn't pay much, and we couldn't guarantee you anything."

The air seeped rapidly from my punctured balloon. It was good morning and goodbye.

What a choice. I could move my family to Los Angeles where I had almost no contacts, and start over completely, and maybe, just maybe New Line would let me start at the bottom. Or, having lost my biggest client, I could continue struggling in New York's low-budget movie world, working for peanuts for fourteen hours a day. I didn't need another decade of false starts and working for idiots with no future. I didn't want to work in New York's booming porno industry, which was always a choice, but a dead end too. John was the only person I enjoyed making movies with, because he really was together, and did what he said he'd do. But he seemed out of the picture now. Everything was out of the picture now. For the first time, I regretted not going to graduate school, getting an MFA in writing and finding a cushy college teaching job.

But then the phone rang. It was Dave Insley again. He had been contacted by a new ad agency that had a large package of TV commercial work and wanted Dave to be their exclusive production company. Could I come down immediately? The budgets were large and the egos were small. People making commercials did not have the cutthroat ambitions, duplicities, jealousies, over-blown egos, inexperience, and delusions of low-budget movie makers. TV commercials were all about money, and the money was good.

I started commuting to Baltimore, taking Amtrak Monday morning and returning to New York Friday night. Our reputations grew quickly and Dave and I started working with other agencies in Baltimore and Washington, DC. Dave stopped shooting for other people and put a full-time effort into building his production company. It was a busy time for me, but my wife was stranded in a village 25 miles from New York City with a one-year old baby and not happy with my being gone so much. Neither was I.

We'd been away from Baltimore for eight years, and it had become a much more attractive place to live and do business. I enjoyed my trips there more than my life in New York. The New York dream had fizzled, and it was time to move on. New opportunities beckoned, and we had to follow the money. We put our house on the sizzling New York area market, and sold it so fast we had to move into an apartment in Baltimore in a week.

I still visited New York fairly regularly because our lab and post-production work was there. I kept in touch with a few colleagues who still struggled in the low-budget world, but they slowly faded away. I never visited New Line, and had no interest in pursuing movie jobs, as I jumped from one TV commercial to another, and good money rolled in. John was becoming a memory. He called me once saying he had quit pursuing Flamingos Forever, convinced after five years that he had to go more mainstream. He was writing a new script, Hairspray, which was an upbeat teen comedy about how Baltimore's TV dance show craze influenced desegregation in the late 50s. What a change.

He asked if I would still work on it. I was busy with the commercials and wasn't so interested. I'd been out of Low Budget Hell for more than a year, and hadn't looked back. I considered John a friend though, felt sorry about his dead end with Flamingos Forever, and didn't want to abandon him at a tough time. But I didn't have much confidence it would go anywhere.

John wanted to raise about two million dollars for this more mainstream film, much of which had to go to music licensing. That amount would allow hiring a full union cast with a few big names and would pay him a six-figure writer/director fee, which he though he deserved by now. He wouldn't have to rely on royalties to make money.

I offered to budget the script for next to nothing, both curious and wanting to help a friend. The script was very different, decidedly marking his exit from the underground: no penis shots or nudity of any kind, no gay sex or gay references, no shoe fetishes, no dead animals, no blood, shit, needles, puke, drugs, drunks, or outrageous dirty gowns for Divine. In fact, there was no outrageousness from Divine. He played a moral, hard-working housewife and dedicated mother. He could display his acting talent and not just his willingness to gross out an audience. It was G-rated tame, like a Hallmark channel movie. It was like Pink Flamingos, Female Trouble, and Desperate Living never existed. Hairspray toyed with edginess with its race theme, but in a kind and silly PG-rated way. John had written in scenes with rats and roaches, but they were done with gentle humor, not horror. He seemed much more interested in the music and fun dances than any of his other films. Even the edgiest scene, the race riot at the Tilted Acres amusement park, was easily removed from the Broadway musical version and the Travolta re-make and replaced with a Kumbaya peace and love protest march—definitely not an "old" Waters touch.

Despite its more mainstream polish, raising money was not easy. Since New Line had passed on Flamingos Forever, we didn't think they would jump at Hairspray. Still, when they read it and refused, it was a depressing replay of John's past five years. It was a good script. It was mainstream, and it made perfect sense for them to do it. Nightmare on Elm Street was a huge hit for New Line, and established them as the big new thing in Hollywood. Five more Nightmares were in the pipeline. Sarah and Bob had moved to their new building in Hollywood, and it seemed that they didn't have time for a new John Waters film that would probably flounder in the underground culture that was morphing into the disco, fern bar and yuppie culture.

New Line's rejection heaped even more devastation on John, but he didn't give up. With a two million dollar budget, he needed a pipeline to big investors, and he hit on every connection he could find to reach them. Suddenly, out of the blue, Stanley "Bucky" Buchthal appeared on the scene. Bucky was a Wall Street whiz kid with $150 shirts and a taste for fine wine, food, furniture, and art—he let you know it. The scruffy Fells Point Dreamlander world was not his, which said a lot about John's direction too.

Bucky paid John for an option on the script, feeling he could raise money from Wall Street pals who wanted to get into the movie business. Bucky was totally unknown to the movie business, and though John girded himself against another disappointment, in our conversations he was desperate. Buying an option and actually finding funding was a big leap. But then again Bucky did promise to invest his own money if his potential investors fell through.

I made many budget variations for John. I sent a letter to Stanley on November 5, 1986, about six months before actual production, saying the film could be made for $1.18 million. But to present a number that low, John and I left out his fees, insurance, legal fees, and music licensing. It was a desperate ploy. I felt like a car salesman working a bait and switch deal. After adding the various additional pieces, the budget was closer to $2.6 million.

I set up a meeting with John and Bucky at Insley's building in Fells Point. It was a renovated small factory that had been outfitted with offices, editing rooms, and a 2,500 sq. ft. studio, that grossed a million dollars a year in TV commercial production. I wasn't sure I'd actually do the film, or that Insley wanted to either, especially since no money was on the table yet. New Line had already rejected it, and Bucky did not fit the low-budget profile. It didn't seem worth shelving the successful TV commercial business for several months in Low Budget Hell. John nudged me very insistently to trim the budget to make it more appealing to Bucky and his friends. I was very cautious because I knew the movie would need tons of good luck and good breaks to get done for the existing budget, much less an even tighter one.

John urgently wanted me to commit so he could start getting money from Bucky. Pre-production had to begin soon to get the movie shot in the summer, and thousands of details had to be arranged. The weeks dragged on as Bucky frantically searched for money. I had an inkling he wasn't interested in making the film, but only looking to make a big profit by flipping the option to someone else. He never seemed interested in day-to-day decision making. He wanted to be a middle man, and his hands-off approach and Wall Street attitude reminded me of Rocky with Violated.

A subplot in this drama was that the economy was nose-diving due to the Savings and Loan crisis that began in 1986.

Insley Films' main clients were S&Ls and car dealers, and there was an immediate halt in commercials for them. Insley Films was suddenly struggling. Dave quietly considered selling the building and down-sizing, but the real estate market was crashing along with the stock market. Two months earlier, Dave wasn't so interested in taking two months away from his lucrative TV commercial business. Now, it might be a different story.

John called me one day while I was doing renovation work on an old country farm house I had bought because the business was going so well (big mistake). He said Bucky had decided to fund Hairspray on his own, but the budget had to be reduced. He was ready to commit, but needed to cut $100,000. Could I do that? I groaned that anything was possible on paper, but everyone had to cooperate with the financial realities—a nearly impossible task as I had proven now on more than five movies. John said no problem; he would call Bucky and tell him. Fifteen minutes later he called back to say Bucky agreed to the new deal and would wire $10,000. We could start tomorrow. I looked at the paint brush in my hand and thought, "What have I done now? This will have to wait a while."

Dave's fear to commit was still an issue. My earnings had shrunk drastically over the past two months, so suddenly the idea of 18 weeks at a good salary looked better than the empty schedule at Insley Films. I definitely had to do the film and suggested a deal to Dave. He would be hired as DP for a flat eight-week salary. I would hire his wife, who ran the business end of Insley Films as the production accountant. I would rent Insley's offices and studio for the production. I would also rent Insley's camera and editing machine. I promised to hire only our local crew friends, who had served Insley Films well, to help them through the production drought. I would work full-time on Hairspray for the next three months, and if a commercial came in, he could still make it by hiring a freelance producer for a few days. He and his company would only be out of business for eight weeks. Dave would come out well, and the package price and reduced hassle level was good for John and Bucky.

I began pre-production in earnest. Business cards were made, locations scouted, Waters' standard art, costume, and wardrobe crew were hired, scripts were copied, casting began, and short term rental apartments and hotel deals for out-of-towners were tracked down. I negotiated with crew, began setting a shooting schedule, arranging insurances, bank accounts and more. The $10,000 went quickly, and I started to get the old Low Budget Hell feeling in the pit of my stomach. John felt the undertow too. Where was Bucky with another cash infusion? This time we'd need $100,000, and $100,000 more a week later.

Ten days into pre-production, when we were nearly out of money, the phone rang. It was John with a blockbuster bomb. Bucky had sold his option to New Line, and they were taking over the production. What in the holy hell?

Sarah and Bob Shaye called me an hour later to discuss their involvement. They were very chipper on the phone, and happy to be with the Dreamlanders again. Hollywood had been good to them and they had learned quite a bit since Alone in the Dark. They liked what they'd heard of my work so far, were happy to have the standard Waters crew, and would be hands-off the production for the most part. Only two things needed to be done. First, I should send the budget to Rachel in their office. Ironically, Rachel, my free production assistant on John's last movie, who I had hired on two other movies, was now their senior production manager, and she had to review it.

Second, I had to cut $200,000 from the budget. Bucky would still be an executive producer and need to be paid $125,000, and New Line would need a production overhead fee of about $80,000—plus a few weeks salary for Rachel.

Cutting $200,000 from the production budget unlocked the door to Low Budget Hell. It meant begging for free locations, cutting essential office personnel, hiring inexperienced crew and using free PAs who'd never been on a set. I had to whittle down the crew salaries and size, cut back the art budget, transportation, catering, and editing staff and gear. Everyone would be angry and resentful—and it would all be aimed at the line producer. I thought I had left that behind me. I might have walked away, except the economy really sucked now, and I honestly needed the money.

Baltimore's film production industry was hurting badly and everyone offered a job on the movie was glad for a three-month gig, even if the pay was half what they'd make on a TV commercial—if they could find one. I stressed to the crew that it was a very tight budget, and if we were to make it through, they would have to cooperate with budget realities. What I offered is what I had. There might be rough patches, but throwing money at a problem was not an option.

Rachel returned my budget with few changes saying it was comparable to her LA budgets, and she had no worries. She would come to Baltimore for a few pre-production weeks, but wouldn't stay long, having plenty to do in Hollywood. I said I would be happy for the help, and welcome any pointers. I honestly felt proud she was doing so well. I had no dreams of moving to Hollywood. I was content with my two kids and family in our little cottage in the country, and figured I would continue making lucrative TV commercials for the rest of my life.

After Rachel arrived the budget was a different story. It became as elastic as a rubber band. She said New Line told her to stay as long as she felt comfortable. If they were paying her off-budget, I was fine with that. But suddenly she became a budget item, and the above-the-line budget expanded. John and New Line chose many names including Jerry Stiller, Pia Zadora, Ric Ocasek, Ruth Brown, and Debbie Harry, even for day players. Though famous in their time (for most nearly 10 years earlier) none were current box office stars, and I doubted they justified their expense. Union rules required they travel first class, stay in first-class hotels, be paid a per diem, be chauffeured everywhere, and be paid overtime, and penalties. We were flirting with big budget categories, and dividing the production into haves and have-nots.

I did manage a deal with the local Screen Actors' Guild which had quietly instituted a low-budget "affirmative action agreement." If we hired a certain number of African-Americans, they gave us breaks on extras and expensive union rules. At the end of the film, SAG totaled the number of white and black working hours, and if you did not hit the right ratio, you would have to pay an additional $150,000. No one at New Line had heard of it, but it saved the production a fortune. Being a film about race relations, hitting the race ratio should be an easy thing, but it was close. I kept a close eye on the running totals, and at the end, to meet our quota I kept several of the minority actors sitting around extra days. Better to spend $2,500 than $150,000. Also, the budget had to stay under the "low budget" ceiling of $2 million. That was becoming difficult, and it became obvious that many expenses would have to be "off budget."

Rachel researched the music rights and determined that my $150,000 budget wasn't nearly enough. She hired a music licensing agent who said $450,000 was more like it. I said, in keeping with the low-budget sacrifices of others, we could create a great original score for $150,000, but suddenly, and without a fuss, the budget increased to accommodate the music rights. To accommodate the SAG contract budget limit, the music could not be added to the production budget. It would be inserted into the budget well after the SAG contract had been forgotten. In the meantime, I had to juggle two sets of books. I didn't get the idea of increasing the budget by nearly 50% for forgotten novelty songs any more than I got that Pia Zadora was a box office draw. I would have killed to get that kind of increase for the crew. In another sign of the budget bulge, New Line decided that Rachel should stay a few weeks longer to protect New Line's commitment, which increased the budget even more.

As the budget started snowballing, a pattern became clear. Since we had such expensive music, we had to have good dancers. Good dancers meant good choreographers from New York. Good choreographers meant good rehearsal space. Rehearsals meant paying union actors for rehearsal days. Next, Insley's studio was deemed too small for the TV studio set. Because so much was being spent on dancing, we had to rent Baltimore's largest sound stage, fill it with expensive extra props, and more extras wearing more costumes, requiring more make-up, catering, transportation, lights, and more people to put up the lights.

Since we were now spending more on production values, why not keep going? It was decided to fly the entire crew and cast to an amusement park in northern Pennsylvania. Baltimore's most expensive ballroom would be rented, a flying exploding wig would be constructed along with a futuristic little electric car. How fun!

When Rachel realized New Line was willing to spend almost anything to build Hairspray into a mainstream movie, she decided she should stay to oversee the whole production. I couldn't get a tiny increase in the catering budget, but she announced $10,000 budget increases daily. One day, she said she realized that she was actually producing the film, not John, and she was considering changing her title from New Line Production Supervisor to Producer, and what did I think of that? I said I had no plans to go to Hollywood, and didn't need the credit. I said go for it. It was a heart-warming story: Production Assistant moves to Producer in one movie. What an astounding career she could have. Maybe she'd own New Line in a few years. John had no problem with the money New Line was pouring into his movie. His fee was secure. Budget, what budget? If New Line was happy with Rachel's new title and salary, he was too. He agreed that Rachel should be the producer too.

With her new title secure, Rachel promptly left the office to be on the set as "producer." Ultimately she wanted to be a director, so why not? A friend of hers from Hollywood, Aaron, appeared one day. He had been a production coordinator in LA on several New Line films, but pointedly said he was a consultant and didn't do much to help our overwhelmed office staff. Though he was credited as Production Coordinator, I never figured out Aaron's purpose as he glided around the production office in Hawaiian shirts and sandals humming the Brady Bunch theme, and calling out the names of A-list directors like Marty, Steve, and Francis, while he gossiped with his buddies in LA rolling up our long distance charges. Maybe he was really Rachel's spy. In the midst of regular calamities he would dispense airy comments like, "the secret is remain blameless." I nearly died when I saw him on TV years later accepting an Oscar for producing Shrek, which, besides him, had about nineteen other producers by the way. Maybe he was the only one to remain blameless.

Rachel complained bitterly about the shooting pace as the production fell behind. For this she squarely blamed the assistant director, Steve. It was Steve's first movie, though he had been AD on many commercials, and worked closely on video assist with John on Polyester. He was a long shot, but so were John and everyone else—especially when Hairspray was a low-budget film. Rachel wanted to fire Steve and brought in a second AD from Hollywood, probably thinking she could take over, when Steve finally broke. Rachel decided her new main job would be on set pushing Steve through the day. I'd been through this before on Alone in the Dark, when Bob Shaye assigned Benni to hurry along the director, Jack. Steve complained to me that Rachel's barbed complaints and constant meddling slowed things down and created needless stress. We had long soul-searing conversations in the evenings as Steve tried to figure why things were so difficult. In the end, he survived, possibly because the risk of changing assistant director so late in the game would be worse. He was also a known entity to John, who didn't like surprises. Rachel finally gave in and concluded that thought through sheer will power she could get the shoot done and let Steve stay. Not that it stopped the carping to me about him.

Steve went on to become a very successful New York assistant director, with dozens of big films and TV series to his credit, including Michael Clayton, The Adjustment Bureau, and The West Wing.

The editing was the biggest calamity. Coming in at the beginning, Charles, who had edited John's previous three films for next to nothing, agreed to work on this one for a very low rate, in the spirit of its low budget. He set up his editing room rent-free in a friend's house, required minimal equipment, and accepted that he could not have a paid assistant, but only a free intern he would have to train first.

Rachel and New Line decided they needed a Hollywood editor in keeping with the production's new status. Money magically appeared for an imported editor, and an assistant, including hotel and per diem. They refused to work in the house in the suburbs. We found a downtown office suite and obeyed their commands for more equipment, more furniture, two phone lines, and stocked coffee service. Furthermore, as soon as the production wrapped they would whisk the film back to a decent editing suite in Hollywood. John would move there, all expenses paid. Charles did not get along with the new editors, who criticized everything, and told him he had no business working on a movie of this scale. A day later, Charles came into the editing room to find the new editor at the editing machine. When he asked what she was doing, she said she had been charged by New Line to be the principal editor and "save the movie." Charles turned on his heels, walked out, and called me.

He said he had put aside his busy freelance editing business and agreed to work with John for little money. He considered John a good friend. How could John do this to him? I said it wasn't John, but Rachel and New Line. They had taken over everything and doubled the budget. He refused to go back and be insulted for a few hundred dollars a week, and was angry at me too for letting this happen. I drove to the set to tell John in person that Charles was walking. John immediately called him. In the beginning, he had demanded that Charles be the editor. Charles was a big security blanket, and with all the pressures and changes on set, John did not need this.

"He quit," John said returning a half-hour later, stunned and blinking back tears. "I couldn't talk him out of it."

John was learning with some pain the price of moving up in the world, of having to take orders from others, that ties had to be cut, and that he could be hurt in the process. Back at the office Rachel, somewhat coldly, claimed Charles was in over his head editing Hairspray, that the Hollywood editors could teach him a lot, and he should just sit back and learn. If he wanted to leave the production, that was his decision and not her fault. She wasn't going to risk the movie because of John's friendship with someone she barely knew.

The theme of the production at this point appeared to be Rachel gets whatever she wants, and I do all the dirty work. I delivered all the bad news to the crew, I negotiated all the vendors to the slimmest profit. I twisted the arms of the unions, ignored promises, and apologized when things went wrong at locations. I begged the city film office for concessions, free police, and forgiveness when citizens complained about our blocking sidewalks and creating humongous traffic jams. I was being paid to do this, and it needed to be done, so at the time I figured it was just part of the job and I'd be forgiven at the end if feelings were hurt. I took the heat so John and Rachel wouldn't have to.

The local crew, whom I'd cajoled to cut their rates to work on John's low-low budget film, watched the production expand. The new faces from Hollywood and New York were not working for free, they knew. To soothe things, I made a deal with the NABET film union, but it only caused more grumbling. The union agreed to waive most of its rules on overtime and penalties if we paid a minimal health/pension fee contribution, which most of the crew would never see anyway. It was a huge concession by the union, and the union was dumped a few years later by its members for being too easy on producers.

The most nagging problem was the food. John had made a deal with a caterer friend who specialized in tasty grazing food. The film crew wanted pot roast and mashed potatoes with a big hunk of chocolate cake for lunch, but they got a dollop of crab salad on a bed of arugula with a thin baguette slice and an apple—and no seconds. My complaints to John and Rachel were ignored. Both were skinny worriers, for whom a few tasty, fashionable bites were an excellent lunch. John refused to change caterers, not wanting to hurt his friend's feelings, and the caterer refused to make the pot roast, fried chicken, and pork chops that the crew craved. I got the heat.

Eventually the crew ignored the catered lunch and headed to the nearest carry out for sub sandwiches, cartons of lo mein and garbage wagon pizzas. This set up quite a friction. John and Rachel blamed me for not controlling the crew. The crew blamed me for screwing them, while giving the cast and the Hollywoods the world. I was beginning the death march. The tone was set, sides taken, and I was squeezed in the middle.

Equipment damage was a large issue a couple times. In one set-up a heavy light was mounted on a hydraulic crane arm which lost pressure for a few seconds. The arm dropped fifteen feet, but stopped before it hit the ground and the actors beneath it. The light bulb, which cost $3,500, shattered from the shock, and the steel housing and stand were both seriously bent. I received a $10,000 insurance claim which covered the damage and some overtime caused by the failure.

Another day, a gaffer presented me with a bill for one of his ruined $3,500 light stands.

"What the hell happened?" I asked.

"A truck ran over it," he answered.

"Whose truck?"

"My truck."

"Who the fuck was driving it?"

"I was."

"You want me to pay $3,500 for your light stand that you drove your truck over, and trashed? Forget it." He got angry, and went to Rachel, who was buddy-buddy with him and she said, "Pay it."

I said, "OK, bring me the bent stand I just bought. I'll put it in a corner as a sculpture."

"Can't do that," he answered.

"Why not?"

"I'm going to fix it and re-use it."

I looked at Rachel with a WTF on my face, but she said, "It's OK, I'm approving it." I hoped she would remember this $3,500 gift when the next over-budget report came out, but with Hollywood people, I would learn memory losses are endemic. Any remaining authority I had was gone.

The worst part was that Dave and his wife sided with the crew, assuming I was getting special treatment by New Line, that I had gone Hollywood, and was screwing the crew. That might be the appearance to some, who didn't know the back story, but the deal I had made a deal with the Insleys paid them and their company very well, and I was shocked that they were giving me a hard time. I even thought briefly about leaving the film, like Charles, but wanted to be loyal to John who I considered a friend above all. We had been friends for twelve years. I had made many good deals for the film, saving hundreds of thousands of dollars, and John needed someone like that; someone to do the dirty work—which is usually the role of the production manager.

I didn't realize how deeply I was cutting my own throat by being the bad guy. Usually the production manager is backed by the executive producers, because the budget is so important, and they need a tough person to control spending. Once again I was in a position similar to my other movies; not enough money, and people on all sides making irrational and unfair decisions, and holding the production manager accountable. It was burn out time.

Hairspray came to a grateful end for everybody. It was shot during an extremely hot summer that roasted everyone. Ferocious thunderstorms that rolled through many afternoons wrecked the production schedule. Despite the heat, difficulties, and hard work, which are normal in most productions, there were no disasters, except for the few people who were let go. To save a few dollars, I was ordered to fire one of the favorite production assistants, a sweet young girl on her first movie, which confirmed my reputation among the crew that I had become the spawn of Satan. There were no serious injuries or deaths like I had experienced on other productions, so it was fine with me.

One minor injury was sustained during the Dorney Amusement park riot scene. Ironically, it was friend of Buckey who had come to be an extra was accidentally hit on his forehead by another extra's camera. It was a small cut, but he demanded to be taken to a hospital. Bucky called me outraged because his friend was a high-dollar model, and his face would now be scarred—due to the production's negligence (meaning me—not John, not Rachel, not the AD, not the Hollywood production coordinator). They were busy remaining blameless. His friend would need extensive plastic surgery so his modeling career wouldn't be ruined. He threatened to sue the production company, but would settle for a $10,000 cash payment for the surgery. I thought it was ridiculous, and surely the guy would only pocket the money. It was too much of a coincidence. Bucky was a smooth operator, I knew that. Of course, Rachel ordered me to write a check, and that was that.

I saved plenty of money in another instance at the amusement park. It was an expensive day with travel, stunts, major cast, and location fees. I suggested to New Line we get rain insurance. Being from Hollywood, rain wasn't a big issue, and they didn't think much of it. The deal was we would buy a policy for $5,000 that would pay $20,000 to the production if more than .25 inches of rain fell in the park on the shoot day between 7:00 a.m. and 5:00 p.m. New Line balked, but when I showed them their potential loss, they let me buy it. It was bright and sunny all day. Then, at 4:51 p.m. as the crew was wrapping, a drenching thunderstorm rolled in. No big deal, we had gotten all the shots. Nevertheless, I went to the guy who had been hired to measure the rain, and he had recorded that .27 inches had fallen on the park before 5:00 p.m. Not only had we gotten all the shots, but we made a profit of $17,000. New Line was impressed, but not enough to give me a bonus (not that I had expected one).

One fun aspect of the amusement park location was escorting Debbie Harry and Sony Bono on a US Air flight from Allentown to Baltimore. The small plane was coach only so Debbie couldn't sit in first class. As she had done in New York when I escorted her to the pharmacy, she wore a blousey jacket and pants, a black scarf covering her hair, and huge sunglasses hiding her eyes. It was a good disguise, and not a soul recognized her. Once again I was cheated out of being the envy of everyone on board because I was sitting next to Debbie Harry. She said few words and fell promptly asleep covered in a blanket.

Sonny, on the other hand not only sported his bushy trademark mustache, but wore a baseball cap with "Bono" embroidered on the front, for those who couldn't quite place his face. He chatted, signed autographs, and posed for photos with anyone who asked. He was happiest with a crowd of gawkers around him, but he'd been out of entertainment for a while, and the matronly crowds he drew were manageable.

I didn't go to the wrap party. I was too exhausted and burned out. Who wanted to be around the spawn of Satan anyway? John called the next day saying he was sorry I missed the only part of the movie that had really been fun. Despite all the troubles, he was grateful for all I did. He recognized what a hellish job I had, and never dreamed Hairspray would take the direction it did after New Line took over. But it certainly benefitted his career. I said not to worry, I would be fine after a little break. He said he might not be seeing me much, since he would be in LA for the editing, but would call me when he was in town again. We remained friends.

By now, in my career, I expected difficult situations. Though they were uncomfortable, they were like birth pains. They would be forgotten, and for the most part bygones would be bygones, especially if the movie was a success. The definite bright spots in the film were the bright, young, energetic cast, hoping this would be a big break for them. Ricki Lake had literally come out of nowhere at the last minute. The script called for the female ingénue lead to be very overweight, like her mother, Divine. John and the New Line folks were getting very nervous about finding a heavy-set teen who could act and be the great dancer the script demanded. At that time, young, fat ingénues were unheard of. They were in the closet, or never stood a chance. John could have had his pick from hundreds of young, cute, and sexy actresses to take the lead of Tracy Turnblad, but refused to compromise his vision of the pleasingly plump beauty.

New Line was getting a little concerned that John's quirks were getting in the way of the film's box office potential with the mainstream. Why did Tracy have to be fat? Why couldn't she be thin, sexy, and beautiful? To them, it was Waters' unprofitable underground ethos raising its head ugly again; just when they thought they had squashed it.

By some miracle, after hitting every casting and talent agent in the U.S., one of them suggested that Ricki should audition for the part. Though she was a locally successful teen singer, she had never acted professionally or released a record, so she was under the radar during most of the frantic search. Ricki was pretty. She was chubby enough for the part, but it was just a padding of baby fat. Her personality was magnetic, and she was a natural actress. She carried herself with a confidence that over-shadowed the more cover-girl/cover-boy looks of the rest of the teen cast.

When Ricki arrived at the chaotic production office in Baltimore, she was a sweet, unassuming teenager who only wanted to please. She would shyly ask me for things like where to get her laundry done, or find a more comfortable pair of shoes. Between rehearsals she would politely ask to use a phone in the production office to call her parents. She had no idea of the fame and success that would flood over her in the next few years.

Ricki was so happy and bubbly, she thought she had died and gone to heaven. This was true with all the youngsters. They were having the time of their lives learning the corny old 50s dances, hamming it up for the camera, and delighted to show off their spiffy 50s wardrobe. I'd say they were the glue that held things together and overcame the backstage egos and dissention that are common in many movies.

Despite the troubles, I thought my relationship with Rachel and New Line ended up being pretty decent. Sarah expressed her appreciation for my sticking it out, and admitted they had contributed to the chaos and bad feelings, but everyone would recover, and if the film were a hit, they would be proud to have worked on it. Rachel said a rushed goodbye. She had to get to LA immediately to oversee the editing. I don't remember her saying thanks for getting her started in the business or getting her in with New Line, or encouraging her to take the producer title on the film. At that point, I didn't care so much. I was tired.

My relationship with Dave, his wife, and his company was the biggest casualty. Right or wrong, I felt abused and unappreciated for bringing the work to them. But Dave's wife complained it had been a big pain in the neck, had lost them money, and I had burned too many bridges for them by being New Line's boy. Who needed me anyway? She could be just as good a producer as I was, and could save her business $100,000 a year.

I was so burned out, that I packed my personal things and walked out the door without saying a word. Dave called me a few days later asking where I was. I said I was finished with the stress and friction. I would start my own production company, and explore new opportunities. He didn't exactly beg me to stay, and I was so ready once again to re-invent myself on my own terms.

13
Crybaby

. . . .

New Line paid me for a few more weeks to wrap up Hairspray's business: approve final bills, sell leftover film stock in New York, liquidate the props and costumes, settle location damage claims, and facilitate the return of everything from porta-potties to commercial hair dryers. It was a blessed relief to get on with my life. I had no plans, but I did call a few clients I was especially close to when with Insley. One told Dave I was trying to steal his business, and he called to tell me to lay off, which I did. I toyed with going back into sound and worked part time at a friend's tidy suburban recording studio. He just made insipid local radio jingles, and I did not want to go back into ad work, so that didn't last.

Then, one day the phone rang. The retired marketing chief of CSX Transportation (the big railroad company) had $100,000 to make a short dramatic movie about the historic B&O Railroad station that would soon be demolished and replaced by the Camden Yards baseball stadium in downtown Baltimore. I had come highly recommended (I always wondered by whom, since I'd never directed a drama before) and was hired to be its producer/director. The 20-minute movie was a collection of historical vignettes about great moments in the railroad's history. It was a period piece requiring costumes, beards, a small herd of horses, carriages, props, sets; the works.

I was confident, because having worked on many period films I knew all the tricks. Van Smith, John's make-up artist was available and I hired him for a decent salary. The period make-up was a far cry from Divine's wild get-ups, but Van was an amazingly talented and versatile artist who never quite got the recognition he deserved. Vince wasn't available to work on this one, but a colleague, John Mills, a department store toy-buyer turned set designer worked tirelessly to make the sets look 150 years old.

As usual there wasn't nearly enough money. The actors were from amateur theater groups, the sets were spare, and the crew was short. One grip working too hard and too fast snapped his forearm almost in half when he reflexively tried to grab a spinning winch on a light stand. I'm glad I didn't cheap out on worker's compensation insurance because the hospital bill was into the tens of thousands of dollars. After months of therapy, he was fine, and we worked together many times after.

We had free access to the Railroad Museums' historic trains, one of which, the priceless Tom Thumb, hadn't been used for 100 years. Somehow I got permission to try to fire it up and ride it down the tracks. The antique steam engine was full of valves, boilers, gauges and other mechanical artifacts, but we got it up and going and shot great footage of it roaring down the tracks. Suddenly there was a sharp metallic crack, steam shot from the boiler, and the carriage ground to a halt. The engineer looked at it for a minute and said, "I hope you got it, 'cause she won't run no more, never."

We pushed it quickly back into its place in the museum. When the curator saw us later and asked how it went, I said "fine, fine, got great footage, wait 'til you see it," and rushed off, not mentioning the breakdown. Well they didn't expect it to run in the first place, so no loss.

Another scene required a team of six horses to pull an antique train carriage down the track. I hired a real "teamster" and her big white trained horses. She brought them down from her farm to the city location and spent the night in a camper so they'd be good and ready for the shoot the next morning.

I arrived on set to find a fleet of police cars and the frantic horse wrangler.

"There are reports of loose horses running down Pratt Street. Traffic's all tied up," said a cop.

No, no please, not that, I thought.

Yes, our rented horses were galloping through downtown Baltimore on one of its busiest streets at rush hour. The poor horse owner didn't know how she would catch six horses by herself. It would take a while. I was experienced enough in the ways of Low Budget Hell to shrug my shoulders and say, "Take your time, we'll shoot around the horses."

This short movie was my first directing job in more than ten years, so of course I over-spent the budget and there was little left for me. Afterwards, I scraped together other little jobs, but my new mortgage, and the lack of lucrative TV commercial work drained my savings fast. The marketing executive who hired me for the CSX film had promised an endless number of film projects, now that CSX had dismantled their in-house production unit.

They required safety training films, PR films, updates of existing films, etc. They had "gazillions to spend," and I was fortunate indeed to have hooked up with him. Nothing new came up, though he claimed to be working very hard drumming up new business. Van Smith, who had done the costumes on the movie, said he saw him every day drinking wine and playing a penny slot machine in the neighborhood gay bar. Great.

The local film business was hurting big time because of the deepening recession. Banks were hurting, car dealers closed, and unemployment skyrocketed. Vince Peranio's props and sets business was closing. Ad agencies drastically downsized and closed TV departments. The crash astounded everyone. Those who thought they could count on $100,000 a year salaries for the rest of their lives now made a tenth of that.

Hairspray meanwhile had completed its editing and a premiere was held in Baltimore. I went to a party with all the Dreamlanders, including Divine. I hadn't spoken with John or Rachel much in the previous nine months, but we sat together at the premiere, and never mentioned Hairspray's difficulties. Charles had hired an attorney to sue New Line and John for breach of contract. They claimed he had quit, and had no grounds for the suit. I had spoken to New Line's attorney, and the whole thing revolved around my giving a deposition about who promised what. Though asked by Charles' attorney, I had not given a deposition, knowing it would be the end of my relationship with John and New Line, and I wasn't ready to cut that cord yet. At the same time Charles was one of my best friends—he and John were the only people I invited to my secret wedding, just after Desperate Living, and for years we were completely in sync. It was devastating.

After the premier, we went out later, for old times' sake, to Bertha's and were the center of attention. All the gawking was uncomfortable for me, but John had mastered dealing with it. I sat on a bar stool between Van and Divine, and Divine started to cuddled up to me. He was like a big teddy bear. Divine stood up and began massaging my shoulders. He asked if I was feeling tense, and cooed that I worked awfully hard, and deserved a break. He asked if I would like a nice massage back at his place, and I began to giggle and edge away.

"No thanks Divvy, you know me, I'm straight as an arrow."

"Well, that's the best kind," he grinned back.

"Oh no, I'm a happily married man with two kids, you don't want to be a home wrecker do you?"

"Oh pooh," he pouted, "you're no fun."

"I know, just an old stick in the mud. Old and in the way. You just go ahead and have fun without me. I'll understand."

Not angry, he just gave me a sweet smile and a hug and glided down the bar to visit with someone else. Van leaned over and whispered.

"You just turned down an amazing opportunity. You don't know what you missed."

"Oh I'm fine, I love Divine, but I'm just not into him that way."

We both laughed. I'd known Divine for ten years, working, at parties, sitting in bars, smoking pot in his apartment, and he'd never come on to me. I guess I was a little flattered, but had no regret. I had no idea it would be the last time I'd speak with him.

A few weeks after the premiere we got the shock of our lives when Divine died from heart failure in his bed in Los Angeles. His performance was a big part of Hairspray's glowing reviews, and box office success. John and Divine had finally hit the big time, and now John would be the only one to relish it. I went to the funeral in Towson, our home town. The funeral home and streets were jammed, and police had to direct the traffic. It was both Divine's largest reception, and the biggest tragedy ever to rock the Dreamlanders' world.

At the Dreamlanders-only wake, I sat with John and quietly talked about the past. Rachel didn't make it. John didn't know where he would go at that point, but with the box office and critical success he was experiencing, it was certainly up. I wasn't sure where I stood with him at this point. We didn't say much about future work, I think we both just suddenly felt old.

Then the phone rang. It was an old buddy from UMBC days, Robert Mugge. Bob had taken a different path and created a niche making Americana music documentaries for PBS and foreign distributors. He had made a film about Hawaiian music, Hawaiian Rainbow, a year before for the State of Hawaii. They liked it so much they contracted him to make one about Hawaiian Dance, Kumu Hula, with a larger budget. I had kept in touch with Bob over the years, because he really wanted to make dramatic feature films, and I was a connection with that world. Kumu Hula had a large enough budget so he asked me if I would go to Hawaii for a month to shoot hula dancing. I was nearly broke, and the idea of getting away for a few weeks was wonderful. I'd never been to Hawaii. He'd even pay for my wife to go too. Bob was extremely generous, maybe to a fault, because, like me, he lived project to project, and couldn't afford to be considerate and generous. But he was. It was so unlike the movie people I had been working with for the past five years.

The Hawaiian shoot was a dream. Money was not a problem. We had three cameramen, a sound man, and a 24-track sound rig to produce a CD. There was no art department, no cast, no executive producers, no assistants to assistants, no costumers, no locations to wreck, no light trucks, no caterer, no parking or traffic nightmares—and no unions to work around. I spent mornings on my hotel room balcony overlooking Waikiki making phone calls, then shooting small hula groups at breathtaking sites. Bob hosted nice dinners at the best restaurants for the crew and their spouses most nights. It convinced me to get out of the movie business and pursue documentaries. The idea of making films with just three or four people travelling to exotic places was a revelation. Documentaries of Bob Mugge's caliber were rare, though he promised to hire me on many more because we got on so well, and he felt his career was taking off.

Returning from the Hawaiian Shangri-La was a rude wake-up call. There was no other work. I was behind on my mortgage, and started paying credit card bills with other credit cards in a death spiral. We finally decided to sell our newly renovated house and downsize to a rental until it became clearer where the economy was headed, and all this promising new work materialized.

To pay credit card bills, I decided to sell the Jean-Michel Basquait painting I had bought five years earlier. I called Sotheby's in New York, which was having a new art auction soon. I took a Polaroid of the painting, including the back, where Jean-Michel signed it, and they'd let me know if they were interested. They called back estimating a sale price $9,500. Nice profit even considering Sotheby's 30% commission. I had paid $100 for it. But it all went to creditors to get them off my back.

We moved into the rental house, and I looked for work, without much success. I even tried working for a caterer, making chicken salad by the gallon, and washing huge pots. It was exhausting and I made in a day what I had made in an hour as a producer. No future there. I was beginning to doubt I even had a future in Baltimore. Hairspray left a lot of smoking bridges.

It seemed everybody was burned out; depressed by the recession, and discouraged by the sudden decline of the local film business. We looked for houses to buy in the Baltimore area, but the prices were too high. Not having a big cash reserve or a full-time job, it would be impossible to get a mortgage. My wife was from North Carolina. We had visited her family regularly for years, and we began to contemplate moving there, where the economy seemed better and my wife could be near family who could help with the kids when I was away on shoots—hopefully more documentaries.

The Crybaby Shock

Trying to keep connected to my old Fells Point world, I invited Vince Peranio and his wife Delores, who I still considered best friends, to dinner at our rented country home. Sitting by the fire, sipping glasses of wine, I asked Vince if he was up to anything new.

"I've been working on John's new film."

"What?" I said. "John's new film?"

Pause.

"You don't know about it?"

"Uh, no…. He hasn't called me.

"We've been working on it for a few weeks. Rachel's producing it. It's a big budget. $9 million. Maybe you should call him," he said.

I stopped breathing for a minute. John never stopped calling me before Hairspray started pre-production. This was really weird. What was going on?

First thing the next morning I called John, slightly panicked, and very bewildered.

"I've been meaning to call you," he said. " I can't talk now, let's have lunch today."

That sounded good, he's been meaning to call me, just too busy, he was probably going to call me today anyway.

Early as always, John sat by himself in a corner of the restaurant, ironically across the street from where my wife and I were married. He greeted me with a forced smile and said, "Hello Bobby."

I sat down.

"This is going to be one of the worst lunches of my life. I've been dreading this," he said almost in a whisper.

Innocently, I answered,

"Why, what's going on, John?"

"Well, I am doing another movie. It's backed by a big Hollywood company. They're approving everybody working on it, and I don't have any control over it. I was just hired to write and direct it."

"I heard Rachel is producing it?"

"Yes…"

"But… um ah, John, we've done four movies together."

With an edge to his voice I'd never heard, he answered. "I know, but this is different. My career's different now. Those were my first movies, and they don't have anything to do with where I'm going now. Rachel is an experienced Hollywood producer. They picked her, and I'm behind that."

"Vince is the art director, right?" I asked.

"Yeah."

"Who's shooting?"

"Dave."

"Hair and Makeup?"

"Chris," he said.

"Is Pat involved?"

"Of course, she's casting... and associate producer."

It sounded so far like this movie had a lot to do with his older ones.

I asked who else was on the crew. John recited the name of every single person who had been hand-picked by me to work on Hairspray, and my head started to spin. It was everyone who I had begged to work at a cut rate on Hairspray, and who had begged me to work on Hairspray. Everyone from Dave, the DP, to the free apprentice editor Charles and I had found. It was like they had copied my contact list from Hairspray and started dialing numbers.

"Sounds like everybody but me."

"Well, they want the production staff from Hollywood, but are trying to keep the rest local to save money."

"Who is they?"

"Brian Grazer and Jim Abrahams. Universal is backing it, so the budget is much bigger. I had to join the Directors Guild. I'm finished with low budget."

"What is the budget?"

"It's nine million dollars, but music and overhead are really high—you know, Hollywood."

"Nine million? Is there anything for me?"

"I'm afraid not, Bobby. Rachel has her own people. I think it's better to skip this one. It's different now. I don't think it would be right for you, and you wouldn't be very happy with it."

But it was right for everyone else? Even those whose first movie ever was Hairspray? As much as it hurt to be the only one left out—and that Rachel, who I started in the business, and had nursed through three low budget movies had nothing for me—to preserve my sanity, I convinced myself that yes, I probably didn't deserve anything. Yes, it was over my head, and I should give John my blessing and say a fond farewell as he moved to his newly re-invented life. This was just a stupid dream anyway, and I would probably wake up in a few seconds.

The other me, the one who had worked hundreds of twenty-hour days out of loyalty and friendship was beyond angry. It was one thing to be screwed. It was another thing to be screwed by someone you considered a good friend, when you desperately need a job because you were broke. That was the real bottom line.

"Isn't there anything for me?" I asked again. "Maybe a consultant—assistant production manager? What about location manager?"

"I think they have someone for that already."

"Who?"

"Wally, the guy who did it on Hairspray."

"Well that's nice, that was Wally's first location manager job too. I hired him."

John stared back at me blinking. He was not great at confronting people with bad news, and went on the defensive.

"Look, you had every chance to benefit from my movies. You learned a lot, just like I did. You got in with New Line, and all the others in New York. It was up to you to take it to the next level. I don't think I owe you anything. I can't take you with me on this or any more movies."

"John, I'm not asking for line producer, or production manager. I need work. It's been very difficult since Hairspray. I could do a great job as location manger, and that has to be a local. I've done ten movies supervising location managers, I mean come on. Hairspray was difficult, but no worse than Desperate Living or Polyester. Why get rid of me now?"

"People complained to me all the time about you during Hairspray, I can't put up with it on another movie," John said.

"John, people always complain about the production manager. I deliver the bad news, so you don't have to. I fire people, I cut their budgets, and I refuse their requests. I'm the bad guy; you're the good. Of course they'll complain about me. That's how we've always played it. If you had a problem with it in Hairspray, why not tell me then? Why wait 'til now? Every decision I made was for your benefit, to protect the budget, to protect you, and New Line, and Rachel, and that was incredibly difficult. It cost me a lot of friends and work. Why am I a problem now?"

Freaked out by my desperation, John gave up.

"Maybe there's something. If you were location manager, wouldn't you feel like it's a demotion?"

"I wouldn't do it if I did. It's great that you and everyone are moving up. Location management is a great job. I'll give 110%. I always have."

"I'm afraid you won't like having to work under Rachel," he said.

"I'm fine with Rachel. We got along fine on Hairspray—I thought. We sat together at the premiere."

"I just have a bad feeling things won't work out, and you might be very sorry you did it."

"I think I need to take that risk John."

After a long pause, he said, "I'll talk to Rachel."

After he had spoken with Rachel, John called me later to say she would hire me as the location manager. She said she would have offered it in the beginning, but thought I would turn it down, because it might be beneath me. Sounded nice, but a little fishy.

I was on the crew, and happy to be working on a $9 million movie. Karen, Rachel's production manager choice had good credits, as did her choices of assistant director and second assistant director. But at the end of the day their allegiance was to Hollywood, and they did not mix well with the Baltimore crew. Arrogance was part of their makeup, but worse a sneakiness permeated them, and unnerved the production. For example, second assistant director, Jeffrey Wetzel, a big name in Hollywood now, was nicknamed by the crew, Jeffrey Weasel, in the first week of shooting. Maybe they didn't trust the unknown Baltimore crew, and feared for their jobs if something went wrong. There was also an atmosphere of shifting blame when something went wrong. The competitiveness of the Hollywoods was so intense that it seemed they cared little about the movie, and much more about looking good to the executives to ensure they would be hired on the next film. Frequently this meant stabbing other people in the back or secretly undermining them to move up in the pecking order.

At an early pre-production meeting, when I first met Karen, she looked over my shoulder, limply shook my hand, and then made believe I was invisible for the rest of the meeting. When it broke-up, she said I should come to her office tomorrow and talk. At that meeting, salary was the first topic. She had budgeted $1,000 a week for a location manager. That was flat rate, unlimited hours, seven days a week, no benefits. I made $1,800 a week as line producer on Hairspray. I felt that out of loyalty or gratitude, they would have pushed that up to at least what I had made on Hairspray. Out of a $9 million budget, paying the important job of location manager on a location film less than a 2nd grip was laughable. When I asked for more, Karen said Wally Hall would do it for $1,000 a week. She had already interviewed and decided to hire him, except John had stepped in. He would take it if I didn't. It was take it or leave it. I needed the money, so I took it.

An assistant location manager was budgeted at $400/week; less than a PA. When I complained, she said that was the going rate in LA. I asked Wally if he would do it, and he refused because of the low pay. When I told Karen to find someone else, she said it was my problem. I finally found someone who was smart and enthusiastic, but had never worked on a movie before. For expenses, I had to use my own car, and would only be reimbursed for gas receipts. Figuring I'd put 4,000-5,000 miles on the car, it was a pretty bad deal. They did pay for a pager—not a cell phone—which was ridiculous. I had to visit the bank every morning for two rolls of quarters, and stop at nearly every payphone on my travels to check-in with the dozens of locations I was trying to procure and manage.

If I had been more astute about the ways of Hollywood, I would have realized they were making the job so miserable that I would turn it down. At the end of the meeting, I told Karen that even though I was just the location manager, I had been shooting in Baltimore for more than ten years and was even a Directors Guild production manager. If she wanted help with anything else, I'd be happy to assist.

"Please let me know if I can help. I'm sure something will come up," I said.

"I doubt it," she answered coolly.

Crybaby was a tempest. It was a big movie that made Hairspray look like a student film. It was period, requiring 1950s buildings, decoration and furniture, vehicles, wardrobe, and makeup. It had many big names including Johnny Depp, Iggy Pop, Patty Hearst, Polly Bergen, Troy Donahue, and Tracey Lords who needed private dressing room trailers, personal drivers, and first class hotel accommodations. There were 23 different locations which frequently required additional nearby staging areas for dozens of extras, parking for 15 large vehicles, plus cast and crew parking. It was all union, with no special low budget breaks.

Nevertheless, the production fell behind from the first day. As director of photography and camera operator, Dave Insley was overwhelmed and took the heat. Instead of hiring someone locally, a second cameraman was quickly dispatched from LA, and Dave was nudged aside, which started the first low grumble from the crew. Although we weren't that close anymore, Dave and I exchanged commiserating glances. The Baltimore crew was too slow for the Hollywood production team. The truth was the production was extremely complex, and even at $9 million was under-budgeted. The crew was insufficient for the demands of an all-location, period, dancing movie. Rachel and the production team jammed too much into a day, falsely shortening the schedule and budget. John was not the most effective at picking angles and getting shots done fast. He did not have anywhere near the hours of set experience of any of the key crew, and they saw it. A storyboard artist (the whole movie was storyboarded, so there was little need for discussion about shot coverage), sharp assistant director team, and excellent continuity person eased the load, so it wasn't so bad for him, and he was happy to concentrate on his favorite job, working with the actors.

Fortunately for me, the locations were nearly always ready. Shoot days averaged 14 hours, and I was on location hours before anyone to be sure direction signs were posted on the roads, parking was secured, and the caterer could be ready for breakfast for 50 by call time, which was frequently 5:00 a.m. I was always last out, to be sure no trash was left, or see if there was obvious damage, and often slept less than four hours a night. The art department was beaten to a pulp, building one set, shooting on another, and wrapping another. Vince's wife, Delores, the art director, was responsible for everything to be ready on the set. It was nearly impossible due to the constantly shifting schedule, and she lashed out at everyone. Towards the end of the day, new schedules were printed every 15 minutes, because the day's scenes weren't getting done.

The scenes were difficult. John wrote several complex stunts, moving car shots, and big night scenes. Many scenes had hundreds of extras. We shot in the giant 19th century Maryland House of Corrections prison, and were locked in with prisoners walking around us and whistling at the women. I was shocked to find that prison guards carried no weapons when going into the prison common areas, like we did. If they wanted to, the inmates could have jumped and held us for quite a while until a SWAT team could come and rescue us. But this was not a high security prison. They made license plates there, so violent prisoners were a very remote possibility; still, it was something to think about.

Maryland's afternoon thunderstorms ended many days too early. They made me happy, because it meant a few hours extra sleep, but it also meant re-scheduling locations.

The assistant directors were equally mean to everybody. I had daily run-ins as they listed their complaints. The catering truck was too far away, John had to park too far away. The extras area wasn't air conditioned enough. There weren't enough porta-potties. The directions weren't detailed enough. I had to go tell nearby construction crews to stop their work because of the noise. They would inform me at the last minute that they needed three more hours to finish a location, so I had to negotiate with the owners for more time.

Schedule changes were a nightmare, because changing locations sometimes required alerting entire neighborhoods at the last minute. I dealt with a dozen municipalities for permission to use public spaces, parking, closing streets and sidewalks, and trimming trees. Night shoots, with their noise and stadium lights drove neighbors crazy. The big location question was could we get the needed shots before we wore out our welcome? Usually the answer was yes, if we paid more money for the inconvenience—sometimes a lot of money. For this, the Hollywoods blamed me. Their inability to complete a scheduled day played no role. It was the same old song.

On one location I left my car open while I was inside dealing with some business. Jeffrey, the 2nd AD plopped down in the driver's seat, and plugged his mammoth Motorola cell phone into the cigarette adapter to chat with his people in LA about his next job. I came out, and he was still on the phone and gestured he needed a few more minutes. I had plenty to do, so no problem. Delores was having a tense moment dishing everyone about how they were treating the beautiful historic mansion location. I don't think she nor Vince were ever the same after Crybaby either.

I returned to my car, and Jeffrey was still yakking away in a loud voice, impressing everyone in earshot with what a busy, popular guy he was in Hollywood. It was Friday, so he was dressed in pajamas, his trade mark touch of eccentricity. Maybe people in LA people thought it was clever to wear pajamas to work. In Baltimore, he was an embarrassing dork.

"Jeffrey, I gotta go. I'm late for an appointment," I said.

He waved me away like a pesky mosquito, and I politely moved out of earshot.

After shifting on my feet for a minute, I approached my car, with a pissed off look on my face. Jeffrey bounded out, still on the phone ignoring me. I got in, turned the key, and nothing. His phone had drained my car battery. The little prick. It would take another half-hour to get a jump start, and I was already a half-hour late. Hollywood vampires, taking you for all you're worth, even sucked your car battery dry.

When I had a few minutes, I'd wander through the set, which was like a travelling carnival. Crafts service had a lavish spread of snacks and drinks, and crew people hung out there to exchange gossip. The stars wandered from private dressing room to dressing room, partying and gossiping in the air conditioning for hours until their scene came up, while everyone else suffered in the 98 degree heat. It was a happy, relaxed camp. Johnny Depp was everyone's pal. He was a randy teenager having the time of his life, and many of the girls were dying to get him in bed. One day inside the make-up trailer,

I saw an actress point to a hickey on her neck, and whisper to the artist, "Johnny."

To get through the stresses of the day, the crew started drinking even before wrap. A teamster-driven truck would pull up with a few cases of cold ones, and dispensed to any crew member who had thrown a few bucks into the beer kitty. I disposed of bag after bag of empties when they cleared the location. In John's early films, this would never have happened.

Unlike any of my previous films, Crybaby became a large factory, where people appeared to care less and less about the project. They just wanted to keep on the job, do as little as possible, and get blamed for nothing. I was surprised that several of the Hollywoods actually ran businesses like Subway sandwich shops and liquor stores back in LA that they managed with cell phones while on set. The transportation coordinator was insane about the schedule changes, because he had a very sick friend he wanted to visit in Las Vegas, but didn't dare leave for a few days, because the schedule changed daily, and he was terrified of putting the quicksand of a schedule into the hands of an underling.

John was especially picky about locations. On the old films, when it was his money, he was always willing to compromise, but with a $9 million budget, he turned quite persnickety. One big scene required a 50s era shopping mall, where we could stage a grand opening. That's a huge location. It was impossible to find, because even in Baltimore, they had all been torn down. Maybe a 50s style awning was left in a re-furbished shopping center, or slanted roof line, but neither exterior or interior existed, and I drove hundreds of miles scouring small towns and suburbs within 40 miles of Baltimore to discover that.

I suggested that John change the location from a mall to a theme park. Baltimore's Enchanted Forest, a tacky kiddie amusement park with exhibits, dinky rides, and snack bars based on the theme of a fairytale village, had been a huge hit in the 50s, 60s, and even 70s, before kids' cable TV channels and video games made going outdoors obsolete. It still looked very 50s, and was the only large scale period public place that would have a believable grand opening.

John balked. Messing with his script these days was like re-writing the Bible, even when I suggested it would save tens of thousands of dollars in set decoration. Vince loved it immediately, not in the least because it was essentially unchanged from 1955 when it opened, and required almost no set dressing. His art department was near collapse from exhaustion, changed schedules, and general overwork. Vince's prodding eventually swayed John, and Rachel and Karen dragged their feet, probably because they didn't like the idea of the location manager affecting the script so dramatically. There was no choice. They knew I had been looking for months for the mythical shopping mall, and the scene was scheduled for next week. Vince gave me a big hug on the way out.

I was pleased, and even a little proud that so many of the locations had worked out. There had been a few unhappy neighbors, but nothing serious; no law suits, no injuries, no damages, no fines, no fires, nothing that a little more money wouldn't cure.

Of all things, Karen began giving me problems about my personal expenses. I went through a tank of gas a day, which she felt was impossible, and accused me of hanging around gas stations to buy receipts from people filling up at the pumps. I laughed, saying who would think of such a thing? She informed me it happened all the time in LA.

The Hollywood approach to money was bewildering. Their dislike of Baltimore went beyond the crew. They didn't want anything local. Cartons of office supplies were shipped from LA. All stationary printing was done in LA. Computers were rented from LA. Crates of production expendables like gaffer tape, lighting gels, and bulbs came from LA. A few years later while working at a studio in North Carolina, and dealing with Hollywood movie supply companies, I was clearly offered kickbacks to buy from them. A Hollywood production manager assured me that was always the case. The production staff's compensation included a hefty salary, plus "all you can steal." Maybe that explained my new battle with Crybaby.

Karen called me into her office again with a new pile of my receipts on her desk.

"I finally caught you this time."

"Caught me at what?"

"Look at these receipts, where are they from?"

They were for things like maps, toilet paper for locations, and a case of beer to placate an irate location owner. There was a restaurant receipt for another irate neighbor who I told to take his wife out to dinner and we'd be gone when they returned. Most were little things like batteries for my flashlight and photocopies made at a convenience store.

"They're my work receipts. I'm out on locations all day. I don't sit in the office," I said.

"What does that mean?"

"Nothing. So what's wrong with them?

"You're turning in receipts from California."

"What? I haven't been to California in years."

"Look at this receipt. It says CA, that's California. You're in big trouble mister."

"Wait. CA, that means cash. It means I paid cash, not credit card. Look, at the top it says Catonsville, Maryland. What are you trying to do?"

Now I had caught her red handed. How was her budget looking? Not too good I'd guess. Accusing me of stealing pennies from the production? No wonder the movie was falling behind.

"You're the worst location manager I've ever met. You've cost this production tens of thousands of dollars," she said.

Right. Blame all the problems on me. It was ridiculous, because everyone on the crew was ready to put the heads of the ADs on sticks. They knew where the problems were.

"I'll resign right now if you want me to."

It was the last week of the production, and one final location was still to be shot. It was a small, easy exterior night in a public park. All the arrangements had been made with my buddies in the police and parks departments. But Karen had no idea of the status of the location, or any of the previous ones for that matter.

"Don't you dare leave. You have a contract."

I didn't have a contract. She never bothered with one, figuring I'd be out the door in the first week.

"I'll make your life miserable if you quit."

"We'll see. I've got a meeting, and I want my petty cash reimbursement check ready when I come back. It's been two weeks."

I left the office hoping I had scared her good. It was like, who do you have to bribe to get off this film? I met with my assistant location manager. She had survived the whole film, and learned many things, like never work in the location department again. On extremely long days, I put her in charge of the wraps so I could get some sleep and still arrive at the next morning's location by 5:00 a.m. She would arrive around 9:00 a.m. after her few hours sleep.

I surprised her when I said I was resigning from the film that afternoon, and she would have to see it through the night. There were no extras, just two actors and a short crew. Since the shoot wasn't expected to last more than two hours, we didn't even bother with the caterer. I gave her my information sheets; she already knew the police contacts personally. She said my resigning on the last shoot was "awesome," and I would be a hero. I said I didn't want to hurt the film or John; I just wanted to make a statement.

I went back up to the Crybaby office to drop off some files as my last act. Karen saw me and pounced out of her office. The office staff listened intently.

"Where are the location files?"

"Right here in this file cabinet and the production coordinator has a copy of everything."

"I want to see every page of your notes and agreements."

"That's a couple of hundred pages. I don't have the time right now."

"Well, just make time."

"Is my petty cash reimbursement ready?"

"No."

"Then I resign. Right now. I'm out of here."

"You can't. You can't resign."

I kept walking past the other saucer-eyed staff.

"Come back here.... You can't resign.... You can't resign because you're fired!"

"Mail me my petty cash check, or you'll hear from my lawyer," I said as I walked out the door.

I went home, immensely pleased that it was over, had a beer, and then played with my kids whom I'd hardly seen in two months. John called in a panic, the first time we had spoken on the phone for months. What had I done? Was I sabotaging the film? I said don't worry. I had arranged with Kristen to oversee the last shoot. All the permissions were signed, and the police and parks were ready. It was an easy shoot. She could handle it. He said he was sorry I left, but understood. He did mumble, "I told you so." But John was totally burned out, and wanted to just go home too.

Kristen called to say that Karen had visited the set and announced loudly that I had been fired and appointed her to be the location manager for the last three hours shooting. So my final act on my fifth John Waters film was to get fired. That was what everyone would remember.

What a hoot, I was reminded of the Lipstick Beauty Salon scene in Female Trouble, when Divine gets her husband Gator fired and he throws acid in her face. I did not go to the wrap party, though John called specifically to invite me—saying Karen and Rachel had already gone back to LA. I never felt he was angry or disappointed. The film was so big and I was so busy off set, we rarely saw each other. I doubted he knew what was going on in the office, and I didn't want to bum him out with it. I still felt that after fifteen years, we were still friends.

It was a short conversation, since we both seemed very ready to move in different directions, and surely would never work together again. I never heard from Rachel again, not a word. Ironically I wrote a book two years later called Location Scouting and Management for Focal Press that was quite successful, so the movie was ultimately worthwhile for me.

Fortunately I had money in the bank, but on the other hand, no solid work prospects. Bob Mugge was optimistic about new films, and I had an offer to teach a few production management seminars at my Alma Mater, American University, but it wasn't a career.

I was excited when I found an ad in The Baltimore Sun for a National/International Production Coordinator at my other Alma Mater, Maryland Public Television. I sent a resume, and had a good initial phone interview with the Executive Producer, Leo Eaton. I spoke about my experiences in Baltimore and New York over the past eight years, and he thought they were perfect for his National/International Productions unit. He loved the combination of feature films, period pieces, and PBS documentaries. He specialized in complicated, long form international co-productions, and needed a budget-conscious person who had traveled, could manage historic re-enactments, and juggle multiple crews in different parts of the world. He liked me, and said he felt lucky that I was in Baltimore. We made an appointment where I would be interviewed by the hiring committee.

The appointment went well, except I balked at the disappointing $45,000 a year salary. I had made close to twice that with Insley, and union production managers made over $2,500 a week. Leo gushed compliments, and at the end said don't worry about the money, he could probably work out a compromise if I could bend a little too. I was sure the job was mine, and returning to documentaries with a steady job with a major PBS producer was just the ticket I needed to escape Low Budget Hell once and for all.

A week later, not having heard anything, I called, but Leo said no decision had been made. Feeling guilty about my objecting to the salary in the interview, when I asked if money was an issue, he said no. Disappointed, and having no firm contact about next jobs, I started to have an overwhelming urge to get out of Baltimore for something new. I had left New York hoping for a better life. Maybe if I had stayed there, I'd be in a better situation. Was returning to Baltimore a stupid thing? Above all I craved stability after moving on average once a year for the past ten years.

I visited Vince in Fells Point knowing his difficulties during Crybaby and hoping to commiserate. Vince and I had been good friends and neighbors in Fells Point, and talked through many bad times. He had worked on many movies, but this one had really worn him down. On top of that, his sets business, which was lucrative and fulfilling during the TV commercial boom, had split apart leaving some bad feelings among the partners. He was deeply discouraged, maybe clinically depressed. I certainly was feeling that.

He didn't want to discuss Crybaby, at all, while I hoped to figure out what happened. I wanted to know if he thought John had changed. I wanted to know if the Hollywoods were as antagonistic to his crew as they were to me. Or was it just me? Vince answered he didn't care about Crybaby. He didn't care about anything anymore, and not caring made him very happy. He didn't want to hang out, but just go home and watch TV alone. I wondered if he was on anti-depressants. I sure could have used some.

I thought I was in bad shape, but didn't want to sit home and watch TV alone, and didn't want to get to that point either. I had two wonderfully happy little kids and I needed to do something about that quick.

Baltimore was grim. My best friend Charles blamed me for getting canned from Hairspray. John saw me as leftover meatloaf to be tossed out before it made a stink. Vince wanted to be alone. My relationship with Insley was irreparable. The economy was a disaster. Even all my credit cards had been cancelled.

I interviewed with the new Discovery Channel in Washington, DC, several times, but was beaten out by people with more network TV experience, no matter how fascinated the executives were with my work on low-budget movies. I tried to get a job with the new America's Most Wanted series, but after several interviews they picked someone with more network experience too. Low budget movies hadn't prepared me for much else, it appeared.

My hopes were pinned on the Maryland Public TV job. Just back from the America's Most Wanted rejection, I played back this message on my answering machine:

"Hello, this is Leo Eaton at MPT. I'm sorry to leave an important message like this on your answering machine, but after a very difficult decision, we have selected another candidate for the production coordinator position. I would prefer to speak to you in person, but I know you have other plans, and didn't want to hold you up. And please Bob, know that the decision had nothing to do with salary. I wish you the very best in your career, which I am sure will be super, and we will keep your resume on file in case something else comes up."

Crap.

They had hired someone with several years unit managing experience at NBC News in New York. Hard to beat that; my specialty was gore. Looking at every nook and cranny, I had already called several production companies in the growing

Sun Belt city of Charlotte, North Carolina, because of my wife's family roots there. They were actually encouraging, replacing the discouragement I'd been getting in Baltimore. One even flew me in for a day of interviews. They weren't hiring at that very minute, but they said if I were in Charlotte, I'd surely find good work.

After the rejection by MPT, we called my wife's parents and said we were now seriously considering moving to their little college town. I would likely be travelling for work on Bob Mugge's documentaries, possibly short stints back in New York. My wife was tired of me travelling for weeks at a time, and with two very young children, being close to her parents would make life so much easier. Besides, the opportunities in Charlotte appeared good too.

Her parents were delighted, and said they had just bought a small rental house around the corner from their home. They would sell it to us cheap and hold the mortgage. Considering everything, it was an offer we couldn't refuse, so we made a very fast decision to go south. It was the week after Christmas, and the next day I hired a 24 foot U-Haul truck, had a few neighbors help load our furniture, books, and kids' toys, and took off. My wife drove with the kids in our car, and I drove the truck with the family cat in a cage beside me mournfully meowing all four hundred miles.

14
North Carolina
. . . .

I purposely only told Charles I was leaving. He understood my situation, and made me promise to stay in touch. As a farewell present to him, I said I would speak to his attorney and agree to give a deposition in his lawsuit against John and New Line, which he still pursued. I never even gave the deposition. New Line quickly settled, figuring I had no reason anymore to support them in my deposition, and it was easier to pay Charles some cash and get it over with.

I didn't want to say goodbye to anyone else—not John, not Dave, not Vince. I didn't want a party or farewells. I wanted to disappear. It was far from New York, from Baltimore, and DC. It was the Bible Belt. It was like going to a different country. It was a pretty desperate move.

The move to North Carolina however wasn't a dead end. Though I secretly wanted to buy the old-fashioned soda shop in the village, I stayed in production as a production manager, and increasingly as a writer/director—which is always what I wanted to do anyway. In my first few months there, I stumbled into managing southern B-movie maker Earl Owensby's run-down studio out in the boonies forty miles west of Charlotte. A low-budget Hollywood producer had leased the place and wanted me to be his eyes and ears on the ground in North Carolina, while he stayed in LA to drum up money and business for the 100,000 sq. ft. studio complex. It seemed like a dream come true, and ironically positioned North Carolina, along with Dino DeLaurentis' giant studio complex in Wilmington, NC, to be a major player in the movie making industry.

But true to Low Budget Hell rules, it turned out to be a scam. Six weeks after I started, my paycheck bounced. The next day a message appeared in the fax machine saying the company had suspended its North Carolina operations, and all workers were immediately terminated. Minutes later the electricity went off because the bill hadn't been paid. Earl Owensby's son escorted us out the door by flashlight.

It turned out that none of the bills the studio had racked up had been paid—neither rent, water, phone, furniture rental, office supplies, nor copier. I had to sneak one of the associate producers out of the motel where he had stayed for a month, because they were hounding him to pay the bill. At the airport, he promised he'd get to the bottom of this, and he would be back from LA soon. I never saw him again.

In what must be the weirdest irony of my career, nine months after the move, a producer at Maryland Public TV called saying they were looking for an experienced production manager for a complicated six-hour PBS series that would have crews travelling around the world for a year. It sounded familiar. They were anxious to get going, and flew me to Baltimore the next day. After a brief interview, I was immediately hired for $1,500 a week for a five-day week for nine months. I didn't get the staff job, but I got a dream producer job instead. I had to start in three days.

After being burned so many times, we decided my wife and the kids would stay in North Carolina. I would commute to Baltimore, flying from Charlotte Sunday night, and returning on Friday afternoon. A sharp LA travel agent found loopholes that got me round trip flights for less than $100. Nor could I face packing up and moving again. What if the series went bust? We'd see how things went for a few months before making another big change.

Besides becoming an expert on the 55 minute flight between Charlotte and Baltimore, the series was fascinating, but getting a good night's sleep was hard. During the day I worked with the office staff and producers who were planning their shoots in twenty different countries. My phone rang all night long as crews checked in from ten different time zones around the world. They shot in Europe, Kenya, South America, Russia, Fiji, Vietnam, and Indonesia. One crew member travelled from Japan to Vancouver on a giant freighter. Another spent a lovely week on a Caribbean cruise ship. One was stuck in the ice on a research ship in Antarctica for more than a week. He would check in with me on a scratchy satellite phone and I'd relay to his frantic wife that he was OK, they had plenty of food, and would surely get out of the ice pack in just a few more days. The ship's cook was also a superb pastry chef, and he was actually gaining weight as the chef tried out all sorts of delicacies on the bored and captive audience.

I got along with the American and British executives very well. They trusted me implicitly. It was such a refreshing change from the Hollywoods. Of course the series had problems. We replaced three of the four producers. In that chaos, I was asked to produce several stories on a Norwegian Coast Guard Cruiser 1,500 miles above the Arctic Circle, and spent two weeks with a another crew travelling from Portugal to France and Monte Carlo.

One of the most intriguing locations was a spiffy Norwegian oil rig in the North Sea that was so high tech, I felt like I was riding on a luxurious space ship. On a one-week patrol with the Norwegian Coast Guard, I boarded a Russian fishing trawler, had tea with the captain, and gave him a present of a few Hershey bars I had brought from the U.S. In return, he gave me his old Soviet Union flag (hammer and sickle). When I said, oh no sir, I can't take your flag, he replied,

"Why not, the cold war's over, and you won, so take it, you deserve it."

The series screened at the MIP-TV festival in Cannes, France with a party on a Russian battle ship hired by the British partner. It was the first Russian warship allowed in French waters since before WWII. The nervous French government tried to shoo them out after the party, but the poor Russians had only enough fuel to get to Cannes, and were so broke they couldn't afford food to feed their crew. The sailors pulled us aside to sell their hats, belts, and medals so they could buy bread ashore. The producers felt terrible, and to avoid an international incident, the French and British governments gave the captain enough food, water, and diesel to limp back to mother Russia. I had witnessed the end of the cold war first hand in two very different situations. God, I loved documentaries.

Despite living in Baltimore for over a year while working on the series, I never saw John once. We exchanged phone messages, promising each other to do lunch. I rarely had a minute free, because in the evenings I wrote my Location Scouting and Management textbook (for which I had been paid a $2,000 advance, and was way behind delivering). I occasionally spent a weekend in Baltimore and though I kept missing John, I got the nerve to call Vince. It had been two years, since I'd run off, but he and Delores were very welcoming. Things were looking up. John had made another film with a different group and it was very pleasant. Vince moved from film to film, and a new

HBO TV series that promised years of work in Baltimore was in the planned. It became a ritual to visit Vince and Delores for lunch on every trip to Baltimore thereafter, but John never seemed available.

Near the end of the MPT series, Leo was optimistic about future work together. He had written a grant to PBS for another big series, this time about world religions, and figured he had enough work for the next ten years. I even started looking for houses for a potential move back to Baltimore. Alas, PBS hated his proposal. He had nothing else in the hopper, so I put the brakes on returning to Baltimore. Leo left MPT about a year later, and though we stayed friends, we never worked together again. That's showbiz.

I helped Bob Mugge on four more Americana music films. One hosted by Dave Stewart (The Eurhythmics) and the late New York Times rock writer, Robert Palmer, was a tribute to the blues artists who had inspired the 60s British rock scene. We made a two week magical mystery tour through the down and out juke joints of the Mississippi Delta from Memphis to Jackson. One memorable night I was accidently left behind in a little half-collapsed country bar where we had filmed for several hours. The owner offered me a ride back to town, but was stinking drunk. Trying to lock up for the evening, he pulled the door right out of the frame and it crashed to the floor, leaving it wide open for anyone who happened by.

"N'mine," he said, weaving his way to his car, "I getta t'morrah."

We ran over several trees and mail boxes, and sideswiped two parked cars before I grabbed the steering wheel and begged him to just push on the pedals while I steered. We made it to town, but I never again felt comfortable driving with someone who had been drinking.

Work in Charlotte didn't amount to much. Mostly a day here and a day there. I got restless and made trips back to DC hoping my international documentary experience would land me a job at Discovery Networks or the new National Geographic Channel. It was promising, but I had to live in DC to freelance and grab a big job when it opened up. It was hard to figure how to juggle a family 400 miles away with freelance work in DC. What to do? Some said I should move to Orlando, which was becoming a production giant.

Then I saw an ad in the Charlotte paper. The local public TV station, which had a newly renovated facility, was looking for a production director. By that time, my resume was pretty thick with PBS credits. At the group interview, the station manager treated me with compliments and praised the good fortune for them that I had landed in Charlotte. He offered me the job before the interview finished. They paid me the highest salary level, which was half what I'd been making in Baltimore, but the cost of living in North Carolina was about half. It had the benefits of a government job, was the most secure thing I'd done since I met John at UMBC. With two kids in elementary school, I was ready for it.

I stayed in touch with John sporadically. We exchanged one set of letters beginning with one I wrote in my lowest moment where I accused him of betraying a best friend and ruining my life by exiling me to Nowheresville, North Carolina. In a furious letter back to me, he replied I was responsible for my life, it was stupid of me to sneak out of Baltimore without saying goodbye to him or anyone, and it served me right for not taking his advice about not working on Crybaby. He recognized that some of his old colleagues were badly handled by the Hollywoods, but answering my accusation that they were ruthless back-stabbers he wrote, "What do you expect?

Who do you think are attracted to a nine-million dollar movie? They are ambitious people who can be ruthless. That's how it is."

So movie making was merely survival of the fittest. It made me feel better that I had left it behind.

He also was mystified that I suddenly decided to testify against him and New Line in Charles' lawsuit against them. I wanted to answer, "What do you expect?" I took these to be our last words. He was right that I had to make my own path and it was up to me to make the best of the opportunities I had. There was no pension plan at Dreamland. He had gone one way and I another. Best to leave it at that.

But I knew John still felt some loyalty from several examples. When Love Letter to Edie was released on DVD, I sent him a copy, which he called to thank me for. He recommended it in his lectures, and I occasionally noticed an uptick in sales orders from places he spoke. On my regular visits to Baltimore I'd still occasionally call and we'd speak briefly, hoping to make time for lunch, but never could. His office staff knew me well, and was always cordial. They gave me his cell phone number when I had a question and he was out of town. I'm still on his Christmas card list, and have an open invitation to his Baltimore Christmas party, though I haven't made it since 1987.

In the late 1990s, we were booked to appear together on a panel at the Chicago Underground Film Festival, because they had booked Love Letter to Edie along with several of his films. It was daunting, having not seen him for ten years. He called out of the blue a few days before the event to check if I was "doing all right"—meaning was I a psychotic threat? He didn't want me screaming or throwing a chair at him and turning it into a Jerry Springer Show. I assured him I was fine, would be a gentleman, and looked forward to catching up with him.

Life was good outside of Low Budget Hell. He was relieved. He showed up with several tough looking guys, who, someone told me, were his bodyguards. I thought that was funny—and fit with his mission to be a fop. We had dinner with Mink Stole and Elizabeth Coffey who were also on the panel, had good calm conversations, and promised to get together more.

On another occasion, my son Philip wanted to interview The Locust, a noise band featured in Cecil B. Demented, for a fanzine he published in high school. I asked John if he would contact them and make an introduction. John made the connection right away, and Philip had a great time going to the show and hanging out with the band late in the evening.

John would call out of the blue with bits and pieces of information. One sad call was to tell me Tom L'oizeaux, the cinematographer I had brought to Desperate Living and worked on a few of John's later films, had unexpectedly died of a heart attack. Another time John's office called to invite me to a lecture John was giving in North Carolina, but I was travelling at the time and missed it.

At the end of the day, though I frequently had doubts, my work with John has opened doors that were a great benefit to my career. Even better it has started many good conversations. The memories and stories are great, like his shouting into my ear for hours while sitting on Fells Point bar stools, and pacing around theater lobbies smoking a pack of cigarettes before the premiers are priceless.

Following John's advice, I have made my own way along a winding roller coaster path. In one phone conversation, he said he had heard I had become a Bible-Belt religious fanatic snake handler. I wish I could have said yes, absolutely, but he was relieved when I said I was most definitely not. He couldn't believe my son Evan had willingly joined the Army. He was again relieved when I told him Evan was most definitely not a Jarhead, but was nicknamed "fuckin' liberal" while he disarmed land mines in Afghanistan.

Now, nearly 40 years later, I have come full circle. I teach video at a small college to a handful of hopeful filmmakers. They're hoping to set the world on fire with their movies, but have no idea what that entails; and maybe that's a good thing. Most of my students and friends don't know anything about John Waters and underground movies. They have no clue about the downtown New York art scene, globe-trotting documentaries, or old films about fat weirdos. I am frequently surprised how few people have even heard of John Waters. It's like that whole experience happened on another planet. And that's not just in the south where I live. I've found many "culturally aware" people who never go to the movies, watch late night TV, or read edgy books.

I'm never sure how to approach my fifteen years working with "the prince of puke" with strangers. I do tell people I worked in film and television, but John is so far out and complicated for most people, I have little desire to introduce them to the intricate wit and irony of Pink Flamingos, Desperate Living, or Polyester.

When I meet a stranger who asks, "What movies have you done?" I ask them, "Have you heard of John Waters?" If they haven't, I'll say, "PBS programs, mostly educational stuff, documentaries, things you probably haven't seen." They nod politely and the conversation moves on. If the answer is, "Oh my God, yes, I love his films!" then I'll proudly say I made five films with him. I start reeling out the stories, and they are riveted. I'm a little un-nerved when I pause and catch them staring wide-eyed at me. I see them wondering, "If I reach out my hand, will he shake it or lick it?"

Afterward

· · · · · · · · · · · ·

In case you were wondering, this book is unauthorized. It is a personal memoir. It is my story of what I saw, and what I thought about an interesting time with interesting people. I purposely did not make this book a researched biography of John Waters. I worked with him for fifteen years, but this book covers much more. Nevertheless the time with Waters and the Dreamlanders was always an influence.

I did not consult with John about this book, but I did tell him I was writing one. When I sent him the full manuscript draft as a favor before it was published, his reaction was not positive. He found no humor in it, and made several comments that were so negative and ironic I was tempted to put them on the front cover to help sell the book. As you now know from the book, John and I frequently disagreed and argued quite a bit, but we were never mean. They were productive arguments that helped shape some wonderful works of art, so never mind.

I wanted to write a funny book, not a mean one. But it was important to tell it the way it was. Several people had already read the manuscript and said they loved it. If they admired Waters, their opinion was enhanced, and they were inspired to see his movies again. Those who knew little or nothing about him thought he was a fascinating character, and they would look for his movies and books to learn more.

This book could upset some others who appear in it. But I think anybody who appears in any book will be horrified if they don't see exactly their own self-image. Celebrities and public figures, or anyone working in show business may feel this more than anyone else. But their fans are dying to know if their heroes are unreachable gods, or mere mortals like the rest of us. Can we aspire to their greatness in any little way, or are they absolutely flawless?

After thirty years working in film, I felt that I had learned some helpful truths that could be shared. I felt these truths were also entertaining. People love the movies and they want to know what goes on behind the scenes.

I don't regret anything in the book. It's history, and I learned to handle the good and the bad. I'm still walking; I don't need professional counseling (unless you count a monthly visit to my masseur). I'm not in rehab and I don't live in a cardboard box or give my money to cults. I love my work and family, and look forward to the next adventure.

I hope this book is ironic. I hope it changed and enhanced your view of the movies and the characters that inhabit them. Everybody has their faults, and faults are funny. Truth is funny too. Good sides aren't so funny, and praise gets boring pretty fast.

Maybe the favorite comment I've had about the book was that it is not about John Waters, but about the strange and complicated journey of life, about good and bad decisions, about surprises, survival, friends, business, and the struggle to make art. And, that sometimes things do actually turn out well. John and the other characters in the book help tell the story. I thank them for being there and for being who they were, and for making it such an amazing trip

About the Author

Robert Maier grew up in Baltimore and has worked more than 30 years in film and TV production. He started working with John Waters when he was 23 and continued through five Waters movies: Female Trouble, Desperate Living, Polyester, Hairspray, and Crybaby, moving from soundman to line producer. He has worked on many other high and low-budget productions from Hawaii to New York to Afghanistan, authored several film production books, published magazine articles, and taught college-level courses in audio and video production. He has two grown sons and lives in North Carolina with his wife who has been with him since the beginning.

CPSIA information can be obtained at www.ICGtesting.com
Printed in the USA
BVOW02s0024310715

410918BV00001B/176/P